This book is a study of Paul's response to the financial help he received from the church in Philippi whilst he was a prisoner in Rome. Philippians 4.10–20 has always puzzled commentators because of its seemingly strained and tortured mode of thanks. Word studies, psychological studies and literary studies have all failed to provide insight into the text, which is unique in the Pauline corpus. Using contemporary sources Dr Peterman re-examines this difficult passage in the light of Greek and Roman practices and language regarding the exchange of gifts and favours in society. He concludes that 'gift exchange' or 'social reciprocity', with its expectations and obligations, permeated every level of society in Paul's day, and that Paul's seemingly ungracious response was an attempt to create a new, Christian attitude to gifts and to giving.

SOCIETY FOR NEW TESTAMENT STUDIES

MONOGRAPH SERIES

General editor: Richard Bauckham

92

PAUL'S GIFT FROM PHILIPPI

Paul's gift from Philippi

Conventions of gift-exchange and Christian giving

G. W. PETERMAN

Pastor, Osceola Evangelical Free Church,
Osceola, Iowa

CAMBRIDGE
UNIVERSITY PRESS

Published by the Press Syndicate of the University of Cambridge
The Pitt Building, Trumpington Street, Cambridge CB2 1RP
40 West 20th Street, New York, NY 10011-4211, USA
10 Stamford Road, Oakleigh, Melbourne 3166, Australia

First published 1997

Printed in Great Britain at the University Press, Cambridge

A catalogue record for this book is available from the British Library

Library of Congress cataloguing in publication data

Peterman, Gerald W.
Paul's gift from Philippi: conventions of gift-exchange
and Christian giving / G. W. Peterman.
    p.   cm. – (Monograph series / Society for New Testament studies: 92)
Revision of thesis (Ph.D) – Kings College, London, 1992.
Includes bibliographical references and index.
ISBN 0 521 57220 7 (hardback)
1. Bible. N. T. Philippians IV, 10–20 – Criticism, interpretation, etc.
2. Christian giving – Biblical teaching.   3. Gifts – Rome.
4. Rome – Social life and customs.   I. Title.   II. Series.
III. Series: Monograph series (Society for New Testament Studies): 92.
BS2705.6.C53P48   1997   227'.6067–dc20   96-7897 CIP

ISBN 0 521 57220 7 hardback

CE

CONTENTS

PREFACE

This book is a revision of a doctoral dissertation submitted to the Department of Theology and Religious Studies at King's College London in 1992. The work was completed under the careful supervision of Professor Graham N. Stanton with further comments given by the examiners Dr Judith Lieu and Dr Loveday Alexander.

I should like very much to thank Professor Stanton for generosity with his time during the course of my study, for his thoughtful reading of the work (along with his indefatigable correction of split infinitives), and for his written comments recommending it for the Society for New Testament Studies Monograph Series.

I am indebted to the Tyndale House Council and especially to the warden of Tyndale House, the Revd Dr Bruce W. Winter, for their partnership in this undertaking from the first day until now. Without their generous support, financial and otherwise, the work would never have progressed. Thanks go also to Ian Hodgins and Heather Richardson.

The Morley congregation of Eden Baptist Church, Cambridge, has provided my family and me with Christian encouragement during our time in England. We are thankful to them for their financial support and prayers.

My colleagues at Tyndale House have been more helpful than they realize. Over tea in the common room, I often solicited their reflections on various issues. My inadequate memory allows me to name only a few: Daniel Bailey, Anthony Bash, Robert Burrelli, D. A. Carson, Andrew Clarke, John Craig, Peter Dunn, Peter Head, Randolf Herrmann, Philip Kern, Brent Kinman, Randal Massot, Brian Rosner, Ian Smith and Kim-Huat Tan.

This work is dedicated to my wife, Marjory, with gratitude for partnership.

ABBREVIATIONS

ANRW	*Aufstieg und Niedergang der römischen Welt*, ed. Wolfgang Haase, Berlin: Walter de Gruyter
AusBR	*Australian Biblical Review*
BDF	F. Blass and A. Debrunner, *A Grammar of the Greek New Testament and Other Early Christian Literature*, translated and revised by R. W. Funk (Chicago: University of Chicago Press, 1961).
Bib	*Biblica*
BJRL	*Bulletin of the John Rylands University Library of Manchester*
BSac	*Bibliotheca Sacra*
BTB	*Biblical Theology Bulletin*
BZ	*Biblische Zeitschrift*
CBQ	*Catholic Biblical Quarterly*
CPR	*Corpus Papyrorum Raineri, Griechische Texte IV–V*, ed. H. Zilliacus et al., Wien: Hollinek, 1979–83
CQ	*Classical Quarterly*
CurTM	*Currents in Theology and Mission*
EvQ	*Evangelical Quarterly*
EvT	*Evangelische Theologie*
ExpTim	*Expository Times*
Fs.	*Festschrift*
HTR	*Harvard Theological Review*
IE	*Die Inschriften von Ephesos*, ed. H. Wankel et al., Bonn: Rudolf Habelt, 1979–
Int	*Interpretation*
IVP	*Inter-Varsity Press*
JAC	*Jahrbuch für Antike und Christentum*
JBL	*Journal of Biblical Literature*
JETS	*Journal of the Evangelical Theological Society*
JJS	*Journal of Jewish Studies*

JRH	*Journal of Religious History*
JSNT	*Journal for the Study of the New Testament*
JSOT	*Journal for the Study of the Old Testament*
LCL	Loeb Classical Library
NEB	New English Bible
NIV	New International Version
NJB	New Jerusalem Bible
NTS	*New Testament Studies*
NIC	New International Commentary
NovT	*Novum Testamentum*
OGIS	*Orientis Graeci Inscriptiones Selectae*, 2 vols., Lipsiae: Apud S. Hirzel, 1903
RAC	*Reallexikon für die Antike und Christentum*, ed. T. Klauser, et al., Stuttgart: Anton Hiersemann, 1941–
RB	*Revue Biblique*
ResQ	*Restoration Quarterly*
RevExp	*Review and Expositor*
SB	*Sammelbuch griechischer Urkunden aus Aegypten*, ed. F. Preisigke et al., 1913–
SEG	*Supplementum Epigraphicum Graecum*, ed. J. Hondius et al., 1923–
SIG²	*Sylloge Inscriptionum Graecarum*, ed. W. Dittenberger, 2nd edn, 3 vols., 1898–1901
TBT	*The Bible Today*
TDNT	*Theological Dictionary of the New Testament*, 10 vols., ed. G. Kittel and G. Friedrich, trans. G. W. Bromiley, Grand Rapids: Eerdmans, 1964–76
TynBul	*Tyndale Bulletin*
VT	*Vetus Testamentum*
ZNW	*Zeitschrift für die neutestamentliche Wissenschaft*
ZPE	*Zeitschrift für Papyrologie und Epigraphik*

1

INTRODUCTION

Every reader of the New Testament brings to the text a set of presuppositions about social behaviour. These general assumptions about the normal or proper way that individuals interacted in ancient society are inevitably drawn from the reader's own experience of personal relationships. A reader's evaluation of the meaning and significance of any particular ancient text is heavily influenced by these presuppositions.

Problems may arise when the reader operates with a set of social assumptions which differs from that of the writers of the New Testament. If cognizance is taken of the social distance between a modern reader and an ancient text, one becomes aware of pitfalls in interpretation.

Insight into the meaning of a New Testament text also requires an understanding of first-century social conventions which must be derived from study of relevant ancient documents.

Exploration of the social conventions underlying New Testament texts is a relatively new activity. In his seminal work, *Light from the Ancient East*,[1] Adolf Deissmann gave the New Testament scholarly world a healthy injection of reality and opened many avenues of opportunity, but scholarship since Deissmann has only slowly gained momentum in its attempt to locate the New Testament in its Greco-Roman environment. Abraham Malherbe refers to Helmut Koester's observation that the Hellenistic background to Paul has been brought into ill repute.[2] Malherbe goes on to assert that there

---

[1] Adolf Deissmann, *Light from the Ancient East*, trans. Lionel R. M. Strachen (London: Hodder and Stoughton, rev. edn, 1927).

[2] Malherbe contends that 'there is still a tendency on dogmatic grounds to deny any real Hellenistic influence on Paul ... Paul's indebtedness to Jewish traditions, however, is accepted as somehow preserving his theological integrity' (Abraham J. Malherbe, 'Greco-Roman Religion and Philosophy and the New Testament', *The New Testament and its Modern Interpreters*, ed. E. J. Epp and G. W. MacRae (Philadelphia: Fortress Press, 1989): 7). Koester cites as causes of this trend 'the discovery of new material to illustrate the Jewish background of the

has been no general improvement in the situation since then.[3] While advances are being made with literary, form and redaction critical, feminist and reader-response methods, the fertile soil of the Greco-Roman background to the documents is still not being cultivated as intensively as it should be.[4]

The Greco-Roman background of the New Testament has not been ignored. Philosophical, religious and rhetorical issues have received considerable attention and produced valuable results. Yet the social conventions which dictated the interaction between individuals in the Greco-Roman world have not fared as well.[5] This neglect is explicable, for the delineation of the convention depends upon data which have not been assembled in a form readily accessible to New Testament scholars.

Some New Testament scholars have braved the task, giving themselves to an examination of certain aspects of Greco-Roman social issues. At the risk of drawing a false dichotomy, we see that their studies have operated with one of two methodologies. First, an exegete may attempt to reconstruct the workings of a particular aspect of first-century society by using ancient documents. This reconstruction is then used to clarify the meaning of New Testament texts. Leaders in using this method include Judge, Hengel, Malherbe and Theissen.[6] Many others, however, could be named.[7]

NT' and the 'deplorable decay of students' knowledge of the Greek language' (cf. Helmut Koester, 'Paul and Hellenism', *The Bible and Modern Scholarship*, ed. J. P. Hyatt (Nashville: Abingdon Press, 1965): 187).

3 Malherbe, 'Greco-Roman Religon', 7.

4 Malherbe offers several factors as reasons for this neglect of the Greco-Roman background ('Greco-Roman Religion', 3).

5 See, e.g., David L. Balch, Everett Ferguson and Wayne A. Meeks, eds., *Greeks, Romans, and Christians: Essays in Honor of Abraham J. Malherbe* (Minneapolis: Fortress Press, 1990). Parts 1 and 2 are titled respectively 'Schools of Hellenistic Philosophy' and 'Hellenistic Literature and Rhetoric'. These comprise 234 pages. By contrast, Part 4 titled 'Hellenistic Social Behavior' comprises only thirty-five pages.

6 In addition to scores of articles, see the following monographs: Edwin Judge, *Rank and Status in the World of the Caesars and of St Paul* (Canterbury: University of Canterbury Press, 1982); Martin Hengel, *Gewalt und Gewaltlosigkeit: Zur 'politischen Theologie' in neutestamentlicher Zeit* (Stuttgart: Calwer, 1973) and *Eigentum und Reichtum in der frühen Kirche* (Stuttgart: Calwer, 1973); Abraham Malherbe, *Social Aspects of Early Christianity* (Philadelphia: Fortress Press, 1983) and *Paul and the Thessalonians. The Philosophic Tradition of Pastoral Care* (Philadelphia: Fortress Press, 1987); Gerd Theissen, *Studien zur Soziologie des Urchristentums* (Tübingen: J. C. B. Mohr, 1983), *The Social Setting of Pauline Christianity* (Philadelphia: Fortress Press, 1982) and *The Sociology of Early Palestinian Christianity* (Philadelphia: Fortress Press, 1978).

7 Again citing only monographs, see Ronald F. Hock, *The Social Context of Paul's*

Secondly, in contrast, several scholars of the New Testament have seen value in using sociological or anthropological models developed by specialists in the respective disciplines.[8] They assume that the generally unchanging nature of human life allows the development of universal models of behaviour which are founded on evidence from several centuries and various cultures. These models may then be brought to bear on the historically particular events of the New Testament. Those scholars using such methods realize the possibility of misapplication, but this awareness has not always preserved them from questionable conclusions.[9]

This study employs the former method. It is an attempt to use ancient documents in order to establish what were the common conventions regarding certain aspects of social interaction in the first century and to apply these conventions to a study of selected passages in Paul. The particular aspect of the social world to be investigated is the role that gifts and favours played in interpersonal relationships, that is, the convention of social reciprocity, which we will explore and define presently.

Social reciprocity in the ancient world

In our study we shall use the term social reciprocity (or simply reciprocity) to refer to a convention that operates in the interpersonal relationships of some societies. Speaking generally, this convention dictates that when a person (or persons) is the recipient of good in the form of a favour or a gift, the receiver is obligated to respond to the giver with goodwill and to return a counter-gift or favour in proportion to the good received.[10]

Ministry (Philadelphia: Fortress Press, 1980); Robert M. Grant, *Early Christianity and Society: Seven Studies* (New York: Harper and Row, 1977); Wayne Meeks, *The First Urban Christians* (New Haven: Yale University Press, 1983); J. Paul Sampley, *Pauline Partnership in Christ. Christian Community and Commitment in Light of Roman Law* (Philadelphia: Fortress Press, 1980).

[8] John G. Gager, *Kingdom and Community: The Social World of Early Christianity* (Englewood Cliffs: Prentice Hall, 1975); Bruce J. Malina, *Christian Origins and Cultural Anthropology: Practical Models for Biblical Interpretation* (Atlanta: John Knox Press, 1986); John H. Elliot, *A Home for the Homeless. A Sociological Exegesis of 1 Peter, its Situation and Strategy* (Philadelphia: Fortress Press, 1981); Francis Watson, *Paul, Judaism and the Gentiles: A Sociological Approach* (Cambridge: Cambridge University Press, repr., 1989); Jerome H. Neyrey, *Paul, In Other Words. A Cultural Reading of his Letters* (Louisville: Westminster/John Knox Press, 1990).

[9] E.g., pp. 13–14 for comments on Malina's view of verbal gratitude.

[10] Lawrence C. Becker, in his work on philosophical ethics, considers reciprocity to

Social reciprocity is a general convention and may operate at many levels and between various groups and individuals within a society. Thus friendship and patronage relationships are different manifestations of the same underlying phenomenon. Mutual obligations may be formed between economically equal individuals, between a rich and a poor individual, between one person and a group, between groups of persons or between countries, to name a few possible combinations. Reciprocity as a phenomenon has attracted much scholarly work from sociologists and anthropologists. Some have studied industrialized and others have studied archaic societies.[11] Not surprisingly, there is disagreement on the social or psychological mechanisms which cause reciprocity.[12] We shall not concern ourselves with these specialized questions. Rather, proceeding from the definition offered above, we shall show that social reciprocity existed in the Greco-Roman world and shall delineate some of its characteristics which will be helpful in our exegesis of Paul.

Social reciprocity in Greco-Roman society

It has long been known among classicists that social reciprocity operated at many levels of Greek and Roman society.[13] In recent

be a moral virtue and not a purely social one. See his discussion of the rational basis for reciprocity in *Reciprocity* (London: Routledge and Kegan Paul, 1986): esp. 73–144.

[11] A seminal and readable introduction may be found in Marcel Mauss, *The Gift: Forms and Functions of Exchange in Archaic Societies*, trans. I. Cumnison (London: Routledge and Kegan Paul, repr., 1974). See also Karen S. Cook, ed., *Social Network Theory* (London: Sage Publications, 1987); Jack N. Mitchell, *Social Exchange* (New York, 1978); Clyde J. Mitchell, 'Social Networks', *Annual Review of Anthropology* 3 (1974): 279–99; P. W. Holland and S. Leinhardt, eds., *Perspectives on Social Network Research* (New York: Academic Press, 1975).

[12] See, for example, the view of George M. Foster, 'Peasant Society and the Image of Limited Good', *American Anthropologist* 67 (1965): 293–315 and the criticisms of this view expressed by James R. Gregory, 'Image of Limited Good, or Expectation of Reciprocity?' *Current Anthropology* 16 (1975): 73–84. Also see the responses offered by several scholars following Gregory's article on 84–93.

[13] See, e.g., A. C. Pearson, 'Gifts (Greek and Roman)', *Encyclopedia of Religion and Ethics*, 7 vols. ed. James Hastings (Edinburgh: T & T Clark, 1908–26): 6.209–13 and more recently H. Bolkestein, *Wohltätigkeit und Armenpflege in vorchristlichen Altertum* (Utrecht: A. Oosthoek, 1939); Ernst Badian, *Foreign Clientelae (265–70 B.C.)* (Oxford: Clarendon Press, 1958); Albrecht Dihle, *Die goldene Regel; eine Einführung in die Geschichte der antiken und frühchristlichen Vulgärethik* (Göttingen: Vandenhoeck & Ruprecht, 1962); Gabriel Herman, *Ritualized Friendship and the Greek City* (Cambridge: Cambridge University Press, repr., 1989).

years several scholarly monographs have detailed various aspects of reciprocity.[14] What we must stress here, and intend to demonstrate below in chapter 3, is the way in which social reciprocity was embedded in all aspects of Greco-Roman society. Donlan asserts that in ancient societies, there is an economic element in every social relationship and a social element in every economic relationship.[15]

Social reciprocity and the New Testament

The recognition of such social networks operating in the Greco-Roman world has crept into some works in the biblical field.[16] Yet even books specializing in New Testament backgrounds give us little or no introduction to the conventions of social reciprocity.[17] There has not been widespread recognition of the significance that this convention might have on the exegesis of the New Testament.

There have been several recent works which, to some extent, make reference to social reciprocity and how the convention helps enlighten exegesis of Paul. F. W. Danker has considered how social reciprocity sheds light on a few New Testament texts.[18] His

[14] E.g., Andrew Wallace-Hadrill (ed.), *Patronage in Ancient Society* (London: Routledge, 1989); E. Gellner and J. Waterbury (eds)., *Patrons and Clients in Mediterranean Societies* (London: Duckworth, 1977); A. R. Hands, *Charities and Social Aid in Greece and Rome* (London: Thames and Hudson, 1968).

[15] Walter Donlan, 'Reciprocities in Homer', *Classical World* 75 (1981–2): 139. Donlan builds on the work of Sahlins who likewise asserts that, 'A material transaction is usually a monetary episode in a continuous social relation' (M. Sahlins, *Stone Age Economics* (Chicago: Aldine Publishing, 1972): 185).

[16] John E. Stambaugh and David L. Balch (*The New Testament and its Social Environment* (Philadelphia: Westminster Press, 1986)) make reference to the convention. Peter Marshall (*Enmity in Corinth: Social Conventions in Paul's Relations with the Corinthians* (Tübingen: J. C. B. Mohr, 1987)) applies in a limited way some findings regarding reciprocity to Paul's difficult relationship with the Corinthians. See also John H. Elliott, 'Patronage and Clientism in Early Christian Society. A Short Reading Guide', *Forum* 3 (1987): 39–48.

[17] The revised edition of C. K. Barrett's *The New Testament Background: Selected Documents* (London: SPCK, 1986) gives no document to illustrate such conventions. Similarly, the otherwise thorough treatment of Ferguson provides only one paragraph on patron-client relations, making no mention of reciprocity that operated between social equals (Everett Ferguson, *Backgrounds of Early Christianity* (Grand Rapids: Eerdmans, 1987): 45).

[18] F. W. Danker, 'Reciprocity in the Ancient World and in Acts 15: 23–9', *Political Issues in Luke-Acts*, ed. Richard J. Cassidy and Philip J. Scharper (Maryknoll: Orbis Books, 1983): 49–58; 'Bridging St Paul and the Apostolic Fathers: A Study in Reciprocity', *CurTM* 15 (1988): 84–94; 'Paul's Debt to the De Corona of Demosthenes: A Study of Rhetorical Techniques in Second Corinthians', *Persua-*

treatments, however, though illustrative for the texts considered, have not marked out the characteristics of giving and receiving in Greco-Roman society through a broad study of primary documents. David Register has produced a short study on giving and receiving,[19] but his concerns are quite different from ours.[20] Register is concerned to compare and contrast the place of charitable giving in Paul's letters with Greco-Roman and Jewish practices. Therefore, he is not concerned, as we are here, with Paul's relationship to his churches nor with the apostle's personal relationship of giving and receiving in Philippians 4. Similarly, the work of Chow focuses on Paul's relationship with the Corinthians as seen in 1 Corinthians, leaving the Philippian material untouched.[21]

The most significant recent study in the general field of this dissertation is that of Peter Marshall. In the first part of his monograph Marshall cites primary literature to illustrate the reciprocal nature of Greco-Roman friendship and the role that gift giving played in that society. He seeks to demonstrate that gifts were used to establish friendships and that the refusal of a gift could be taken as an insult. The second part of Marshall's work focuses on why Paul's initially positive relationship with the Corinthians so quickly turned to enmity. He asserts that Paul's refusal of the Corinthian offer of support (1 Cor. 9.12; 2 Cor. 11.9–12, 12.13), while accepting support from the Philippians, is the most useful key to unlocking the mystery of enmity at Corinth. Marshall stresses repeatedly that this contradiction on Paul's part was not only the primary cause of later hostility,[22] but also contained the basis for what would become a developed invective which portrayed Paul as a chameleon-like flatterer.[23]

Marshall devotes a few pages to Philippians 4.10–20. According to his own words, the discussion of the Philippians' gifts is 'of

---

sive Artistry. Studies in New Testament Rhetoric in Honour of George A. Kennedy, ed. Duane F. Watson (Sheffield: JSOT Press, 1991): 262–80.

[19] In our study, 'social reciprocity' and 'giving and receiving' are used interchangeably.

[20] David R. Register, 'Concerning Giving and Receiving. Charitable Giving and Poor Relief in Paul's Epistles in Comparison with Greco-Roman and Jewish Attitudes and Practices' (M. Phil. thesis, University of Sheffield, 1990).

[21] John K. Chow, *Patronage and Power: A Study of Social Networks in Corinth* (Sheffield: JSOT Press, 1992).

[22] Marshall, *Enmity*, 255.

[23] Ibid., 281.

special importance', and the relationship which is allegedly implied therein is 'critical' for his study.[24] Unfortunately, Marshall's cursory treatment of Philippians 4.10–20 cannot bear the weight he places on it. Though his comments on this text are helpful, he fails to give this key passage sufficient treatment and to use it to delineate the nature of Paul's relationship with the Philippians.[25] This text and relationship deserves fuller treatment because of the information we can gain from it on Paul's financial support and relationships of giving and receiving, to which we now turn.

Introduction to the issues

The life of the apostle Paul was a life of hardship and, to a certain extent, he brought troubles upon himself. For, while preaching and establishing churches, rather than requesting financial assistance, he worked night and day to support himself (1 Thess. 2.9). Frequently he went without sleep and was hungry (2 Cor. 11.27). According to the writer of Acts, at times he worked with his hands not only to supply his own needs but those of his companions (20.34).

Though Paul does not himself make the connection, this stress and deprivation certainly came about, at least in part, because of his renunciation of financial support. Though Paul emphatically states that he has the right to be materially supported by his churches (1 Cor. 9), it nevertheless appears to be his general practice to refuse support and to supply his own needs.[26] Therefore, as a free artisan and one who travelled extensively, he put himself in one of the most financially unstable situations.[27] If he had

---

[24] Ibid., xii, 165.

[25] Pheme Perkins ('Philippians: Theology for the Heavenly Politeuma', *Pauline Theology I: Thessalonians, Philippians, Galatians, Philemon*, ed. Jouette M. Bassler (Minneapolis: Augsburg Fortress, 1991): 89–104) and L. Michael White ('Morality Between Two Worlds: A Paradigm of Friendship in Philippians', *Greeks, Romans, and Christians*, 201–15) merely take over Marshall's conclusions into their work and do not forward the discussion on Phil. 4.10–20.

[26] Owing to the paucity of evidence, however, one could just as easily contend that it was his general practice to accept when assistance was offered, and the Corinthians merely proved to be an exception to this rule (as argued by Wilhelm Pratscher, 'Der Verzicht des Paulus auf finanziellen Unterhalt durch seine Gemeinden: Ein Aspekt seiner Missionsweise', *NTS* 25 (1979): 284–98). See our discussion of social obligations and the Corinthian conflict, pp. 162–72.

[27] Hock, *Social Context*, 35; Alison Burford, *Craftsmen in Greek and Roman Society* (London: Thames and Hudson, 1972): 124: 'Without a patron, the craftsman was literally and figuratively at a loss.'

accepted support, he doubtless could have avoided some of the hunger, thirst, cold and sleeplessness he mentions.

If indeed Paul suffered greatly owing to a lack of financial means, it is all the more surprising that he should obstinately refuse aid from the Corinthian church. For the Corinthians had apparently offered him aid several times, and his refusal offended them. Yet, despite their feelings of rejection, he pledges that he will never accept their support (2 Cor. 11.9). Perhaps it is even more surprising in some ways that when receiving aid from the Philippians (apparently his only financial partner), Paul gave such a laboured, and indeed some say aloof, response.[28] It seems as though he received their gifts grudgingly.

What could motivate such behaviour on Paul's part? Was there a theological, ethical, pastoral or a social reason for his renunciation of financial support? Scholars have recognized one or more of these reasons.[29] To focus on only one of these considerations would be reductionistic, for the decision probably arose from a number of factors. One of these factors will concern us in the pages that follow: the social reason. We will argue that a deeply embedded system of social obligations was basic to the fabric of the society in which Paul worked, both on the Greco-Roman sides as well as the Jewish side. Yet the demands of social reciprocity did not have the power to usurp the supreme place of the gospel in the apostle's life. When issues of social reciprocity arose in his dealings with his converts, Paul always gave the gospel top priority. He does not repudiate social reciprocity or its language. Indeed the phrase ἐκοινώνησεν εἰς λόγον δόσεως καὶ λήμψεως of Philippians 4.15, a social metaphor denoting friendship, becomes a Christian appellation for financial fellowship in missionary work. Nevertheless, the advance of the gospel message, both its geographic spread and the obedience to it rendered by individuals, was of the utmost importance.

This top priority was worked out in the apostle's life in a particular way. Knowing the power of social reciprocity, rather than contract unhealthy obligations, Paul made the sacrifice of his own personal pain. Though the reception of support from congregations with which he was working would have given him more

---

[28] Several theories are offered to explain what is perceived to be the uneasiness of Paul's response to the Philippians' support in Phil. 4.10–20. See the overview of these theories below, pp. 11–15.

[29] E.g., Hock, *Social Context*.

physical comfort, Paul maintained that this reception would hinder the advance of the gospel. Therefore, he chose to support himself, knowing the hardships that would result.

There is, however, one exception to Paul's general practice to be self-supporting. He received aid from the Philippians and we have a record of his response in Philippians 4.10–20.[30] Our study of biblical material begins with this text, since it presents a window to view a unique relationship which the apostle enjoyed with one of his congregations.

The biblical material

Philippians 4

In our study of giving and receiving in Paul we shall devote most of our time to Philippians 4.10–20. The reader may reasonably ask why this study should focus so much attention on one small, mundane and apparently insignificant part of one chapter.[31] We offer the following reasons:

First, Philippians 4.10–20 provides an example of a direct response to a gift received. Paul has received financial help from the church in Philippi. Therefore, these verses may be profitably compared with direct responses to gifts found in the papyri and with texts in the literary sources which describe or prescribe the proper social conventions regarding the reception of gifts.

Secondly, Paul's relationship with the Philippians was an essentially positive one, whereas, though there is perhaps more material to work with, the Corinthian correspondence provides an example of a negative relationship. The fact that Paul accepted the Philippians' gifts, and refused aid from the Corinthians, is one piece of evidence that reflects the different relationships.

Thirdly, little scholarly work has been done on Paul's financial relationship with the Philippians. In this area we have basically

---

[30] We call this an exception, though it does follow Paul's practice not to receive *while present* with a congregation. See our discussion on types of support below, pp. 163–7.

[31] This question becomes particularly acute when we compare the number of words commentators give to other parts of Philippians. In his recent major commentary, O'Brien devotes 107 pages to 2.1–11 and 65 pages to 3.1–10. 4.10–20, however, receives only 37 pages. Such disproportion gives one the impression that this text is relatively insignificant.

only Sampley's *Pauline Partnership in Christ*.[32] In comparison, much ink has been spilled in the study of Paul's financial relationship with the Corinthians. This neglect of the Philippian material deserves redress, especially since, as mentioned above, the apostle's relationship with the Philippian congregation was an essentially positive one.

Fourthly, Philippians 4.10–20 contains several phrases and words that are commonly called 'commercial-technical terms'.[33] Most commentators draw attention to terms which are sometimes found in commercial transactions: εἰς λόγον δόσεως καὶ λήμψεως (v. 15), εἰς λόγον (v. 17), ἀπέχω (v. 18).[34] Here is where the agreement of scholars ends, for it is far easier to point out the presence of these terms than to explain their significance.

Finally, there is one term which is expected, yet absent, in Philippians 4: εὐχαριστέω.[35] Why did Paul not thank the Philippians for the gift? Was returning thanks unacceptable culturally, or did Paul desire to avoid the denotations or connotations of the word? Are there social and cultural factors which can help explain his use of so-called commercial terminology? These questions have yet to be answered convincingly, though several views have been propounded. We cannot summarize all the views taken on the issues which confront the interpreter of Philippians 4, but a short survey of the most prominent theories will bring the relevance of these questions into perspective.

---

[32] Jouette M. Bassler devotes a small section to Paul's financial dealings with the Philippians in *God & Mammon. Asking for Money in the New Testament* (Nashville: Abingdon Press, 1991): 75–80. Though it reaches a few of the same conclusions drawn here, as a popular level book primarily concerned with stewardship and fundraising in the church it is not able to interact extensively with primary literature. See our references to Bassler in chapters 4 and 5.

[33] Although Marshall is basically correct in calling the phrase of 4.15 (ἐκοινώνησεν εἰς λόγον δόσεως καὶ λήμψεως) an idiomatic expression indicating friendship (Marshall, *Enmity*, 163), because of the particular emphases of his study he has not clearly defined the apostle's relationship with the Philippians nor examined all the ways that this positive relationship can help us in our understanding of the negative one in Corinthians.

[34] Gerald F. Hawthorne, *Philippians* (Waco: Word, 1983): 204; Ralph P. Martin, *Philippians* (NCB; Grand Rapids: Eerdmans, 1976): 167; J. H. Michael, 'The First and Second Epistles to the Philippians', *ExpTim* 34 (1922–3): 107–9.

[35] Hawthorne (*Philippians*, 195) states that 'it is remarkable that in this so-called "thank-you" section (Phil. 4.10–20), Paul does not use the verb εὐχαριστεῖν'. But we might expect Paul to omit εὐχαριστέω if he intends to avoid the obligations which may attend the word (see the comments on gratitude as solicitation, pp. 86–8).

A view that is popular and has much to commend it is that there is a psychological reason for the words, namely that Paul was embarrassed about money.[36] By drawing a synthesis of the data which show that Paul preferred to be self-supporting and thereby self-reliant and independent, some scholars conclude that Paul was embarrassed about money matters. According to Beare, Paul's embarrassment is essentially a sense of shame, for he always felt he was demeaning himself by accepting support.[37] With Martin, this discomfort results from a conflict between his desire to express appreciation for the gift and a concern to show himself superior to questions of money.[38] According to Dodd, we can infer from 1 Corinthians 9.15–18 that Paul really hated taking this money from the Philippians.[39] Receiving support stripped him of his boast, leaving him painfully embarrassed.

Against this view, however, we see that when Paul gives explicit reasons for refusing support, it is to avoid being a burden (2 Cor. 11.9; 1 Thess. 2.9), or because somehow acceptance would hinder the gospel (1 Cor. 9.12). This view appears to take the evidence into account and to give a reasonable explanation for the one personal reason Paul gives for refusing support, i.e., it would remove his boast and put him on a par with those who want to look equal with Paul (1 Cor. 9.15–16; 2 Cor. 11.12–13). Yet the assertion that Paul was embarrassed about money matters is nevertheless a conjecture which is based primarily on passages other than Philippians 4.

Another approach finds the explanation in Paul's unique dealings with the Philippians. This view is defended on the basis of four lines of argumentation.

[36] This is an aspect of Pauline psychology not mentioned by Gerd Theissen, *Psychological Aspects of Pauline Theology* (Edinburgh: T & T Clark, 1987).

[37] F. W. Beare, *The Epistle to the Philippians*, 3rd edn (London: Adam and Charles Black, 1976): 152. A sense of shame or embarrassment when receiving gifts or favours is certainly not unknown to those in the twentieth century and apparently also to the ancients (Arist. *Eth. Nic.* 4.3.24; Seneca *Ben.* 2.2.1), but that in itself cannot establish Paul's motives.

[38] Martin, *Philippians* (IVP), 176. Martin does not define what it means to be 'superior to questions of money'. In his earlier commentary the wording is 'superior to questions of depending on others for financial support' ((NCB), 161). Unfortunately this statement is likewise difficult. Apparently Martin believes that concern with money (or support) would be taken as greed and a lack of concern would be godly indifference. Consequently the detachment the apostle conveys shows him to be 'free from the love of money' and thus godly.

[39] C. H. Dodd, 'The Mind of Paul: I', *New Testament Studies* (Manchester: University Press, 1953): 71.

First, some assert that Paul had already informed the Philippians that he intended to be self-supporting and the coolness of this text is a result of it being a reminder not to infringe on this self-reliance. Hawthorne and Buchanan agree that the lateness and the ambiguity of Paul's thanks result from the apostle's disappointment in the congregation for violating his stated principles.[40]

Certainly Paul told the Corinthians of his resolution to refuse support from them, but it is an assumption unsupported by the evidence that he told the Philippians not to support him. If the Philippians had violated a stated principle of Paul, it is hard to see how he could praise them for their action (καλῶς ἐποιήσατε, 4.14).[41]

Secondly, Michael contends that the only reasonable way to understand Philippians 4.10–20 is to see it as the second statement of thanks which has been sent to the congregation.[42] He asserts that it is unlikely Paul would leave mention of the gift to the last and that, even there, no direct thanks should be given. Further, Michael states that there would not be such an emphatic pronouncement of independence, unless there had been a previous letter of thanks sent, and this one is only supplementary. Therefore the history of the process is: the Philippians sent a gift, Paul responded with a letter of thanks, but this letter was perceived as inadequate by the church. Piqued at the lack of appreciation on Paul's part they had written again. Our canonical epistle is Paul's second reply.

In response we ask: if Paul's second letter of thanks (the canonical epistle) is a strained or inadequate expression of thanks and is best understood as a reiteration of the contents of a first letter of thanks which was strained or inadequate, then why cannot the canonical epistle be the first letter of thanks?[43]

Thirdly, close to that of Michael is the view of Collange who sees the book as a compilation of three letters. Originally 4.10–20 was a thank-you note. The reasons Collange gives are typical: the peri-

---

[40] Hawthorne, *Philippians*, 195; Colin O. Buchanan, 'Epaphroditus' Sickness and the Letter to the Philippians', *EvQ* 36 (1964): 162.

[41] See the comments on this phrase on pp. 144–5.

[42] Michael, 'Philippians', 107. Recently, the same view is given by D. A. Carson, Douglas J. Moo and Leon Morris, *An Introduction to the New Testament* (Grand Rapids: Zondervan, 1992): 322.

[43] That Phil. 4.10–20 is the first acknowledgment of receipt seems clear from ἀπέχω, which would be at least redundant otherwise (so correctly Joachim Gnilka, *Der Philipperbrief* (Freiburg: Herder, 1968): 179).

cope is loosely connected to the context, thanks at the end is unlikely, 2.19–30 implies a length of time between receipt and thanks, and 1.3–11 and 2.19–30 seem to imply that thanks have already been given.[44]

Finally, Kennedy suggests that in this text Paul maintains a 'half-humorous' or 'more or less playful tone' which is 'thoroughly in keeping with the bright and vivacious character of the Epistle, in which he converses so frankly and charmingly with the best loved of all the Christian societies'.[45]

Some see a theological reason for Paul's terms: Paul is too heavenly minded to give earthly thanks.

Dibelius asserts that 'everything whether "spiritual" or "secular" (according to later distinctions), is important only "in Christ". Hence Paul damps his feelings where we should have expected purely human affection, as in the case of the "thankless thanks" for monetary assistance in Philippians iv, 10–20.'[46]

Even though Vincent maintains that 'only the most perverted and shallow exegesis' can describe Paul's words as a 'thankless thanks', nevertheless his view fits best here. For this author, 'It is characteristic that there is no formal expression of thanks beyond his recognition and commendation of the moral and spiritual significance of the act . . . The best thanks (Paul) can give them is to recognize their fidelity to the principle of Christian love, and to see their gift as an expression of that principle.'[47]

Glombitza asserts that Paul does not actually thank the Philippians for their gift but expresses thanks for the common sharing that their gift implies.

---

[44] Jean-François Collange, *The Epistle of Saint Paul to the Philippians*, trans. A. W. Heathcote (London: Epworth Press, 1979): 5, 148. Although for Collange the lateness of Paul's thanks is a problem to be solved, for Gnilka it is in keeping with Paul's evaluation of the gift: 'Es ist nicht forderlich, daß der Dank für die Gabe schon am Anfang von Brief A (1.1–3.1a; 4.2–7, 10–23) expresse hätte abgestattet werden müssen. Wenn ihn Paulus für den Schluß aufspart, stimmt das durchaus mit der sachlichen und seelsorgerlich Beurteilung zusammen, die die Spende nunmehr erfähren' (*Philipperbrief*, 172).

[45] H. A. A. Kennedy, 'The Financial Colouring of Philippians 4: 15–18', *ExpTim* 12 (1900–1): 43–4; cf. Deissmann (*Light*, 110–12) who uses the term 'humorous', Moisés Silva (*Philippians* (Chicago: Moody Press, 1988): 238) who calls Paul 'playful', and even O'Brien (*Philippians*, 540) who also uses the term 'humour'.

[46] Martin Dibelius, *A Fresh Approach to the New Testament and Early Christian Literature* (Hertford: Stephen Austin and Sons, 1936): 149.

[47] Marvin R. Vincent, *A Critical and Exegetical Commentary on the Epistles to the Philippians and to Philemon* (Edinburgh: T & T Clark, reprint 1979): 145–6.

Although not referring to the Philippian letter, Malina contends that expressions of gratitude were used to call a halt to exchange relationships. A 'thank-you' means the relationship of mutual obligation is over.[48] He asserts that most people in the gospels do not thank Jesus for healing them; instead they praise God, the giver of health, further implying that they might have to interact with Jesus again should illness strike later.[49] Malina's assertion regarding this lack of verbal gratitude is based on his 'limited good' model, which is unsupported by evidence in his writings.[50] Further, besides conflicting with the context in many instances (esp. Luke 17.16) Malina's theory does not take into consideration the literary and epigraphic sources.[51] For example: during the course of Judas Maccabaeus' military exploits he 'pressed hard on to Scythopolis, seventy-five miles from Jerusalem. But as the Jews who had settled there assured Judas that the people of Scythopolis had always treated them well and had been particularly kind to them when times were at their worst, he and his men thanked them and urged them to extend the same friendship to his race in the future' (εὐχαριστήσαντες καὶ προσπαρακαλέσαντες καὶ εἰς τὰ λοιπὰ πρὸς τὸ γένος εὐμενεῖς εἶναι παρεγενήθησαν εἰς Ἱεροσόλυμα τῆς τῶν ἑβδομάδων ἑορτῆς οὔσης ὑπογύου, 2 Macc. 12.29–31; NJB trans). Demosthenes refers to a decree (*Or.* 18.90–1) which gives as its purpose that the Greeks may know the εὐχαριστία of the Byzantines. In *Oratio* 18.92 Demosthenes refers to honours given the Athenians by the people of Chersonesus, who pledge never to fail thanking them and doing them whatever good they can (ἐν τῷ μετὰ αἰῶνι παντὶ οὐκ ἐλλείψει εὐχαριστῶν καὶ ποιῶν ὅ τι ἂν δύνηται ἀγαθόν), cf. Plut. *Vit. Fab. Mai.* 13.2.[52]

Though basically right in asserting that an expression of grati-

---

48 Glombitza, 'Der Dank des Apostels. Zum Verstandnis von Phil. 4: 10–20', *NovT* 7 (1964–5): 135–41.

49 Bruce J. Malina, 'Limited Good and the Social World of Early Christianity', *BTB* 8 (1978): 169; *The New Testament World: Insights from Cultural Anthropology* (Atlanta: Scholars Press, 1981): 79. Malina cites no evidence which explicitly supports this assertion though he does list some New Testament examples (Mark 2.12; Matt. 9.8, 15.31; Luke 5.26, 7.16, 17.16; Gal. 1.24).

50 Malina, *NT World*, 79.

51 Malina adopts the conclusions of Foster, 'Peasant Society', 293–315. For an evaluation of Foster's view see Gregory, 'Image of Limited Good?' 73–84.

52 In this short response to Malina we restrict ourselves to εὐχαριστέω (although in the sources ἀποδιδόναι χάριν often appears to perform the same function as εὐχαριστέω). We shall study further the place of verbalized gratitude in chapter 3.

tude could be taken as solicitation, Bassler incorrectly states that Paul uses business terminology to temper his gratitude and to indicate that the Philippians' debt to Paul for spiritual benefits has been fully discharged.[53] We shall see in chapter 3 that such 'business terminology' is often used to describe relationships of social reciprocity in the Greco-Roman world.

Brief responses have been offered to most of the above views. In addition, it is important to note that several of them share a common assumption: twentieth-century conventions regarding gratitude are appropriate criteria by which to evaluate Paul's thanks.[54] Thus, understandably, these authors have detected something socially inappropriate in Paul's 'thanks'. They have then looked for evidence in Philippians 4.10–20 itself or in the broader context of the Pauline corpus to explain this social oddity. The resulting theories have differing probabilities, yet all, with the exception of Sampley, have no moorings in the apostle's social world. If we are not to run adrift, then Paul's unique dealings with the Philippians must be anchored to a social context.

As we mentioned above, one crucial mistake has been made by several scholars dealing with the texts we shall treat in Paul: they have assumed that the terms commonly called 'commercial-technical terms' are in fact just that. They have failed to take into account the reciprocal character of many relationships in the ancient world and failed to see that these relationships can often be described with financial terminology.[55] The nature of these relationships lends itself to the use of this type of speech. Since Paul's relationships with his many converts and fellow workers took place in this social matrix, they must have also experienced this type of interaction. Thus, we should not be surprised to see him employ such terminology.

[53] Bassler, *God & Mammon*, 79. Against Bassler, compare Paul's statement to Philemon that the slave owner owes the apostle his very self (v. 19). Such a great debt on the part of many in Philippi could hardly be discharged through a material gift, no matter how large (see the treatment of Phlm 17–19 on pp. 185–91).

[54] Criticisms of this assumption are made by Loveday Alexander, 'Hellenistic Letter-Forms and the Structure of Philippians', *JSNT* 37 (1989): 98 and D. E. Garland, 'The Composition and Unity of Philippians: Some Neglected Literary Factors', *NovT* 27 (1985): 153 n. 44.

[55] See chapter 3, especially the treatments of Arist. *Eth. Nic.* 4.1.1–25; Cic. *Amic.* 16.58; Philo *Cher.* 122–3, pp. 58–9, 63–5.

Other Pauline passages

In addition to our treatment of Philippians 4.10–20, we shall also study the first two chapters of Philippians in order to help us define more fully the unique relationship of giving and receiving which the apostle enjoyed with this congregation.[56] Philippians 1.3–11 is especially important. For, as the introductory thanksgiving, it introduces the central themes of the letter and begins to define the nature of the Philippian partnership. Paul reports on the gospel's advance, despite his imprisonment, in 1.12–26. These verses show us the missionary concerns of the Philippians. This concern is consistent with their financial support. In 1.27–2.18 Paul begins to define conduct worthy of the gospel. Such conduct is urged as congruent with the Philippians' position as a missionary church. Finally, 2.19–30 shows us further the reciprocal character of the apostle's partnership with the Philippians: they both serve each other sacrificially. The Philippians with the θυσία of their gifts and prayers, the apostle with the θυσία of himself.

Paul's opportunities for giving and receiving were certainly not restricted to his relationship with the Philippians. Therefore, we shall also discuss several other Pauline passages which refer to the practice of giving and receiving. First, we shall consider together a group of texts which refer to Paul's financial and social relationship with the Corinthians (1 Cor. 1.16, 9.11–15, 16.6; 2 Cor. 6.13, 11.7–15, 12.13–16). Here Paul's rejection of support from the Corinthians is in sharp contrast to his acceptance of aid from the Philippians. We shall focus our attention on the motivations Paul gives for this varying behaviour. Secondly, Romans 15.25–31 is included because of its conspicuous language of obligation and its clear assumption that a relationship can be formed on the basis of giving and receiving. The relationship described in Romans 15.26–7 is quite illustrative of that found in the Philippian letter. Thirdly, Philemon 17–19 provides us with another example of mutual obligations arising between Paul and his converts. In this example, Paul calls for the repayment of a benefit. Fourthly, whoever penned

---

[56] Omission of material from Phil. 3 does not indicate our belief in a partition theory of the letter (see our discussion of Philippian unity below). Phil. 3 offers a negative example of service to God in contrast to the positive examples given for imitation in 1.21–6, 2.6–11 and 2.20–2. The generally negative character of the material in Phil. 3 does not serve our purposes in this study.

it, 1 Timothy 5.4 gives us an example, unique within the New Testament writings, of early church teaching which is common to the Greco-Roman world: persons are required to pay back the many benefactions they have received from their parents. Finally, Romans 5.7 is included because of the powerful way the unspoken assumptions of the text speak of the feelings of social obligation that motivate the receiver of benefactions.

We shall not discuss these texts in as much detail as Philippians 4. Several of them could well be the object of a monograph in themselves and they raise many issues not of direct relevance for our study. These additional texts will be studied with a view toward illustrating and filling-out the conclusions which have been reached regarding the Philippian material.

Working assumptions for Philippians

The question of unity

In our study of the Philippian material, we will operate with the assumption that canonical Philippians is a unity. In the current scholarly environment this is a reasonable presupposition with which to work. Although many scholars have argued, or accepted the argumentation of others, that the letter is an edited collection of several pieces of Pauline correspondence,[57] the arguments given are not conclusive. The two strongest arguments in favour of partition theories may be summarized as follows.

It is claimed that a harsh change of tone in 3.2, the use of τò λοιπόν in 3.1, and a change in subject matter in 3.1–21, all mark out these verses as belonging to correspondence different from that contained in 1.1–2.30. Against this view, however, we assert, first, that the threefold occurrence of βλέπετε in 3.2 should not be understood as 'look out for' but as 'consider' or as 'see'. The imperative has this meaning when followed by the accusative (cf.

---

[57] E.g., Beare, *Philippians*, 4, 150; Collange, *Philippians*, 8–14; Wolfgang Schenk, *Die Philipperbriefe des Paulus* (Stuttgart: W. Kohlhammer, 1984): 334–6; B. D. Rahtjen, 'The Three Letters of Paul to the Philippians', *NTS* 6 (1959–1960): 167–73; Günther Bornkamm, 'Der Philipperbrief als paulinische Briefsammlung', *Neotestamentica et Patristica* (Leiden: E. J. Brill, 1962): 192–202; C. J. Peifer, 'Three Letters in One', *TBT* 23 (1985): 363–8; John Reumann, 'Contributions of the Philippian Community to Paul and to Earliest Christianity', *NTS* 39 (1993): 438–57.

Mark 13.9; 1 Cor. 1.26, 10.18; 2 John 8).[58] It has the meaning 'look out for' when followed by ἀπό or a similar preposition (cf. Mark 8.15, 12.38; Luke 21.30). Secondly, τὸ λοιπόν need not be taken to mean 'finally', but can be used merely as a connecting particle with the meaning 'furthermore'.[59] Thirdly, there is a greater correspondence between the subject matter and vocabulary of 3.1–21 and the rest of the letter than is admitted by the advocates of a partition theory.[60] Among many points of contact we refer to rejoicing (1.4, cf. 3.1), destruction and salvation (1.28, cf. 3.19–20), humility (2.2, 7, cf. 3.3, 8) and suffering (1.29, 2.17, cf. 3.10).[61] These parallels point to development in Paul's central themes rather than to fresh topics belonging to a different letter.

It is claimed that the location of 4.10–20, the thank-you note for the Philippians' gift, is unacceptable. Some assert that it is very odd to have thanks reserved for the last and that we should therefore conclude that this text was not originally located at the end of a letter. This assertion of oddity is based on modern, western criteria about the appropriate way to give thanks.[62] These criteria are falsely applied to the apostle's thanks. Further, Alexander has shown that Hellenistic letter structure does not support this alleged evidence for partition. In papyrus letters thanks might be reserved to the end or omitted.[63]

Besides being able to offer good arguments against the strongest evidence in favour of a partition theory, there are several studies which defend the unity of the letter, and these studies have been undertaken from different perspectives.[64] Watson employs the

---

58 G. D. Kilpatrick, 'ΒΛΕΠΕΤΕ, Philippians 3: 2', *In Memoriam Paul Kahle*, ed. M. Black and G. Fohrer (Berlin: A. Töpelmann, 1968): 146–8.

59 Margaret E. Thrall, *Greek Particles in the New Testament. Linguistic and Exegetical Studies* (Leiden: E. J. Brill, 1962): 25, 28; O'Brien, *Philippians*, 13; Alexander, 'Hellenistic Letter Forms', 96–7; cf. 1 Cor. 4.2, 7.29.

60 See W. J. Dalton, 'The Integrity of Philippians', *Bib* 60 (1979): 99; R. C. Swift, 'The Theme and Structure of Philippians', *BSac* 141 (1984): 234–54; D. E. Garland, 'The Composition and Unity of Philippians: Some Neglected Literary Factors', *NovT* 27 (1985): 157–9.

61 See A. B. Spencer, *Paul's Literary Style. A Stylistic and Historical Comparison of II Corinthians 11.16–12.13, Romans 8.9–39, and Philippians 3.2–4.13* (Jackson: ETS, 1984): 80–1.

62 See Gerald W. Peterman, '"Thankless Thanks". The Social-Epistolary Convention in Philippians 4.10–20', *TynBul* 42 (1991): 261–70.

63 Alexander, 'Hellenistic Letter Forms', 87–101.

64 See, e.g., Robert Jewett, 'The Epistolary Thanksgiving and the Integrity of Philippians', *NovT* 12 (1970): 40–53; Peter T. O'Brien, 'The Importance of the Gospel in Philippians', *God Who is Rich in Mercy*, ed. Peter T. O'Brien and

methods of rhetorical analysis to demonstrate that the letter systematically develops the proposition found in 1.27–30.[65] Garland notes the extensive use of inclusion which marks out the shorter sections, 1.12–16, 1.27–30, 2.1–18, 2.19–24 and 2.15–30 as well as an overarching inclusion which marks out the paraenesis of 1.27–4.3.[66] Alexander notes that the epistolary conventions of Hellenistic letter structure do not support the arguments typically given for partition.[67] These contributions support our working assumption that canonical Philippians is a unity.

Furthermore, although our study is not directly concerned with the unity question, much of the evidence set out in this thesis will lend support to the argument for unity.[68]

Date, authorship, place of writing

There is little dispute that the letter to the Philippians should be included among the genuine letters of the apostle Paul. Though there have been isolated challenges to this position, they can be ignored.

The date of the letter is bound up with the place of its writing and with its unity.[69] Fortunately, whether the letter to the Philippians was written from Rome, Corinth or Ephesus is not significant for our purpose. Some scholars assert that origin from Rome would imply lengthy travel times and thus lengthen the amount of time between the reception of the gift from Philippi and Paul's response to it. It is asserted that a great gap between these two would be unacceptable, for Paul would never have waited so long to give thanks.[70] But this assertion is based on certain social

---

David G. Peterson (Homebush West, Australia: Lancer Books, 1986): 213–33 and 'The Fellowship Theme in Philippians', *Reformed Theological Review* 37 (1978): 9–18; Swift, 'Philippians', 234–54.

[65] Duane Watson, 'A Rhetorical Analysis of Philippians and its Implications for the Unity Question', *NovT* 30 (1988): 57–88; esp. 66, 84.

[66] Garland, 'Composition', 160–1.

[67] Alexander, 'Hellenistic Letter Forms', 87–101.

[68] See pp. 91–2 for our chart comparing the verbal and conceptual parallels between Phil. 1.3–11 and 4.10–20.

[69] One can hardly speak of 'a date' for the letter, if in fact the letter was originally several bits of correspondence. Thus, for example, Gnilka (*Philipperbrief*, 24–5) and S. Dockx ('Lieu et Date de l'Épître aux Philippiens', *RB* 80 (1973): 230–46) offer slightly different dates for different parts of the letter.

[70] E.g., Beare, *Philippians*, 4.

assumptions about the timing of gratitude.[71] Therefore, we shall follow the traditional view that the letter was written from Rome around AD 60–2.[72]

Method

As was mentioned above, we shall not utilize a sociological model first created by those working solely in the field of sociology or anthropology.[73] We shall be very much concerned with social questions, but this concern is not to be equated with the use of models developed by sociologists.[74] Our study is primarily historical. For the sake of clarity we shall distinguish between sociological analysis and historical research into social phenomena.

Sociological analysis attempts to generalize about the structure of human society.[75] It tends to be synchronic and typically comes to data with a model of dynamics taken from analyses of other groups and other data.[76] Because sociological analysis is comparative, it emphasizes that which is typical in human behaviour.

Historians also study human societies. But by contrast, the historian's emphasis is typically on the differences between societies and on the changes which have taken place in each society over time.[77] Historical study is less concerned to generalize and more concerned with that which is unique to the society under investigation.

In their study of the New Testament documents, New Testament scholars may employ models developed by sociologists. Though

---

[71] We have already questioned this assumption above. See further our discussion of verbal gratitude on pp. 73–83.

[72] Amongst several scholars this view is held by O'Brien, *Philippians*, 25; Silva, *Philippians*, 8; Beare, *Philippians*, 24; B. Reicke, 'Caesarea, Rome, and the Captivity Epistles', *Apostolic History and the Gospel*, ed. W. W. Gasque and R. P. Martin (Exeter: Paternoster, 1970): 277–86.

[73] Such a method is adopted, for example, by Bengt Holmberg, *Paul and Power. The Structure of Authority in the Primitive Church as Reflected in the Pauline Epistles* (Philadelphia: Fortress Press, 1980).

[74] Robin Scroggs does not make this distinction clear ('The Sociological Interpretation of the New Testament: The Present State of Research', *NTS* 26 (1980): 164–79).

[75] Peter Burke, *Sociology and History* (London: George Allen and Unwin, 1980): 13. For a readable essay on the differentiation between sociology and history, see pp. 13–30. Burke also speaks of the dialogue between sociologists and historians and gives an historical sketch of the interaction between the two disciplines.

[76] Scroggs, 'Sociological Interpretation', 168.

[77] Burke, 'Sociology and History', 13.

such a procedure can yield valuable results, it has a basic methodological flaw: the models offered by sociology are often developed on the basis of data taken from twentieth-century societies. These data may or may not be an appropriate basis on which to found a model for the interpretation of first-century human society. This point is made concisely by E. A. Judge. Writing of Holmberg's *Paul and Power*, Judge comments:

> It couples with New Testament studies a strong admixture of modern sociology, as though social theories can be safely transposed across the centuries without verification. The basic question remains unasked: What are the social facts of life characteristic of the world to which the New Testament belongs? Until the painstaking field work is better done, the importation of social models that have been defined in terms of other cultures is methodologically no improvement on the 'idealistic fallacy'. We may fairly call it the 'sociological fallacy'.[78]

Thus, we consider an historical approach to New Testament social questions to be more methodologically sound. Before applying a social model to the interpretation of New Testament texts, the model must be developed from ancient sources. These sources should be socially and chronologically close to the New Testament texts. Perfect data and models are not possible. But in terms of method, this procedure is preferable.

We shall attempt to establish what were the typical conventions of reciprocity which operated in Greco-Roman society at the time of Paul's interaction with the churches he founded. Our task will then be to see how these conventions help us understand the behaviour the apostle exhibited in his relationships of giving and receiving with special emphasis on his relationship with the Philippians. These relationships will be viewed through only a selection of texts which we have judged to be most indicative of the conventions under consideration.

[78] E. A. Judge, 'The Social Identity of the First Christians: A Question of Method in Religious History', *JRH* 11 (1980): 210.

2

GIVING AND RECEIVING IN THE OLD TESTAMENT AND EXTRA-BIBLICAL JEWISH LITERATURE

For a comprehensive view of the social matrix in which Paul's financial dealings with the Philippians are embedded, we must place it in the context of the ancient world. This chapter, which is devoted to Jewish literature, and the one that follows, in which Greco-Roman writings are considered, attempt to do this. These two chapters aid us in detecting the extent to which social reciprocity operated in these cultures and in uncovering the defining characteristics of each.

We have chosen to devote a chapter to Jewish literature for two reasons: as a former Pharisee (Phil. 3.5) living in a Greco-Roman society, the apostle's views regarding the role of money in social interactions would not be wholly formed by the conventions operating in his social world. The teaching of the Old Testament writings would have had a strong influence on Paul. For they were religiously authoritative documents which certainly show much interest in the social life of their community.

Also, this chapter of Jewish material, when viewed alongside the following chapter of Greco-Roman material, allows us to detect if these two cultures had similar or divergent ideas on social reciprocity.

The present chapter is devoted to a survey of two types of texts. First, we shall examine didactic texts which deal with reward for charity or reward for the proper discharge of one's tithing obligations. Secondly, we shall treat narrative texts which record specific examples of individuals entering into social exchange. We shall select examples both from the Old Testament and later Jewish literature. The chapter will focus only on selected texts which are judged to be most helpful or representative of social convention. It will be particularly important for us to note if there is a discrepancy between the conventions assumed in these two groups of texts: that is, to detect inconsistency between the taught morality and the practised morality.

Old Testament

Reward for giving in the Old Testament

The concept of reward accruing to the one who gives is of relevance not only to place Paul's giving and receiving in its broader social context, but also because the apostle specifically mentions the reward which the Philippians will receive because of their generosity (Phil. 4.17, 19). Our concern here will be to concentrate on didactic texts which communicate this belief.

The belief that the righteous will be rewarded for their good deeds is common in the Old Testament.[1] The failure of this doctrine to work itself out in practice is at the very heart of Job.[2] For our purposes, however, we shall be primarily restricted to the issue of financial sharing or the giving of alms. We begin with Deuteronomy.

(i) Deuteronomy

For every Israelite the giving of alms is a duty.[3] One's hand must be open to give to the poor (Deut. 15.8, 11). Surprisingly, we rarely see this duty presented in Deuteronomy as an act of compassion for its own sake.[4] Rather, deeply embedded in deuteronomic literature is the concept of national reward, and it is reward which is the chief incentive employed by the deuteronomic school to induce the nation to observe its teaching.[5] We have selected three examples which mention specifically the aspect of giving and the attendant reward.

14.29: Though not speaking about alms specifically, the tithe mentioned in this text may be labelled an indirect form of charitable

[1] E.g., Deut. 7.12–15; 15.4–6; 28.1–14 (cf. curses in vv. 15–68); Ruth 2.12; 1 Sam. 24.19; Ps. 5.12; 112.2; 128.4; Prov. 13.21.
[2] David J. A. Clines, *Job 1–20* (Dallas: Word, 1989): xxxix; Marvin H. Pope, *Job* (Garden City: Doubleday and Company, Inc., 3rd edn, 1973): lxxiii.
[3] Roland de Vaux, *Ancient Israel: Its Life and Institutions*, trans. John McHugh (London: Darton, Longman and Todd, 1961): 73.
[4] The Israelites should remember that they were slaves in Egypt (e.g., 15.15; 24.18, 22), which could be taken to mean, 'Do unto others as you would have them do unto you; for you were yourselves poor at one time.' This is an appeal to compassion, but only indirectly.
[5] Moshe Weinfeld, *Deuteronomy and the Deuteronomic School* (Oxford: Clarendon Press, 1972): 307. See the section on reward (307–19) and Weinfeld's Appendix A, 345–9, for a table of reward and punishment sayings.

giving. The tithe of the third year was not to be taken to a central location but collected in local towns.[6] That which is given is pooled and made into a fund to help the poor, landless and destitute.[7] One should give this tithe *in order* that the Lord may bless the people (*lema 'an yebarekka*).

15.10: Similarly, this text does not address alms directly but a charitable attitude.[8] Regarding lending, one should not refuse to help another because the year of debt cancellation is near and the possibility looms that the loan will turn into a gift. The motivation clause here is slightly different from 14.29 and 24.19: 'Because of this the Lord your God will bless you.'[9]

24.19: This verse comes closest of the three to charitable giving. While harvesting various crops, one should not be too thorough lest there be nothing left for the poor to gather. It shares the motivation clause found in 14.29 (*lema 'an yebarekka*).

We see that in Deuteronomy social concern, demonstrated in financial sharing, is a serious matter. It is legislated explicitly; it is demanded by the Law. Yet we also see that this charitable behaviour is solicited, not on the basis that it is right, but on the basis that it will bring reward to the nation. This reward is constantly presented as material and has its source in God who will bless the righteous.[10]

(ii) Proverbs

In its pragmatic way this book states that a generous man will prosper (11.24–6), and that a generous man will himself be blessed (22.9).[11] In 28.27, 'He who gives to the poor will lack nothing', and in 14.21, 'Blessed is he who is kind to the needy.'

19.17: Here the wisdom teacher presents alms as a loan which

---

6   Whether the tithe of the third year constituted a new tithe or merely special treatment of the tithe commanded elsewhere (Lev. 27.30; Num. 18.21–28) does not affect our purpose. On the conflict see S. R. Driver, *A Critical and Exegetical Commentary on Deuteronomy* (Edinburgh: T & T Clark, 1902): 169–73.

7   Driver, *Deuteronomy*, 166.

8   Peter C. Craigie, *The Book of Deuteronomy* (Grand Rapids: Eerdmans, 1976): 237.

9   Unless otherwise noted, all biblical quotations are taken from the NIV.

10 The examples might be multiplied. See, e.g., 2.7; 4.26; 5.30; 7.13; 11.9; 12.7; 14.24; 15.6, 18; 16.10; 17.20; 23.21; 26.15; 28.4; 30.9, 16; 32.47.

11 Apparently here the blessing comes from God, though in 11.26 the blessing may be construed as 'thanks' from the people.

puts Yahweh in debt to pay back the giver.[12] 'He who is kind to the poor lends to the Lord, and he will reward him for what he has done.' This text presents two very illuminating details. First, we should note the triangular relationship. Though the material aid passes between two persons, Yahweh plays a part as a third member in the relationship. In a sense God becomes a debtor to the benefactor. Secondly, though the relationships are social, they may be described with financial terminology. The benefactor lends to Yahweh; Yahweh will *repay* the benefactor. Both of these observations will play a significant role in our understanding of Philippians 4.[13]

25.14: 'Like clouds without rain is a man who boasts of gifts that he does not give.' It makes little difference for us whether the man described here merely poses as a greater benefactor than he actually is, or whether he does not give at all. The fact remains that the text assumes social prestige accrues to the one who gives[14] and places others in his debt. This prestige must be what the man seeks to gain through his boasting.

The book of Proverbs shares the same conception of reward for the righteous as Deuteronomy.[15] Social concern demonstrated in charity yields reward from Yahweh. This reward comes as material blessing. The reward is constantly presented as the motivation for benevolence.

(iii) Ecclesiastes 11.1–2

This pericope offers difficulties in interpretation owing to its metaphors and condensed language.[16] Two possibilities exist: Qoheleth is presenting advice about charitable giving or business enterprise. The balance of probability supports the first alternative for the following reasons.

First, there are Egyptian and Arabic proverbs which give similar

---

[12] William McKane, *Proverbs: A New Approach* (London: SCM Press, 1970): 534.

[13] See pp. 146–51, 155–7.

[14] This prestige appears to be at issue with Ananias and Sapphira in Acts 5. That giving may elevate one's social standing see P. J. Hamilton-Grierson, 'Gifts (Primitive and Savage)', *Encyclopedia of Religion and Ethics*, 7 vols., ed. James Hastings (Edinburgh: T & T Clark, 1908–1926): 6.197–209 (and the notes for sources from the nineteenth-century), Mauss, *The Gift*, and the comments on P. Mert. 12 and P. Oxy. 3057 on pp. 74–7, 80–2.

[15] Weinfeld, *Deuteronomy*, 312.

[16] We should not, however, despair of establishing the meaning of the text. *Contra* Graham Ogden, *Qoheleth* (Sheffield: JSOT Press, 1987): 184, 186.

advice: 'Do good, cast your bread upon the waters, and one day you will be rewarded',[17] and 'Do a good deed and throw it into the water; when it dries you will find it.'[18] Though the original understanding of the role of water in these proverbs is now lost to us,[19] what is obvious is their emphasis on charity. Even if these parallels are dependent on Ecclesiastes,[20] we at least have external attestation of the idea of reward coming from charitable giving.

Secondly, as obscure as its use here with water may be, *lehem* frequently occurs as the medium of charity,[21] or as a gift.[22] While a beggar in the twentieth-century west asks for money, those in the ancient east asked for bread. Moreover, 'A generous man will himself be blessed, for he shares his bread with the poor' (Prov. 22.9).

Thirdly, and related to the above, Qoheleth is replete with financial terms and descriptions.[23] *Lehem*, however, does not occur elsewhere as a metaphorical reference to money or investment.

Fourthly, it is hard to see why *kî* cannot be the grounds for v. 1a and 2a, but rather must have an adversative sense.[24] Though *kî* can have adversative force, this occurs typically after a negative.[25] Ogden supports this position by the structure of the pericope. The imperative portions (1a, 2a) have the common theme of distribution, while the concluding halves (1b, 2b) show the contrasting results of this action.[26] After asserting this point Ogden contends that, even though wisdom advice frequently was grounded on reward, the contrasting results of the distributive action in our text

---

[17] Cited by G. A. Barton, *A Critical and Exegetical Commentary on the Book of Ecclesiastes* (Edinburgh: T & T Clark, 1908): 181; J. L. Crenshaw, *Ecclesiastes: A Commentary* (London: SCM Press, 1988): 178; Ogden, *Qoheleth*, 184.

[18] M. Lichtheim, *Ancient Egyptian Literature*, 3 vols. (Berkeley: University of California Press, 1973–80): 3: 174. This text dates to the late Ptolemaic period. Also cited by M. V. Fox, *Qohelet and his Contradictions* (Sheffield: Almond Press, 1989): 274.

[19] Ogden, *Qoheleth*, 185.

[20] As suggested by Robert Gordis, *Koheleth – The Man and his World* (New York: Bloch, 1955): 320.

[21] Gen. 47.15; Deut. 10.18; Job 22.7; Ps. 37.25, 132.15, 146.7; Prov. 25.21; Isa. 58.7; Lam. 4.4; Ezek. 18.7, 16.

[22] 1 Sam. 9.7, 10.4, 25.11, 18; 2 Sam. 6.19; 1 Kgs. 14.3.

[23] James L. Kugel, 'Qohelet and Money', *CBQ* 51 (1989): 32. Mitchell J. Dahood ('Canaanite-Phoenician Influence in Qohelet', *Bib* 33 (1952): 220–1) provides a list of twenty-nine different terms.

[24] *Contra* Aarre Lauhe, *Kohelet* (Neukirchen: Neukirchener, 1978): 210.

[25] Ronald J. Williams, *Hebrew Syntax: An Outline* (Toronto: University of Toronto Press, 2nd edn repr., 1984): 72–3, 93.

[26] Ogden, *Qoheleth*, 184.

are better highlighted by treating *ki* as adversative.[27] This understanding forces the *ki* clauses to serve the presupposed structure, but if taken as causal there is no reason to see them as presenting contrasting results. Moreover, although 1b could easily be construed as a result (the bread is scattered, the bread will be found) it is not so easy to see the same relationship for 2b (the portions are given, the giver will be ignorant of coming hardship).

Fifthly, Delitzsch prefers to translate *natan le* as 'to divide into',[28] and although *natan le* does occur with the meaning 'to make into'[29] it does not appear that the texts cited support his point. The construction does not admit the idea of division, indeed in some cases multiplication is seen (Gen. 17.6, 20; 48.4). Here, the more simple 'give to' is preferable.

Finally, there is no conflict between liberality and Qohelet's general outlook.[30] The writer is not without some concern for the poor and the oppressed.[31] Also, if the *ki* clauses are taken as grounds for the preceding advice, then we see an element of self-protection in these words: give and you will get; give to many because you do not know when you may need help.[32] We also see an attempt to deal with some of the unknowns of life, certainly one of Qoheleth's major concerns.

Although the broad sweep of the Old Testament teaches that those who give to the poor will be rewarded, and although this reward is often presented as material prosperity, yet it is not clear that the giver will receive a reward from the receiver. God is the one who will repay the righteous for his good works. Nevertheless, this truth is employed as motivation to give; the certainty that God will repay should call forth giving.

Social conventions in the Old Testament

We have looked briefly at a few didactic texts which speak of reward coming from God to the one who shares financially. Though in Deuteronomy the expectation is for national reward, in the wisdom literature the expectation is for personal reward. This

---

[27] Ibid., 185.

[28] Franz Delitzsch (*Commentary on the Song of Songs and Ecclesiastes*, trans. M. G. Easton (Edinburgh: T & T Clark, 1891): 393) cites Gen. 17.20.

[29] Deut. 28.13; Isa. 42.24; Jer. 9.10; Ps. 106.46.

[30] *Contra* Gordis, *Koheleth*, 320.   [31] Eccles. 4.1, 5.8, 9.15–16.

[32] 'An enlightened self interest coincides with a proper social concern' (McKane, *Proverbs*, 435). The same idea is reflected in *ANET*, 413.

difference of perspective is significant. For now, as we come to examine examples of social exchange in the Old Testament, we see that repayment is actually worked out in practice with the expectation that men should repay good with good. That is, giving and receiving is viewed on a purely human level; Yahweh has been left out of the relationship triangle.[33]

(i) Genesis 33: Jacob's gift to Esau

Since reunion after long separation from his brother appears imminent, Jacob prepares a generous gift for the stated purpose of gaining his brother's favour (32.20). The key social interaction occurs in 33.4–11. Esau is already willing to forgive,[34] and this willingness should be obvious from his kiss and embrace (v. 4).[35] But Jacob is operating at a different level, as a vassal greets his patron.[36] This difference is seen in that Jacob requests *his lord* to accept the gift that he may find favour with him, whereas Esau refuses, telling *his brother* he has all he needs. Jacob's response of v. 10 shows that the acceptance of the gift will be seen as proof of Esau's favour.[37] Probably also acceptance of this gift will assure Jacob of future favour.[38] The construction is typical: 'If I have found favour in your eyes, then please . . .' Every time this construction occurs in the Old Testament the idea is plainly seen that the granting of a request is proof of favour.[39] Clark comments that the construction places the subject of the verb in a positive but subordinate formal relationship to the grantor, much like a patron–client relationship.[40]

The second time Jacob insists on acceptance the language is different. 'Please accept this gift', or 'take my blessing' (v.11:

---

[33] See our comments on Prov. 19.17 above, p. 25.

[34] Alfred Stuiber, 'Geschenk', *RAC* 10 (1978): 687.

[35] All Esau's actions betray his willingness to accept Jacob: He ran . . . embraced . . . fell on . . . and kissed. The construction appeared in 29.13 clearly as an expression of acceptance and welcome.

[36] Claus Westermann, *Genesis 12–36: A Commentary*, trans. John J. Scullion (Minneapolis: Augsburg, 1985): 524. Stuiber comments: 'Aufrichtig freundliche Gesinnung, Nomadensitte u. orientalische Diplomatie, allen Beteiligten wohlbewußt, mischen sich hier unentwirrbar' ('Geschenk', 687).

[37] S. R. Driver, *The Book of Genesis* (London: Methuen and Co. Ltd., 1904): 298; cf. 2 Sam. 14.22 below.

[38] Driver, *Genesis*, 299.

[39] Gen. 18.3, 19.9, 34.11, 47.29, 50.4; Ex. 33.12–13, 34.9; Num. 11.15, 32.5; Jud. 6.17; 1 Sam. 20.29, 27.5; 2 Sam. 14.22; Esth. 5.8, 7.3, 8.5.

[40] W. Malcolm Clark, 'The Righteousness of Noah', *VT* 21 (1971): 262.

birkati). Elsewhere *beraka* is used as a term for a gift,[41] so it is not difficult to see a possible word play. The source of all Jacob's anxiety arose in Genesis 27.36 where he took Esau's blessing, so now this offer could be taken as Jacob's giving back the blessing he had originally stolen.[42]

Esau's offer to lend aid in return is refused by Jacob, and Esau's lack of insistence on this point shows the fundamentally different view the two men have of their relationship. Jacob must only give for he feels that in this way he can secure the favour he needs. On the other hand, the gift is of no consequence to Esau, for nothing can be gained by it.

(ii)   Deuteronomy 24.13

According to the deuteronomic lawgiver, an Israelite lender should return a borrower's pledge (the cloak) before dusk in order that he may sleep in it. If this is done, the borrower will bless (*brk*) the lender. The assumption here appears to be that blessing is the socially appropriate response, apparently an expression of gratitude.[43]

(iii)   Judges 8.5-9

Gideon and his men, exhausted and hungry from their pursuit of the Midianites, stop to request provisions from the people of Succoth and Peniel (v. 5, 8). When refused aid, Gideon swears vengeance on those who did not show him hospitality (cf. 19.22, 20.17). The narrator gives no explicit justification for Gideon's brutal response (cf. 8.13-17). We know that hospitality was viewed as a virtue in the ancient Near East as it is today.[44] Perhaps we should have in view Succoth and Peniel's failure to supply Gideon

---

[41] 1 Sam. 25.27, 30.26; 2 Kgs. 5.15, 18.31 (= Isa. 36.16).

[42] Westermann, *Genesis*, 526.

[43] See below on 2 Sam. 14.22 and Job 29.13, 31.20, pp. 32-3, 35-6.

[44] de Vaux, *Ancient Israel*, 10. Gray refers to 'the accidental killing of a guest's camel in the Arab tribe of al-Basūs, which occasioned a forty-year tribal war' (John Gray, *Joshua, Judges, Ruth* (Basingstoke: Marshall, Morgan and Scott, 1986): 348). This appears to be at issue behind the narrator's use of Gen. 19 in Jud. 19. The inferior host of Jud. 19 is contrasted with the righteous Lot who excelled in hospitality. See Stuart Lasine, 'Guest and Host in Judges 19: Lot's Hospitality in an Inverted World', *JSOT* 29 (1984): 37-59 and T. Desmond Alexander, 'Lot's Hospitality, a Clue to his Righteousness', *JBL* 104 (1985): 289-91.

with needed provisions in his Holy War for Yahweh. In either case, this is not the only instance of the breakdown of social conventions in Judges, indeed it appears to be a significant theme.[45] Even though the narrator is silent as to whether Gideon is justified in this rage, we still see expectations regarding giving reflected here.

(iv)   Judges 8.35

According to the narrator, even though Gideon brought much good to the people, no sooner had he died than they resumed their evil activity: the Israelites worshipped Baals, forgot Yahweh and set up Baal-Berith as their god. Finally, we are told that they also failed to show loyalty (*ḥesed*) to the family of Gideon for all the good things that Gideon had done for them. This failure of loyalty is seen in their countenancing the murder of seventy of Gideon's sons. The LXX translators, however, appear to make the fault lie in the Israelites' failure to repay Gideon for the good he did to Israel.[46] That is, the crowning sin of the Israelites was their ingratitude. This condemnation is in keeping with the themes of social breakdown found throughout Judges. Failure to repay benefits, even to the descendants of the one who conferred them, is presented as reprehensible.

(v)   1 Samuel 25.1–17, 21

While wandering in the wilderness to escape Saul, David and his men met the shepherds of the wealthy Nabal. The soldiers treated the shepherds well, and during sheep shearing time[47] David sent a delegation to Nabal. David's men requested provisions from Nabal, reminding him of David's kindness and even calling on the testimony of Nabal's own men to substantiate this claim (vv. 7–8). Nabal refused to comply with this request and slandered David (vv.

[45] E.g., 3.12–27; 4.17–21; 19.1–30. This motif was first brought to our attention by Dr R. H. O'Connell.

[46] Jud. 8.35 LXX: καὶ οὐκ ἐποίησαν ἔλεος . . . κατὰ πᾶσαν την ἀγαθωσύνην, ἣν ἐποίησεν μετὰ Ισραηλ.

[47] According to H. P. Smith (*A Critical and Exegetical Commentary on the Books of Samuel* (Edinburgh: T & T Clark, 1912): 221): 'the sheep shearing was a festival . . . At such a time a large hospitality was customary.' *Contra* P. Kyle McCarter (*1 Samuel* (Garden City: Doubleday and Company, Inc., 1980): 397): 'In the present passage, then, it refers not to some official holiday . . . but simply to an occasion of good eating and drinking.' For our purposes it does not appear that the nature of the occasion influences the grounds for the claim made.

10–11), which response brought an outburst of anger (v. 13). David vows to kill every man in Nabal's household (v. 22). Nabal's wife Abigail was informed of David's destructive plan by a servant whose words substantiated David's claim (vv. 14–16).[48] She quickly dispatched a generous gift, delivering it and an apology herself, which had the desired effect of saving (at least from David) Nabal and his men. Her gift is labelled *beraka* (cf. Gen. 33.11).

It appears that the narrator understands David's kind treatment as giving him grounds to request a favour.[49] David complained that the kindness he had shown had been in vain (v. 21, *lasseqer*; cf. Jer. 3.23, 8.8). By implication we can assume David had expected a reward for his unsolicited protection of Nabal's property.[50] Instead of the good he had counted on, he has been rewarded with evil (v. 21b).[51] Though David was informed of Nabal's insults, the narrator presents no other motive for David's anger than Nabal's ingratitude.[52] Thus, Nabal's primary offence is based on his social misconduct, not on his failure to recognize David's authority.[53]

Others see the background of this incident in military diplomacy. Wiseman suggests that Nabal's men had been with David's in the wilderness as co-operating allies and that David's approach can be seen as an act of negotiation, inviting Nabal to enter into a regulated covenant with David.[54] Wiseman suggests that the phrase 'to ask the peace' (25.6) should be understood as carrying a diplomatic meaning. Though 'to ask the peace' can indeed have a diplomatic usage,[55] Wiseman himself admits its use in personal greetings.[56] It does not appear that the context or the greeting used by David's envoys suggests a military relationship.

---

48   Ralph W. Klein, *1 Samuel* (Waco: Word, 1983): 249; Hans W. Hertzberg, *1 & 2 Samuel. A Commentary*, trans. John Bowden (London: SCM Press, 1964): 202.
49   Jon D. Levenson, '1 Samuel 25 as Literature and as History', *CBQ* 40 (1978): 20 n. 17.
50   Yochanan Muffs, 'Abraham the Noble Warrior: Patriarchal Politics and Laws of War in Ancient Israel', *JJS* 33 (1982): 95.
51   Cf. Gen. 44.4; 2 Sam. 14.17; Ps. 7.4; 35.12; 38.20; 109.5; Prov. 17.13; Jer. 18.20.
52   Notice the parallel with Gideon (Jud. 8.5–9) becoming furious over a similar refusal of hospitality.
53   *Contra* Adele Berlin, 'Characterization in Biblical Narrative: David's Wives', *JSOT* 23 (1982): 77.
54   D. J. Wiseman, ' "Is it Peace?" Covenant and Diplomacy', *VT* 32 (1982): 318.
55   Wiseman, 'Covenant and Diplomacy', 323. See, e.g., Jud. 18.15; 2 Sam. 8.10.
56   Wiseman, 'Covenant and Diplomacy', 317. But the examples cited (Jud. 19.20; 1 Sam. 25.6; 1 Chr. 12.18; Dan. 10.19) do not contain *ša'al* as in 1 Sam. 17.22, 20.31; Jer. 15.5.

Muffs contends that according to some ancient near eastern customs the vassal is obligated to provide food and drink for the overlord's troops when engaged in defence of an ally.[57] As with the response given above we may say, first, that we do not appear to be dealing with a military context. Nabal's men are not presented as soldiers but shepherds. Secondly, the evidence Muffs draws from treaties implies previous agreement to abide by the treaty stipulations. Such a case is not presented here. Thirdly, not only is an alliance not given as the grounds for David's request, but the actual grounds are presented in detail: David was good to the shepherds, he did not mistreat them, he took no cattle,[58] and he was a wall around them (25.15–16). Only this last reason may be construed in such a way as to make David an ally, but the text itself[59] suggests that David acted more as a defence against the normal dangers of the country (e.g., bandits, wild animals) than as a military ally. Finally, if the narrator intended to draw an analogy between Nabal and Saul,[60] then it would suffice to present the more basic social failure of returning evil for good (cf. 24.17; 25.21).

1 Samuel 25 is informative for the unassuming way that reciprocity arises between the actors. David gives unsolicited protection to a group of shepherds. Gratitude is owed in the form of material repayment. Everyone depicted in the narrative knows that this return is owed to David for his favours; everyone, that is, except the Fool.

(vi)   2 Samuel 14.22

Joab was keen to see David call Absalom back from banishment and devised a plan to accomplish this (14.1–3). Although it was the woman of Tekoa who persuaded the king (vv. 4–17), David recognized this trick as from the hand of Joab (v. 19). After the king agreed to send for his son (v. 21) Joab expressed his reaction in v. 22. According to 22a, 'Joab fell with his face to the ground to pay him honour, and he blessed the king.' Though *brk* may here be

---

57 Muffs, 'Abraham the Noble Warrior', 89.
58 Hertzberg, *1 & 2 Samuel*, 202. The thrice mentioned fact that 'nothing was missing' seems to be the most important consideration (25.7, 15, 21); cf. the reward Israel should receive for its omissions in 2 Chr. 20.11–12.
59 'Night and day they were a wall around us all the time we were *herding our sheep* near them' (25.16; emphasis added).
60 Robert P. Gordon, 'David's Rise and Saul's Demise: Narrative Analogy in Samuel 24–26', *TynBul* 31 (1980): 37–64, esp. 48.

used as an expression of homage or obeisance,[61] it is probably better to see Joab as expressing exaggerated thanks.[62] *Brk* certainly has this meaning in other texts.[63] Though Absalom's return is apparently very important for Joab, the reasons are not obvious.[64]

Then, in 22b, 'Joab said, "Today your servant knows that he has found favour in your eyes, my lord the king, because the king has granted his servant's request."' We should note that this exchange confirms our findings at Genesis 33.10: the granting of a request is seen as evidence of goodwill.

(vii)   2 Kings 4.8–17

Elisha often enjoyed the hospitality of a well-to-do Shunamite woman and her husband. This couple decided to build private quarters for the prophet's use whenever he visited. We are told that during one visit Elisha asked, 'You have gone to all this trouble for us. Now what can be done for you?' (v. 13a). The woman declines Elisha's offer to speak on her behalf to the king or commander of the army,[65] and finally it is Gehazi who proposes an appropriate recompense:[66] 'Well, she has no son and her husband is old' (v. 14b). Elisha predicts that she will bear a son the following year (v. 16a). In her response she asks the prophet not to mislead her (v. 16b). After the son dies she reminds Elisha, 'Didn't I tell you, "Don't raise my hopes"?' (v. 28), which appears to be a reference to the statement of v.16b.

The woman plays an unusually prominent role in initiating kind treatment of the prophet. It is the woman who recognizes Elisha as

---

[61] Hertzberg, *1 & 2 Samuel*, 334; Stuiber, 'Eulogia', 901.

[62] Gutbrod rightly refers to 'die von Dankbarkeit und Lob überströmenden Worte Joabs' (Karl Gutbrod, *Das Buch vom Reich. Das zweite Buch Samuel* (Stuttgart: Calwer, 1958): 171; cf. Smith, *Samuel*, 337).

[63] Ex. 39.43; Deut. 24.13; Prov. 11.26; see A. Murtonen, 'The Use and Meanings of the Words L^ebarek and B^eraka^h in the Old Testament', *VT* 9 (1959): 168–70 and comments on Job below.

[64] Smith, *Samuel*, 337; Gutbrod, *Samuel*, 171.

[65] 'She replied, "I have a home among my own people"' (v. 13b). According to Gray, 'This truly reflects the temper of the ancient Israelite peasantry, which, as modern Arab peasantry, were settled in kin-groups, where social obligations were clearly defined and seriously accepted, the rights of each being safeguarded by all' (John Gray, *1 & 2 Kings* (London: SCM Press, 2nd ed, 1970): 496). Yet no mention is made of this exchange between Elisha and the woman.

[66] Robert Alter, 'How Convention Helps Us Read: The Case of the Bible's Annunciation Type-Scene', *Proof* 3 (1983): 126.

a holy man of God,[67] which is probably a recognition not only of his moral character but also of his power to perform miracles.[68] It is the woman who initiates hospitality (v. 8) and the woman who proposes the idea to build a room for the prophet (v. 10).[69] As a result of all these efforts, Elisha appears to be very concerned to find the necessary way to return the woman's kindness, to make the required social response.[70] As Alter says, the issue appears to be recompense.[71] Although a man of God may elsewhere refuse a gift (*beraka*, 2 Kgs. 5.15), in the socially different situation with the Shunamite it is acceptable to receive her gift. And yet repayment is also very important, for the prophet seeks to discharge his obligations.

(viii)   2 Chronicles 20.10-11[72]

On hearing that a vast army of Moabites, Ammonites and Meunites was gathering against him (v. 1), Jehoshaphat proclaimed a fast (v. 3) and delivered a prayer before the assembly of Judah and Jerusalem (v. 5). He recalled that Yahweh did not allow Israel to invade these lands on coming out of Egypt (v. 10; cf. Deut. 2.1–19). Although Jehoshaphat's words are themselves ambiguous ('See how they are repaying us', 11a), in the context they can only be taken as a negative evaluation of the enemy's action. The really reprehensible nature of the army's attack is clearly that they are repaying evil for good.[73] Here we see the concept of gratitude or repayment working at a national level just as it does at an

---

67   Although Elisha is frequently referred to as a man of God (e.g., 2 Kgs. 4.7, 25–7; 5.8; 6.6, 9–10; 7.17–19; 8.2) the addition of 'holy' is unique to this text.

68   In the dialogues between the messengers of Ahaziah and Elijah the ability to perform a miracle is proof that the one addressed as a man of God indeed fits the title (2 Kgs. 1.9–13).

69   We can compare the Shunamite's behaviour with that of Lydia, whose persistent hospitality won over Paul and his associates in Acts 16.15.

70   His question, *meh la ʿaśōt lak* (4.13) is in the LXX: τì δεῖ ποιῆσαι σοι. The same construction in Esth. 1.14 (*meh la ʿaśōt*, LXX: δεῖ ποιῆσαι) certainly carries the meaning of necessity. The context alone in Esther makes this clear, however. Compare the gifts offered as gratitude in 1 Kgs. 13.7; 2 Kgs. 5.15; Dan. 2.48.

71   Alter, 'Convention', 126.

72   Since most of the material in 2 Chr. 20 is unique to Chronicles (Raymond B. Dillard, *2 Chronicles* (Waco: Word, 1987): 153), there is some debate about its historicity. Fortunately for our purpose the decision on historicity will not affect the validity of drawing conclusions on the social conventions reflected in the narrative.

73   Edward L. Curtis, *A Critical and Exegetical Commentary of the Books of Chronicles* (Edinburgh: T & T Clark, 1910): 406.

individual level.[74] Moreover, the great gap of time since this good deed originally done by Israel, which occurred some centuries previous, does not relieve the obligation.[75] To put it simply: since Israel did not attack Moab and Ammon, Moab and Ammon are obliged, as an expression of proper social conduct, not to attack Israel.[76]

We should stress the significance of this text. First, the ideology assumed by the writer(s) is clearly one of reciprocity. A good deed done must be remembered and must evoke the goodwill of the receiver. Secondly, this goodwill must be seen in the appropriate action of the receiver. Thirdly, the passing of time is not a serious consideration. Though years elapse, the goodwill should still be evident. Finally, reciprocity is a general convention which operates at several levels in society, not only between individuals, but also between groups and, we could conclude, also between an individual and a group. We shall note these four characteristics again in our treatment of reciprocity.[77]

(ix) Job 29.13 and 31.20

The lengthy discourses and responses in the book of Job are occasioned because of a certain assumption about the activity of God: God will give material rewards and health to the person who is righteous. If a person, such as Job, is destitute and ill, it is obvious that the cause must be sin. Thus, in its entirety, this massive book testifies to common acceptance of the teaching on reward which we saw in Proverbs. Here we focus on two particularly helpful texts.

In defence of his own righteousness before his 'friends' Job called

---

[74] The concept of national debt for a favour conveyed by another nation is a common one in Greek history. In times of war these obligations become critical (e.g., Thuc. 1.32.1; 1.33.1–2; 1.41.1–3; Polyb. 3.98.7–11; 4.23.1; 4.38.8–10; Diod. Sic. 15.26.1).

[75] Whether or not the actual dates of the events presented in Deut. 2 and 2 Chr. 20 can be established is not important. Clearly the narrative as it exists portrays Jehoshaphat's prayer as occurring over 300 years after Israel refrained from invading Ammon and Moab.

[76] Goettsberger rightly refers to 'die Undankbarkeit der Gegner' (Johann Goettsberger, *Die Bücher der Chronik oder Paralipomenon* (Bonn: Peter Hanstein, 1939): 288). This aspect of the social world is not mentioned by Dillard, *2 Chronicles*, H. G. M. Williamson, *1 and 2 Chronicles* (London: Marshall Morgan & Scott, 1982), or Jacob M. Myer, *II Chronicles* (Garden City: Doubleday and Company, Inc., 1965).

[77] See our conclusions to chapter 3, pp. 88–9.

on his good deeds. He mentioned the good reputation he had, that those who heard his name spoke well of him because he had rescued the poor and the fatherless. In addition, the man who was dying blessed Job and he made the widow's heart sing (29.13). The same thought occurs in 31.20: Job would gladly accept the terrible things which were happening to him if he did not help the needy (vv. 16–19), if the man without a garment did not bless Job in his heart because Job warmed him with clothing.

We may draw two conclusions: first, the writer presents Job and his friends as those who believe that there is a direct connection between charity on the one hand and material blessing from God, along with social prestige, on the other. Though material blessing is not called a return or a reward, it clearly has this function. Secondly, though they present hypothetical situations, the two responses the needy offer to Job in these texts present to us the accepted social reaction to generosity: blessing. Here the meaning is clearly one of gratitude.[78] Where we might expect εὐχαριστέω the material equivalent is *brk*.[79]

From the above survey of canonical material we can see that didactic texts of the Old Testament make very clear that Yahweh encourages charitable giving. Further, Israel's God will repay, either in blessing the nation or the individual giver. This teaching creates for us a model of a social triangle, with a giver, a receiver, and God being the third member. There is a complete absence of teaching in the Old Testament which requires the receiver to supply a social repayment for aid received.

When we come to narrative sections of the Old Testament, however, we see that the exchange of gifts and services is a significant aspect of the social life. Although reciprocal obligation (or other aspects of social exchange) is not prescribed in didactic

---

78   Stuiber, 'Eulogia', 901; cf. Deut. 24.13; 1 Chr. 18.9–10; Neh. 11.2; Prov. 11.26. Though expressions of gratitude between individuals certainly occur in the Old Testament, we might observe, first, their surprising rarity, and secondly, the scarcity of εὐχαριστέω in the LXX. Many places would seem to warrant the use of this word-group, yet it figures only in Prov. 11.16 (εὐχάριστος). *Barak* and *beraka* are predominantly rendered by εὐλογέω or εὐλογία even when the meaning of the text appears to be thereby distorted (e.g., Job 29.13, 31.20). This may have arisen in an attempt to avoid *barak*/εὐχαριστέω being misunderstood by non-Jewish readers, since the semantic overlap of the two is small (cf. Stuiber, 'Eulogia', 906).

79   H. Conzelmann, 'εὐχαριστέω κτλ', *TDNT*, 9.410.

texts, its description in narrative texts shows it to have been an assumed and strong social convention.

Further, although expressions of gratitude do seem to exist, these are made, physically, with a counter-gift or favour (1 Sam. 25; 2 Kgs. 4) or, verbally, with a blessing (Job 29.13, 31.20; 2 Sam. 14.22). Typically, when *barak* is exchanged between individuals it functions as an expression of verbal gratitude. Εὐχαριστέω, however, is notable for its absence in the Greek Old Testament.[80] The LXX has rendered these verbal expressions of thanks translating *barak* almost exclusively with εὐλογία.

Extra-biblical Jewish sources

Although Old Testament writers are unanimous in asserting that charitable giving deserves a reward, we may rightly question the status of this teaching in the Hellenistic Judaism of the first century. Has the influence of Greek and Roman thought caused the Jews to depart from their ancient teaching?

Thus, to gain a fuller understanding of the Jewish context in which Paul also had roots, we shall look at a few texts which touch on two aspects of our subject: first, those texts which reveal assumptions about the reward that accrues to the giver of charity and, secondly, those texts which reveal something of the accepted social conventions of Hellenistic Judaism.

Tobit 2.11–14

Some time after Tobit became blind, his wife Anna brought home a goat as extra payment[81] for work as a weaver. Tobit, not believing her, but thinking the goat might be stolen, told her to return it. She responded: 'What about your alms? What about your good works? Everyone knows what return you have had for them' (2.14b).[82]

---

[80] As mentioned above, the εὐχαριστ- group occurs only in Prov. 11.16 in the LXX, although Aquila uses it to render *yada* in Lev. 7.12; Ps. 41.5, 49.14, 68.31, 106.22, 146.7; Amos 4.5.

[81] We notice that she labels the animal a gift (Δόσει δέδοταί μοι ἐπὶ τῷ μισθῷ).

[82] New Jerusalem Bible, cf. J. C. Cancy, *The Shorter Books of the Apocrypha* (Cambridge: Cambridge University Press, 1972): 23; A. Miller and J. Schildenberger, *Die Bücher Tobias, Judith und Esther* (Bonn: Peter Hanstein, 1940): 48: 'Was hast du von deiner ganzen Liebestätigkeit in deiner Blindheit jetzt geerntet?' This is probably the best way to understand the words whether we follow the manuscript BA (ἰδοὺ γνωστὰ πάντα μετὰ σοῦ) or S (ἰδὲ ταῦτα μετὰ σοῦ γνωστά ἐστιν).

Tobit's alms are critical to his story. Their repeated appearance draws the reader's attention to Tobit's righteousness (cf. 1.3, 16; 4.7; 12.9). These righteous deeds call out for a reward from God. Tobit's return, however, is blindness.[83] Thus it appears that 2.11–14 takes up the theme of Tobit's alms and asks the question, which was asked by Job,[84] How can one receive the theologically inappropriate reward of evil for good? Since Anna's words are given to justify having the kid, we can see the significance of it being designated a 'gift': she sees it as a small return for Tobit's alms which he receives back even in the midst of his suffering.

Sirach 3.31[85]

The references to social reciprocity found in Ben Sirach are especially interesting, partly due to the variation between the Hebrew and Greek texts of this work. There are several references which the Greek text appears to make more explicit as a comment on social reciprocity. The Hebrew certainly reflects the idea that alms are an important part of a wise man's life (7.32–3), even that they atone for sins (3.30; cf. 29.12) and that the giver will be rewarded (3.31). Yet it is rarely explicit that this reward will be given by the original receiver. In 3.31 the source of the reward is left unexpressed. It simply states: 'The kindness a person has done crosses his path as he goes; when he falls he finds a support.'[86]

The Greek of this text, however, refers plainly to social reciprocity. It states: 'He who repays favours is mindful of the future; and in the day of his fall he will find support.'[87] Skehan/Di Lella prefer the translation: 'He who repays kindnesses (i.e., God) remembers for the future.'[88] Though this latter rendering is possible, it creates a very harsh transition to the latter half of the verse.

---

83 Contrast Cornelius, whose alms merit him the reward of having his eyes opened to the gospel (Acts 10.4, 30–3, 44–8).

84 Miller/Schildenberger, *Tobias*, 48.

85 Unless otherwise noted the (unpointed) Hebrew text for Ben Sirach is taken from Smend, *Jesus Sirach*, the Greek from Rahlfs, *Septuaginta*.

86 *pwʿl ṭwv yqrʾnw bdrkyw wbʿt mwṭw ymṣʾ mšʿn*. The English translation is from Patrick W. Skehan and Alexander Di Lella, *The Wisdom of Ben Sira* (New York: Doubleday, 1987): 162.

87 Our translation (ὁ ἀνταποδίδους χάριτας μέμνηται εἰς τὰ μετὰ ταῦτα καὶ ἐν καιρῷ πτώσεως αὐτοῦ εὑρήσει στήριγμα). For this meaning of μιμνήσκομαι see Deut. 8.2; Isa. 63.7; Barn. 19.10.

88 Skehan/Di Lella, *Ben Sira*, 163. Skehan/Di Lella cite Tobit 14.10–11 as a parallel.

In addition to avoiding such a transition, our rendering is consistent with very similar ideas found in Ecclesiastes 11.1–2.[89] The one who repays the favour he receives is wise. By repaying he places the original giver in his debt and may expect a return at a later date. Thus he considers the future by preparing a defence for himself against unexpected financial hardship.

1 Maccabees 10–11

In their war Demetrius and Alexander Epiphanes recognized Jonathan as a force to be reckoned with.[90] Both vied for his allegiance. In a letter Demetrius promises kind treatment toward the Jews if they remain steadfast in their friendship (ἐνεμείνατε τῇ φιλίᾳ, 10.26) and that he would requite them appropriately for this behaviour (ἀνταποδώσομεν ὑμῖν ἀγαθὰ ἀνθ᾽ ὧν ποιεῖτε μεθ᾽ ἡμῶν, 10.27). These offers are spurned by the people (10.46–7). Instead they gave their allegiance to Alexander. A few years later, when Demetrius II became king (11.19), Jonathan took gifts to the new king and won his favour (11.24). In an official letter from Demetrius to the Jews he promised to do good to them because of their goodwill toward the king (τῷ ἔθνει τῶν Ιουδαίων . . . . ἐκρίναμεν ἀγαθὸν ποιῆσαι χάριν τῆς ἐξ αὐτῶν εὐνοίας πρὸς ἡμᾶς, 11.33). Later, at the king's request Jonathan sent 3,000 troops to aid Demetrius (11.44). When times of peace came, however, Demetrius proved false to his promises and did not pay back Jonathan properly for his favours (οὐκ ἀνταπέδωκεν τὰς εὐνοίας, ἃς ἀνταπέδωκεν αὐτῷ, 11.53).

The ideology of the narrator is clearly one of recompense: one is obliged to return goodwill with goodwill and favours with favours. As we saw earlier on 2 Chronicles 20.10–11, the same convention which applies to ordinary individuals applies to leaders and nations.

Sirach 4.31

In this text the writer recommends, 'Let not your hand be open to receive and clenched when it is time to give.'[91] This passage is

---

[89] See the treatment of this text above, pp. 25–7.

[90] Sidney Tedesche and Solomon Zeitlin, *The First Book of Maccabees* (New York: Harper and Brothers, 1950): 170.

[91] Skehan/Di Lella, Ben Sira, 174. The Hebrew reads: *'l thy ydk ptwḥḥ lqḥt wbʿt ḥšb*

instructive for its simple use of the terms giving and receiving. Clearly it is a reference to the exchange of good deeds; one should be willing to be both the recipient and the giver of good.

Here the Greek translation appears to be better than the English supplied by Skehan and Di Lella: μὴ ἔστω ἡ χείρ σου ἐκτεταμένη εἰς τὸ λαβεῖν καὶ ἐν τῷ ἀποδιδόναι συνεσταλμένη. For the time to give back in Greek (ἀποδιδόναι) is in Hebrew literally 'in the time of the return' (wb't hšb). That is, one should not withhold the hand when the time comes to repay the earlier favour. As was mentioned earlier, ἀποδιδόναι appears frequently in contexts of social exchange.[92]

Sirach 7.27–8

Unfortunately the Hebrew of these verses has been lost through parablepsis.[93] Yet the thought is congruent with 3.1–16. Here Sirach asserts: Honour your father with your whole heart and do not forget your mother's birth pains. Remember that you owe your being to them. How can you repay them for what they have done for you?[94]

Skehan and Di Lella are correct when they comment that adults are to honour aging parents not only because the Law of God says so, but also because the law of gratitude demands the same.[95] But what is this law of gratitude and to which culture does it apply? Skehan and Di Lella provide no references to the social background of obligation to one's parents. According to some, children owe the greatest debt of gratitude to their parents. This is true, not only because parents have given their children life, but also because they have supplied their children with all the necessary supports of life. These activities are great benefactions which children can never

qpwṣh. Here ptwḥh is the variant reading of Cod. A. provided in Smend's notes. The text reads mwšṭt.

[92] 'Αποδιδόναι often appears with ἀμοιβή or a similar term. See, e.g., Arist. Eth. Nic. 9.1.7; Diod. Sic. 1.90.2; 15.26.1; Dio Chrys. Or. 31.27, 53; 44.5; Philo Spec. 2.234; P.Oxy. 705.61 (c. AD 200). See also our comments immediately following on Sirach 7.28.

[93] Benjamin G. Wright, No Small Difference: Sirach's Relationship to its Hebrew Parent Text (Atlanta: Scholars Press, 1989): 158.

[94] Our translation: ₂₇ Ἐν ὅλῃ καρδίᾳ σου δόξασον τὸν πατέρα καὶ μητρὸς ὠδῖνας μὴ ἐπιλάθῃ· ₂₈ μνήσθητι ὅτι δι' αὐτῶν ἐγεννήθης, καὶ τί ἀνταποδώσεις αὐτοῖς καθὼς αὐτοὶ σοί;

[95] Skehan/Di Lella, Ben Sira, 206.

repay.[96] We shall have further recourse to this aspect of social convention below.[97]

Sirach 12.1–2

The texts we have seen earlier in Sirach have encouraged the giving of alms and promised the reward that will come to the giver. Here we find a caution concerning proper giving. 12.1–2 clearly teaches that when one wishes to benefit another (εὖ ποιεῖν) one should be careful to select the right recipient: 'If you do good, know for whom you are doing it, and your kindness will have its effect. Do good to the just and reward will be yours, if not from him, from the Lord.'[98]

What is the effect of kindness? 12.2 suggests that the desired effect is reward, i.e., social repayment (cf. 20.10). In order for one to receive repayment (ἀνταπόδομα)[99] for his good deed, one must make sure he selects the just man as a recipient. The just man will feel the appropriate social pressure to repay. This is a teaching we do not find in the Old Testament, but which is common in Greco-Roman literature.[100]

Sirach 41.19d

In a list of things the righteous man should be ashamed of, one encounters the exhortation: '(Be ashamed) of refusing to give when asked.'[101] There is nothing here to suggest a commercial context and indeed the Hebrew text clearly refers to the duty of alms-

[96] According to Philo none can be more truly called benefactors than parents in relation to their children (*Spec.* 2.229; *Decal.* 112; cf. Arist. *Eth. Nic.* 8.11.1–4; Seneca *Ben.* 5.5.2; SelPap. 1.121.27–28 (2nd AD); 1 Tim. 5.4: ἀμοιβὰς ἀποδιδόναι τοῖς προγόνοις).

[97] See the treatment of Josephus *AP.* 2.206 and Philo *LA.* 3.10 below (pp. 45, 48), as well as Phlm. 17–19 and 2 Cor. 6.13 (pp. 185–91, 172–4).

[98] Skehan/Di Lella, *Ben Sira*, 242. The Hebrew reads:
v. 1 ʿm ṭṭyb dʿ lmy ṭṭyb wyhy ṭybh lṭwbtk.
v. 2 hyṭb lṣdyq wmṣʿ tslwmt ʿm lʿ mmnw myyy.

[99] Note the use of ἀνταπόδομα in Luke 14.12. There Jesus gives the exact opposite teaching as found here in Sirach 12.2: One should not invite friends to a dinner, lest one receive *repayment* (ἀνταπόδομα) by being invited in return.

[100] See pp. 67, 69–71. According to Seneca, the proper recipient is one who will show gratitude (χάρις, cf. *Ben.* 1.1.2; 1.10.4–5; 2.18.5–6).

[101] That one should be quick to give when asked is a social expectation we see asserted elsewhere (cf. Jud. 8.5–9; Matt. 5.42; Luke 11.5–8; Did. 4.7; Barn. 19.11).

giving.[102] We would expect Sirach to teach that one should be ashamed to refuse (cf. 29.8–13). The Greek, however, presents a slightly different social demand: one should be ashamed of contempt of giving and receiving (ἀπὸ σκορακισμοῦ λήμψεως καὶ δόσεως). In this list of shameful things the pattern has been: One should be ashamed before (ἀπό) someone concerning (περί) something. The structure changes from v. 19c, which reads: (Be ashamed) of resting the elbow at dinner (ἀπὸ πηξέως ἀγκῶνος ἐπ' ἄρτοις). If this is correct, then it is asserted here that one should be ashamed of contempt for (objective genitive) giving and receiving.

The question is what sort of giving and receiving this might be. The answer is made difficult due to the lack of a qualifying genitive to supply the object of the transaction. We can be certain that this passing, unexplained remark is assumed to be comprehensible to the readers and that δόσις καὶ λῆμψις here must be a condensed label for a well-known referent. But is this referent the debit and credit of pecuniary transactions or the give and take of social reciprocity?

The context favours a social interpretation. From v. 17 the emphasis is very much on social sins: immorality, falsehood, deceit, crime, disloyalty, theft, breaking an oath and poor table manners. A reminder to be ashamed of contempt for giving and receiving is more readily understood if this transaction is a social one and not an economic one. Why would one have contempt for receipts and expenditures? For record keeping? On the other hand a contempt for social interaction and the attendant debt is comprehensible.

Josephus

Thus far in our study, the texts that clearly depict the operation of social reciprocity have been relatively rare. We have presented most of those found. By contrast, the material available in Josephus, and also in Philo below, is so abundant that we must be very selective in what we present. In general Josephus reflects the same social assumptions as Philo, though, being more concerned with history, these assumptions are more often displayed in narrative rather than in didactic texts.

We shall follow the same pattern in our presentation of material

---

[102] Skehan/Di Lella, *Ben Sira*, 481. These authors, however, offer no comment on the significance of δόσις καὶ λῆμψις.

from Philo and Josephus as we have followed with earlier texts. First, we shall consider statements on the reward from God which comes to the giver of charity. Secondly, we shall present texts which demonstrate the social conventions operating in the social world of the writer.

(i) Reward from God

Only one passage has been found where Josephus links reward from God to giving. Earlier we had the opportunity to look at Deuteronomy 15.10. That text taught national, material reward for lending to the poor when the prospect of repayment is slim.[103] In *AJ* 4.266, Josephus provides comments on lending at interest, or rather the prohibition against it. Josephus asserts that when one aids another with an interest free loan one should consider as profit the recipient's gratitude (κέρδος εἶναι νομίζειν τήν τ᾽ ἐκείνων εὐχαριστίαν) and the reward that comes from God because of generosity (τὴν ἀμοιβὴν τὴν παρὰ τοῦ θεοῦ γενησομένην ἐπὶ τῇ χρηστότητι). At the risk of appearing redundant we will point out three assumptions underlying *AJ* 4.266: (1) the appropriate social response to aid is thanksgiving, and this is probably immaterial (e.g., verbal as opposed to financial),[104] (2) the original giver is socially profited by expressions of thanks directed to him, and (3) such good deeds will receive a reward from Yahweh.

(ii) Social convention in giving and receiving

There are two further ways we can see social reciprocity arising in Josephus' work. First, we might expect that in Josephus' presentation of history he would refer to gift and service relationships between the actors, especially between the Greek and Roman characters. This he does. But not only that, he presents also such relationships between the Jewish characters. Secondly, we might expect Josephus to make clear from his personal comments or analysis of the interaction between people in his history that he also operates with the same social assumptions. This he does also. He censures the ungrateful, praises the beneficent and calls for the

---

[103] See above, p. 24.
[104] Note that the actual return (ἀμοιβή) does not come from the receiver, therefore the thanks the receiver renders (εὐχαριστία) are probably verbal.

proper discharge of social obligations contracted through giving and receiving.

For example, in *AJ* 19.184, Josephus provides a portion of a speech made by Sentius Saturninus in the senate. Sentius applauds Cassius Chaerea for his work in having tyranny overthrown and adds, 'It is a most noble deed, and such as becomes free men, to requite a benefactor, such as this man is.'[105] Though it is reported speech, we may say that the positive function this citation plays in Josephus' narrative displays this Jew's acceptance of a social convention which is widespread among the Greeks: the one who has received a good deed must express his thanks through a counter deed.[106] That this is indeed Josephus' own opinion is clear from his comments in *AJ* 8.300: since Baasha, king of Israel, did not rule justly, a prophet came to warn him that God would destroy him. The reason for the punishment lies in Baasha's ingratitude. Even after God had made him king, he did not repay the Lord's kindness by ruling justly.[107]

On the other hand, the record of Baasha's reign, found in 1 Kings 15.25–34, says nothing of his ingratitude. But because Josephus has accepted social reciprocity, he feels free to read the appropriate conventions back into the texts of the Old Testament. Even where there appears to be no reference to this type of social expectation, his explanation of the texts refers to the motivations of the actors and sometimes says their motives lay in repayment for benefits received.

For example, Josephus refers to the story of Elisha cleansing the water supply at Jericho (2 Kgs. 2.19–22). Josephus claims that, because Elisha had often been the recipient of the town's hospitality, the prophet requited the city by conferring this everlasting benefit on them (ἀμείβεται καὶ τὴν χώραν αἰωνίῳ χάριτι, *BJ* 4.461). Further, Josephus mentions the hereditary friendship with Hiram which Solomon received from his father.[108] Their friendship is seen in the gifts they exchange. Hiram gave Solomon 120 talents

---

105 LCL trans: ἔργον δὲ κάλλιστον καὶ ἐλευθέροις ἀνδράσι πρέπον ἀμείβεσθαι τοὺς εὐεργέτας.

106 W. C. van Unnik, 'Eine merkwürdige liturgische Aussage bei Josephus (Jos. Ant. 8,111–13)', *Josephus Studien*, ed. O. Betz, K. Haacker and M. Hengel (Göttingen: Vandenhoeck and Ruprecht, 1974): 364.

107 ὅτι βασιλεὺς ὑπ' αὐτοῦ γενόμενος, οὐκ ἠμείψατο τὴν εὐεργεσίαν τῷ δικαίως προστῆναι τοῦ πλήθους καὶ εὐσεβῶς.

108 πατρικὴν φιλίαν (*Ap.* 1.110). On inherited friendship see Herman, *Ritualized Friendship*, 69–72.

of gold and cut timber for the Temple. In return, not as payment but as a gift (ἀντεδωρήσατο) Solomon gave him many other things. But this exchange of gifts was not the main bond of their friendship, which was based primarily on their passion for learning (*Ap.* 1.110–11).

Josephus presents us with another opportunity to mention the unique place of parents as benefactors. In the ancient world parents were considered great benefactors in relation to their children, both in Greco-Roman and in Jewish cultures.[109] In his defence of the Jewish law Josephus appeals to this common conception. He asserts that the Law ranks honour to parents second only to honour to God (*Ap.* 2.206).[110] Though the fifth commandment legislates honour for parents, Josephus goes further in stating that, if a son does not repay his parents, the Law hands him over to be stoned.[111]

We may draw at least two conclusions from this text. First, the repayment of parents for their many benefactions is important for Josephus. Secondly, since *Contra Apionem* is an apologetic treatise directed against Greek detractors, we have reason to assert that Josephus believes his statement in 2.206 will find approval with his audience, that it will help him to win sympathy for the Law of God at this point. Thus, repayment for parents is seen to be a widespread social expectation. As we shall see more clearly in chapter 3, this expectation is based on the more general conventions of giving and receiving.

Philo

In general it appears that Philo has fully accepted Greco-Roman social conventions of giving and receiving. Indeed, he has done so to such an extent that, just as Josephus, he instinctively reads these conventions back into the biblical texts which he seeks to understand. In our study, Philo marks the last stage before a turn to complete Greco-Roman social reciprocity.

---

[109] See Sirach 7.27–28 above, pp. 40–1.

[110] Josephus may find support for his belief in the placement of the fifth commandment immediately after those commandments relating to God (Ex. 20.12; Deut. 5.16).

[111] τὸν οὐκ ἀμειβόμενον τὰς παρ᾽ αὐτῶν χάριτας ἀλλ᾽ εἰς ὁτιοῦν ἐλλείποντα λευσθησόμενον παραδίδωσι. Josephus may be drawing on Deut. 21.18: the rebellious son, who does not obey (viz., give repayment in the form of obedience) his parents, is to be stoned.

(i)   Reward from God

Significantly, we have found no instances where Philo teaches that God will reward the giver of charity. Though Philo has frequent recourse to χρηστότης, these references to generosity do not elicit from him the teaching, which is found in the Old Testament, that Yahweh loves a giver and will repay him. In this respect, Philo is closer to the Greco-Roman than to the Old Testament world.[112]

(ii)   Social convention in giving and receiving

In keeping with common Greek and Roman thinking of his day, Philo asserts that goodwill is created by benefaction.[113] For example, in a proper government differing emotions are created in the people by the differing aspects of a ruler's behaviour. Dignity on the part of the ruler evokes respect from the people, strictness evokes fear, and benevolence creates affection (κατασκευάζει . . . . τὸ εὐεργετικὸν εὔνοιαν, *Praem.* 97). Only the perverse, i.e., the ungrateful, fail to demonstrate this affection by requiting their benefactors (*Leg. ad Gaium*, 60).[114]

Such requital is not only owed to the wealthy benefactor for a great largesse. Helping strangers fetch water at a well may suffice. In his reading of Exodus 2.15–20 Philo fills in the gaps of social explanation. After Moses helped Reuel's seven daughters at the well, they returned home and reported the events to their father. When the daughters tell of Moses' aid, Reuel asks why the stranger was left alone and not invited to a meal. Unsatisfied with the cursory report of the biblical text, Philo asserts that Reuel rebuked his daughters for their ingratitude (κατεμέμφετο γοῦν αὐτὰς ἐπ' ἀχαριστίᾳ) and sent them with all speed to fetch Moses so they could repay the favour to him: καὶ ἀμοιβῆς (ὀφείλεται γὰρ αὐτῷ χάρις) μεθέξοντα, *Mos.* 1.58.

Philo's treatment of interest-free loans is much like that of Josephus, with one significant omission. Philo constantly grounds

---

112 This absence presents one small item that allows us to detract from the view of Sandmel that Philo is thoroughly Jewish in his thinking but Greek in his explanations (Samuel Sandmel, *Philo of Alexandria: An Introduction* (Oxford: Oxford University Press, 1979): 15).

113 See our comments on Seneca below, pp. 66–7.

114 Cf. the same ideas in *Plant.* 90; *Virt.* 60; *Jos.* 99; *Leg. ad Gaium* 268; *Spec.* 1.224–5, 2.234; *Mos.* 1.333.

reward in social reciprocity; no reference is made to the reward of God. At *De Specialibus Legibus*. 2.78, Philo comments that exacting interest is inhumane and savage brutality, but this in itself is not the only reason to prohibit interest. Borrowers should have to pay the principal, but only the principal, 'because in time they will do the same service to their creditors, requiting with equal assistance those who began to show favour'.[115] We see here two types of debt: first, the borrower should pay back the principal of the loan; secondly, the borrower will pay back (ἀμείβομαι) his debt for the favour (χάρις) he owes to the original lender.[116]

How is it that one owes a favour as a result of receiving a loan? Philo has recourse to this subject again in *De Virtute* 82–4. When it comes to loans there are three possibilities: first, one may loan at interest. Since this is prohibited by the Law, a second possibility is better: one should lend expecting only the principal back. The third alternative is best of all, namely, 'without restriction of hand and heart to give free gifts to those in need, reflecting that a free gift is in a sense a loan that will be repaid by the recipient, when times are better, without compulsion and with a willing heart'.[117] The original lender receives back not only the principal, but also the social debt felt by the borrower, κοινωνία,[118] εὐφημία and εὔκλεια. These last two are the benefits sought by the boaster in Proverbs 25.14.

In *Cher*. 122–3 Philo states that those who are said to bestow benefits (χαρίζεσθαι) actually sell rather than give (πιπράσκοντας μᾶλλον ἢ δωρουμένους) while those who receive the benefits (λαμβάνειν χάριτας) actually buy (ὠνουμένους). This is true not only because the givers (οἱ διδόντες) look for repayment of the benefit (χάριτας ἀντίδοσιν), but also because the receivers of the gifts (προσιεμένοι τὰς δωρεάς) endeavour to make a return (ἀποδοῦναι). Thus such givers in truth carry out sale (πρᾶσιν

---

[115] Our trans.: πάλιν γὰρ ἐν καιροῖς τὸν αὐτὸν ἔρανον ἀνταποτίσουσι τοῖς συμβάλλουσιν ἀμειβόμενοι ταῖς ἴσαις ὠφελείαις τοὺς χάριτος ἄρξαντας; cf. Dem. *Or*. 59.8: τούτῳ δὲ δικαίως τὸν αὐτὸν ἔρανον ἐνεχειρήσαμεν ἀποδιδοῦναι.

[116] That the original lender will one day need the same assistance is seen explicitly in Philo's treatment of the same legislation in *Spec*. 1.71.

[117] LCL trans.: ἀλλ' ἀνειμέναις χερσὶ καὶ γνώμαις μάλιστα μὲν χαρίζεσθαι τοῖς δεομένοις, λογιζομένους ὅτι καὶ ἡ χάρις τρόπον τινὰ δάνειόν ἐστιν, ἀποδοθησόμενον ἐν καιρῷ βελτίονι (ἄνευ) ἀνάγκης ἑκουσίῳ διαυέσει τοῦ λαβόντος.

[118] Financial sharing is also seen as the basis for κοινωνία in Philippians, Rom. 15.26 and Arist. *Eth. Nic.* 5.5.14. See our discussion of Phil. 1.5 on pp. 99–103.

ἐργάζονται), for it is the practice of those who sell (τοῖς πωλοῦσιν) to take something in exchange for what they offer.

Although Philo admits a difference between social giving and receiving and commercial giving and receiving (buying and selling), this text also demonstrates two points. First, this plethora of commercial terms (πιπράσκω, ὠνέομαι, πρᾶσις, πωλέω, ἀντίδοσις) indicates that commercial terminology does not mandate a commercial understanding of the relationship described. Secondly, this text shows that the two types of transactions may be compared using similar language because the expectations of the two relationships are very similar. The giver may be called a seller and the receiver may be called a buyer, for in each relationship there is the very real element of debt and repayment.

In keeping with the comments of Josephus, Philo asserts that parents are the greatest of all benefactors.[119] Because they give so much to their offspring, it is impossible for the children to requite them (οὐδὲ τοῖς γονεῦσιν ἴσας ἀποδοῦναι χάριτας ἐνδέχεται, *LA* 3.10). Here we see several assumptions we have seen reflected in other texts: (1) at least an attempt at repayment for benefits is expected, (2) ideally, this repayment should present equivalent benefits, (3) parents build up a great store of benefits over the course of raising children.

Because social reciprocity is a convention near to Philo's heart, he finds grounds for returning gratitude in the Law. Though he cites no text to support his assertion directly, he can see the principle operating in the fifth commandment. We have already seen above that Philo views parents as great benefactors. Further, according to Philo the fifth command gives us the general principle that should operate between old and young, rulers and subjects, benefactors and the benefited, masters to slaves. The former of the above-mentioned pairs are the socially superior, the latter are inferior. Thus the fifth command gives implicit instructions that the recipients of benefits should requite them with gratitude (καὶ εὖ μὲν πεπονθόσιν εἰς χαρίτων ἀμοιβάς, *Decal.* 167).

---

[119] *Spec.* 2.229, 234; *LA.* 1.99; *Decal.* 112, 165; *Mos.* 2.207.

(iii)   God in exchange relationships

In addition to giving us insights into his view of social reciprocity on the human level, Philo has a penchant for drawing God into giving and receiving. Not surprisingly, the God of Israel is constantly presented as the great benefactor of the universe.[120] Since the work most appropriate to God is the conferring of benefits, the work most appropriate to creation is the giving of thanks (*Plant.* 130). Even though offerings and sacrifices are acceptable means of giving thanks,[121] they really are of no account since they consist in merely giving back to God what is his (*Plant.* 130; *Spec.* 1.271). So then, to accomplish this one work of gratitude, which is so pre-eminently obligatory, one must never tire of singing hymns and composing fresh eulogies in prose and poetry (*Plant.* 126, 130–1). The issue becomes one of honour: since the creature cannot give to the Creator a gift which will make a suitable return for his benefits, God must receive honour as the equivalent which balances the ledger.[122]

Furthermore, it is easy for Philo to cast God as one member in a social exchange. We see this interaction between the Lord and Abraham, the paradigm of godliness. Abraham's offer of Isaac was a gift of piety and God repays Abraham for his gift by giving back the beloved son (*Abr.* 177). With a play on words we are told that God marvelled at Abraham's faith and paid him back with faithfulness, swearing with an oath to give the promised gifts.[123]

Conclusion

From the texts we have surveyed we can draw several conclusions. First, in the Old Testament the giving of material help to those in need is considered praiseworthy and deserving of reward. Didactic texts in particular make this clear (Deut. 14.29, 15.10, 24.19). These texts also assert that Yahweh is the one who will reward the giver.

---

[120] E.g., *Cong.* 38, 97 171; *Decal.* 41; *Immut.* 110; *LA.* 1.96; *LA.* 2.56; *LA.* 3.137; *Mos.* 2.256; *Opif.* 169; *Plant.* 87; *Spec.* 1.152, 209, 272; *Spec.* 2.219; *Leg.* 118.

[121] E.g., *Heres.* 174; *Spec.* 1.67, 195, 224, 283, 285.

[122] We will see this aspect of exchange relationships in chapter 3 (pp. 72–3): the socially inferior member of the dyad, being unable to return a material equivalent, must give greater honour to the socially superior member (cf. Philo *Jos.* 267).

[123] (θεὸς) τῆς πρὸς αὐτὸν πίστεως ἀγάμενος τὸν ἄνδρα πίστιν ἀντιδίδωσιν αὐτῷ, τὴν δι᾽ ὅρκου βεβαίωσιν ὧν ὑπέσχετο δωρεῶν (*Abr.* 273).

He plays a special role in the transaction between the giver and the receiver, making it not bipolar but triangular (Prov. 19.17).

Secondly, social reciprocity, the obligation to respond to a gift or good deed, not only with verbal gratitude, but also with material gratitude (a counter-gift or favour), can be detected in the Old Testament, especially in narrative texts (cf. 1 Sam. 25). Yet this social expectation is not taught, even in didactic texts. We see here a point of tension between the taught and the practised morality.

Thirdly, and moving on to later Jewish literature, we see that social reciprocity as a convention is not only described but prescribed quite explicitly. In Ben Sirach, Philo and Josephus, the expectation of a return for good is quite clear. The one who receives the goodwill of another, goodwill that is seen in a favour or gift, is obligated to return goodwill in the same form. Consequently, we have reason to believe that social reciprocity as a convention was at least widespread among Jews of Paul's day.

Fourthly, as we move from the Old Testament to later Jewish literature and finally to Philo and Josephus, we see an ever decreasing reference to God as the one who will repay. Rather, the reward comes down to a human level. In Philo and Josephus references to God repaying the charitable person are rare. These authors are only a small step away from Greco-Roman thinking.

To fill out this picture we will need to treat in detail the relevant Greco-Roman literature. This task is undertaken in the following chapter. We shall lay out the summary of conventions at the end of that chapter.

3

GIVING AND RECEIVING IN THE GRECO-ROMAN WORLD

Thus far we have defined the meaning of social reciprocity and have seen elements of this social convention perceptible in the Old Testament and in Jewish literature. Yet, the social awareness of reciprocity is most clearly seen in Greco-Roman literature. Also, owing to the great body of literature available, the exact nature of these conventions may be defined more precisely. Thus, the present chapter will be of crucial importance for our purposes. Moreover, this is more specifically the case since Philippi is a Roman colony.[1] We should expect that the social expectations which dominated interpersonal relationships in the Roman world will have exerted a strong influence on the Philippian Christians.

There is neither sufficient cause nor space here to draw on all the texts applicable to the subject, for there is an immense number which could be the basis of several monographs.[2] Therefore, to help facilitate the presentation and analysis of material we propose to use Seneca's *De Beneficiis* as a guide.[3] Though others have provided studies which compare the thought of Seneca and Paul, there is a lacuna in this area.[4] Other texts from literary and non-literary sources will be brought into the discussion to support or supplement aspects of social practice drawn from Seneca.

---

[1] On Roman colonies generally see B. M. Levick, *Roman Colonies in Southern Asia Minor* (Oxford: Clarendon Press, 1967). For Philippi see P. Collart, *Philippes, ville de Macedonie depuis ses origines jusqu' à la fin de l'époque romaine* (Paris: E. de Boccard, 1937). See also helpful details scattered through C. J. Hemer, *The Book of Acts in the Setting of Hellenistic History* (Tübingen: J. C. B. Mohr, 1989).

[2] Bolkestein (*Wohltätigkeit*) has collected many texts in his study on benefaction in early Jewish, Egyptian and Greco-Roman societies.

[3] Thus, unless otherwise noted, all texts from Seneca come from *De Beneficiis*, trans. John W. Basore (London: William Heinemann Ltd, 1935).

[4] For example, J. N. Sevenster (*Paul and Seneca* (Leiden: E. J. Brill, 1961)) deals at length with social relations, work, wealth, friendship, and even doing good to others in society. He does not, however, compare Paul and Seneca on the giving and receiving of benefits.

The chapter is divided into five sections. In the first (*De Beneficiis*: Introduction) we present our assumptions regarding the date
and purpose of Seneca's treatise. A study of the particular phrase
δόσις καὶ λῆμψις, and expressions with a similar semantic field, is
presented next (Giving and receiving). In the third section (Aspects
of giving) we look at some of the particular social expectations with
regard to giving. Conversely, the following portion looks at the
expectations regarding receiving (Aspects of receiving). Lastly our
conclusions are drawn from the Greco-Roman material (Conclusions).

Seneca's *De Beneficiis*

Scholarly consensus dates *De Beneficiis* between AD 56 and 62.[5]
Thus in *De Beneficiis* we have a work devoted to the social
convention of giving and receiving benefits (*Ben.* 1.1.1) which was
written within a decade of Paul's letter to Christians in Philippi,[6] a
Roman colony and certainly heavily influenced by Roman social
conventions.[7] Roman social conventions, however, shared much in
common with the Greek of this period, and Seneca himself in *De
Beneficiis* is dependent on Chrysippus and Hecaton.[8] Therefore,
methodologically, we have a quite valuable source to inform us
regarding the social conventions of giving and receiving which
would have prevailed in Philippi.

As the *amicus primus* to Nero,[9] Seneca would certainly have had
many opportunities to see the various aspects of social reciprocity
at work and fine tune his skills in this regard.

---

[5]   The *terminus ante quem* is summer 64 because of the reference to *De Beneficiis* in
     Ep. 81.3 which is inscribed with this date (Miriam T. Griffin, *Seneca: A
     Philosopher in Politics* (Oxford: Clarendon Press, 1976): 399). W. L. Friedrich
     ('Die Abfassungzeit von Senecas Werk über die Wohltaten', *Philologische
     Wochenschrift* 34 (1914): 1406–8, 1501–3) prefers a date between 59 and 60.

[6]   See our working assumptions, pp. 19–20. We hold to a date for Philippians
     around AD 60–62 (cf. Hawthorne, *Philippians*, xxxvii). Yet even if dated to AD
     55 or 56 (so Gnilka, *Philippians*, 24) the case is not significantly altered.

[7]   Levick refers to the prevalence of Latin inscriptions at Philippi, and thus to the
     city's Roman character. Of 421 texts, only sixty are in Greek (*Roman Colonies*,
     161).

[8]   Chrysippus 1.3.8, 2.17.3; Hecaton 2.18.2, 2.21.4. Seneca is not content, however,
     since the great Greek writers have not passed on writings about giving and
     receiving (1.3.6–1.4.6).

[9]   On Seneca's role see Griffin, *Seneca*, 76–103. On the place of patronage in the
     governmental structure of the Roman empire see Andrew Wallace-Hadrill,
     'Patronage in Roman Society: From Republic to Empire', *Patronage in Ancient
     Society*, ed. A. Wallace-Hadrill (London: Routledge, 1989): 63–87.

The aim of *De Beneficiis* is to give a definition of what binds human society together, to give a law for human life.[10] Seneca asserts that in his day people do not know how to give and receive benefits (*beneficia nec dare scimus nec accipere*, 1.1.1). This inability is displayed in different ways: worthy recipients are not chosen (1.1.2), gifts are not given in the proper manner (1.1.4), gifts are not received with the proper gratitude (3.4.1). These errors, among others, Seneca sets out to correct. In so doing he is very helpful for the present discussion since he must make constant reference to the social conventions which are the assumed knowledge of other writers. He must bring to the fore what is obvious, and thus rarely mentioned elsewhere, in order to discuss in detail the finer points of social reciprocity.

Giving and receiving terminology

The phrase 'giving and receiving' had strong social implications in the first century. Because 'giving and receiving' (δόσις καὶ λῆμψις) is a critical phrase in Phil. 4.15, our conclusions regarding it will influence greatly our understanding of Paul's response to the Philippians' gift. So then, we will here go into some detail in order to demonstrate the significance of δόσις καὶ λῆμψις. Word studies, however, are not sufficient to explain the meaning of giving and receiving in the Greco-Roman world. We must also seek to gain a fuller picture of the broad social context before drawing conclusions with regard to δόσις καὶ λῆμψις. Therefore, after first looking at this specific phrase, we will also present other expressions which appear to occupy the same semantic field. Then, we will move on to look at particular aspects of the practice of giving and receiving. We will begin with a short section from Seneca before moving to other authors.

Giving and receiving in *De Beneficiis*

(i)   To give and receive benefits

At the beginning of *De Beneficiis* Seneca refers to the need in his day for instruction regarding the giving and receiving of benefits

---

10   Villy Søresen, *Seneca the Humanist in the Court of Nero*, trans. W. Glyn Jones (Edinburgh: Canongate Publishing Ltd, 1984): 215.

(1.1.1, cf. 1.4.2). Simply put, *De Beneficiis* is all about giving and receiving. It is devoted to unpacking this phrase and showing how this interaction is to be carried out. People need to be taught to give, to receive and to return willingly and to strive to outdo each other in deed and spirit (1.4.3). Correct practice in this matter is critical since giving and receiving are actions that are liable to alter the relationship between individuals.[11] Giving and receiving is social exchange; the giving of a benefit is a social act and it lays the receiver under obligation (5.11.5). Moreover, every obligation that involves two people makes equal demands on both (2.18.1). Thus, friendship can be established (created) through the bestowal of benefits (2.2.1; *Ep.* 19.11–12). In the light of these observations, it is easy to see how Seneca can assert that such exchange constitutes the chief bond of human society (1.4.2). It naturally follows that ignorance of how to give and receive properly is one of the most disgraceful errors (1.1.1). What is not immediately obvious from his remarks is the rich background of cultural ideas which lies behind a reference to giving and receiving. Apart from the phrase 'an exchange of benefits', Seneca also uses other expressions which occupy the same semantic space.

(ii)   The exchange of obligations

The reception of a benefit places the receiver under an obligation (5.11.5). But this obligation should not be viewed as one-sided. For every obligation that involves two people makes an equal demand on both (2.18.1). The reception of a benefit implies the existence or establishment of a friendship (2.2.11; 2.18.5; *Ep.* 19.11–12).[12] In this friendship the parties seek to render to each other the services they require. Thus, Seneca can refer to this relationship as an exchange of obligations (2.18.2). Although with this phrase emphasis is put on the feelings of debt experienced by the parties of the social relationship, it is clear that this expression is another label for social reciprocity. Those involved in giving and receiving are involved in an exchange of obligations or debts. In another text Seneca asserts that receiving a benefit is receiving a debt (2.23.2).

---

[11]   George G. Strem, *The Life and Teaching of Lucius Annaeus Seneca* (New York: Vantage Press, 1981): 138.

[12]   We will discuss the role of benefits in creating friendships below, pp. 66–7.

(iii) The exchange of benefits (or good offices)

It is impossible for man to live outside of human society. Seneca asserts that only through an exchange of good deeds (*officia*) is one able to live in security (4.18.1). For through the interchange of benefits life becomes fortified against unseen disasters (4.18.2).[13] The implication here is that the obligations felt by one's friends will cause them to aid him in the event of his distress. But for our purposes it is important to see the recurrence of such words as interchange and exchange. The giving and receiving of benefits, or the exchange of favours, is reciprocal social interaction, or 'give and take', as it may be called.

Giving and receiving in other literature

Although 'giving and receiving' in Seneca refers to social reciprocity, the reader may ask how prevalent these terms were in other literature. Thus, we will begin here a study of the phrase 'giving and receiving'. Owing to their use in Philippians 4.15, we will focus our attention on δόσις καὶ λῆμψις and cognates. Yet, in addition, we will present several other texts which refer to social reciprocity using different terms.

Δόσις and λῆμψις, along with the corresponding verbs, are used to refer to several different transactions, not only those within the social realm. We shall not present all the various options below, but only those considered most helpful for our purposes.[14] Although δόσις and λῆμψις figure in a wide variety of contexts, of most relevance here are a good number of examples which may be found in contexts which refer to social reciprocity. These texts report an exchange of goods, money or services which does not appear to draw its primary significance from the commercial sphere but from the social sphere.[15]

---

[13] See a similar idea in our discussion of Eccles. 11.1–2, pp. 25–7.

[14] For occurrences of the phrase used in other contexts see Appendix B, pp. 205–7.

[15] We do not wish to imply, however, that there is a necessary disjunction here. Even commercial transactions, which occur between persons who are social creatures, must follow social conventions and may have social implications. An example of a commercial transaction which is socially motivated is found in Luke 16.1–9. On learning that he will be brought to account for his poor management, the shrewd manager calls his master's debtors and reduces the amount owed on their accounts (vv. 5–7). His goal is to be received into their homes when he loses his job (v. 4). Though this debt reduction is in itself a commercial transaction, it arises from a social motivation and causes reciprocal social obligations.

To facilitate the presentation of examples, we turn first to four texts which scholars, without interpretive discussion, have cited as support for a commercial understanding of Philippians 4.15. We will offer discussion on these texts. Then other texts, overlooked by scholars, will be presented which help to establish the significance of δόσις καὶ λῆμψις.

Sir. 41.19: This text is significant for its labelling of social reciprocity with the precise terms the apostle employs in Philippians 4.15. Having already studied this text in the preceding chapter, we shall only summarize our conclusions.[16]

The context and the Hebrew text of this verse give us strong arguments in favour of a social understanding for the giving and receiving mentioned. In a list of things the righteous man should be ashamed of, one encounters the exhortation, '(Be ashamed) of refusing to give when asked.' This is clearly a reference to the duty of almsgiving (cf. 29.8–13). The Greek, however, presents a slightly different social demand. It states that one should be ashamed of contempt for giving and receiving (ἀπὸ σκορακισμοῦ λήμψεως καὶ δόσεως). Here λήμψεως καὶ δόσεως appears to be a shorthand label for the transactions of exchange relationships.

Arrian Epicteti Dissertationes 2.9.12: Epictetus asserts that acts in keeping with the character of a man preserve him in that character. Good acts preserve the good man. Thus, specifically, modest acts preserve the modest man and faithful acts the faithful (2.9.11–12a). Conversely, wicked acts strengthen the wicked man in his wicked character. Thus, faithlessness strengthens the faithless, abuse the abusive, wrath the wrathful. Finally, the greedy man is strengthened by incongruous credits and debits (ἐπαύξει . . . τὸν φιλάργυρον αἱ ἀκατάλληλοι λήψεις καὶ δόσεις, 2.9.12b). Should 'giving and receiving' here be understood in a commercial sense? Taken together the following observations argue to the contrary.

Apart from the words themselves, nothing in the context demands that δόσις καὶ λῆμψις be understood in a commercial sense. Moreover, though the acts mentioned in the context (shamelessness, faithlessness, abuse, wrath) are flexible enough to describe activities in the commercial sphere, they appear to gain their

---

[16] See pp. 41–2.

primary significance from the social sphere. Shame is certainly very much an emotion which operates in one's social environment.

In this context ἀκατάλληλος is best understood to denote disproportion. The greedy man must be anxious to take in more than he pays out.[17] When in actual fact such a case obtains, the greedy man is strengthened in his behaviour. On the other hand, the text assumes at least four conditions with regard to the exchange here mentioned.

First, equity is the goal of giving and receiving. The same amount should be going out as comes in. But, secondly, the greedy man's account does not fit this description. He has a surplus of receipts. Thirdly, other parties are necessary for these transactions to take place, namely, those who give to and receive from the greedy man. It may be further assumed that these other parties ought to aim at equity in debits and credits as well. Thus, fourthly, the transaction mentioned here is reciprocal giving and receiving.

In the structure of the cases Epictetus cites one sees that an evil deed (e.g., faithlessness) strengthens the evil man (e.g., the faithless man). To maintain the parallel with the other examples Epictetus offers, one must assert that disproportionate credits and debits is itself an evil act. And indeed, our second point above has already implied this. Such disproportion corresponds in nature to the greedy man and thus strengthens him in this characteristic. Why this disproportion should be an evil act is not stated. If, however, one assumes that the reciprocal giving and receiving described happens in the commercial sphere, then one must assert that Epictetus views financial gain as an evil. For profit is essentially what must be meant by a greater number of credits than debits.

Yet in this context Epictetus asserts that wealth is a matter of indifference (2.9.15; cf. 2.19.13), being neither good or evil. Elsewhere he states that whether one has wealth is a matter beyond one's control (2.19.32) and that one should be willing to accept the lot that God gives, whether it be wealth or poverty (2.16.42). If, in the light of these statements, it can be assumed that the *acquisition* of wealth is a matter of indifference just as is the *possession* of wealth, then one is constrained to conclude that the 'giving and receiving' referred to here must happen outside the commercial sphere.

---

[17] Thus the Loeb translator supplies, 'a disproportion between what he receives and what he pays out (strengthens) the miserly'.

In conclusion, Epictetus' comments are best understood to refer to social giving and receiving. In his social relationships the greedy man is always ready to take (λῆμψις) gifts or favours from his friends but is slow to give (δόσις) back to them. As a result the social ledger shows that he has more credits than debits. Such imbalance is essentially evil and when it obtains it strengthens the man in his greedy behaviour.

Aristotle *Ethica Nicomachea* 4.1: In his commentary on Philippians Vincent cites Aristotle *Ethica Nicomachea* 2.7.4 when he asserts that δόσις καὶ λῆμψις in Philippians 4.15 is a technical commercial phrase.[18] But the comments in 2.7.4 are given to help explain Aristotle's concept of the Mean and are not given as direct discussion on giving and receiving. Therefore, in contrast to Vincent, our analysis will not begin with 2.7.4, but with Book 4 where Aristotle devotes much time to the discussion of liberality. In his discussion he has frequent recourse to δόσις and λῆμψις as well as to cognate forms.

Liberality is the observance of the Mean with respect to wealth. The liberal man observes the Mean in regard to both giving and getting wealth (περὶ δόσιν χρημάτων καὶ λῆψιν, 4.1.1). Although giving can include spending (4.1.29) the primary focus of discussion appears to be the social interaction of giving and receiving favours or benefits.

First, the liberal man is more concerned to give than to obtain wealth because virtue (ἀρετή) is displayed in doing good rather than in receiving good (τὸ εὖ ποιεῖν ἢ τὸ εὖ πάσχειν, 4.1.7).[19] Obviously, doing good goes with giving (οὐκ ἄδηλον δ᾽ ὅτι τῇ δόσει ἕπεται τὸ εὖ ποιεῖν) while receiving good goes with getting (τῇ λήψει τὸ εὖ πάσχειν, 4.1.8). Thus, in Aristotle's discussion giving and receiving wealth (δόσιν καὶ χρημάτων λῆψιν) occupies the same semantic space as doing and receiving good (τὸ εὖ ποιεῖν ἢ τὸ εὖ πάσχειν). Secondly, Aristotle asserts that the liberal man will give and receive the right amounts from the right sources (4.1.24–5), that the liberal man, being accustomed to giving, does not readily accept favours in return (οὐ γάρ ἐστι τοῦ εὖ ποιοῦντος εὐχερῶς εὐεργετεῖσθαι, 4.1.15). Nevertheless, it is not easy to give to everyone and receive from no one (οὐ γάρ ῥᾴδιον μηδαμόθεν

---

18 Vincent, *Philippians*, 148.
19 To do good (εὖ ποιεῖν) is understood as the social act of benefiting another (cf. 4.3.24, 8.12.5 and Plato *Rep.* 332D; Xen. *Mem.* 2.3.8; M. Aur. 7.73).

λαμβάνοντα πᾶσι διδόναι, 4.1.30). Here again, the giving and receiving of wealth (δόσιν χρημάτων καὶ λῆψιν, 4.1.1) is parallel to an exchange of favours (οὐ γάρ ἐστι τοῦ εὖ ποιοῦντος εὐχερῶς εὐεργετεῖσθαι, 4.1.15) and both of these are being discussed in the context of social relations. Though Aristotle is here dealing with money, he is dealing with a social, not a commercial, transaction.[20] We see that what might be called commercial terminology can be used to describe social relationships.

Plato *Republic* 332A–B: This text occurs within a discussion on the definition and nature of justice (330D, 331C). Plato is said to question whether telling the truth and paying back what one has received (ἀποδιδόναι, ἂν τίς τι παρά του λάβῃ, 331C) is a proper definition of justice. For it is not just for the borrower to return weapons if the lender has gone insane (331C). Thus one ought not to return goods if the return and the acceptance (ἡ ἀπόδοσις καὶ ἡ λῆψις) prove harmful and the returner and recipient are friends (φίλοι δὲ ὦσιν ὅ τε ἀπολαμβάνων καὶ ὁ ἀποδιδούς, 332B). This is true because friends owe to friends to do them some good and no evil (332A).[21] Thus, this text also does not deal with a commercial transaction but a social one.

We turn now to passages which have not been utilized in the discussion regarding the 'giving and receiving' of Philippians 4.

Plato *Epistula*. 309: Plato is presented as sending back a gift to a certain Dionysius. The amount was apparently paltry, given more as a form of insult than of aid. Plato does not accept, since accepting would bring disgrace, and states that, for Dionysius, neither the giving nor the accepting of such a gift is of any consequence (σοὶ δ' οὐδὲν διαφέρει δῆλον ὅτι καὶ λαβεῖν καὶ δοῦναι τοσοῦτον, 309.C.3).

Give and Take (δός καὶ λάβε): In the work of Ps-Plato *Axiochus* (2nd–1st BC), Socrates plays down his personal knowledge, claiming that what he says merely echoes Prodicus, to whom he paid fees for instruction. This Prodicus was fond of citing the axiom of

---

[20] This is of primary importance for our understanding of Paul, where the context is heavily weighted with what are perceived to be financial terms (ἀπέχω, v. 18; εἰς λόγον, v. 15, 17; καρπός, v. 17).

[21] On friendship in Plato see A. W. Price, *Love and Friendship in Plato and Aristotle* (Oxford: Clarendon Press, 1989).

Epicharmus: one hand washes another, give something and take something (ἁ δὲ χεῖρ τὰν χεῖρα νίζει· δός τι, καὶ λάβε τι, 366B–C; cf. Epicharmus *Frag.* 273). In the context we see that giving and receiving refers to the exchange of money for instruction. Prodicus, in citing Epicharmus, brings up the general principle of reciprocity, applying it to the specific situation of fees. Therefore, the exchange is being viewed in the realm of mutual aid and not a business transaction. Prodicus helps Socrates by teaching him. Socrates in return helps Prodicus by giving him money, which in this instance may be called 'fees', since the benefit received is instruction in philosophy.

Nearly the same construction with the imperatives (δός καὶ λάβε) is found in other texts (*Anth. Gr.* 9.546; 12.204; Men. *Monost.* 217, 221). In *Anthologia Graeca* 9.546 Antiphilus is reported as reflecting on the pleasures of life at sea. The condensed nature of the epigram makes its exact meaning difficult to decipher. Apparently, among other things, the writer desires to see 'a game of "give and take"',[22] although the rendering, 'Let me hear the words "Give and take"' is possible.[23] That such a game existed is evident from *Anthologia Graeca* 12.204. This epigram of Strato mentions playing at give and take (δός λάβε παίζει), which plainly refers to an exchange of gifts. Yet, whichever rendering is chosen the basic sense is not greatly altered. Here in 9.546 the phrase is taken to refer to fair exchange, implying the well-known adage: κοινὰ τὰ τῶν φίλων; that is, the voyagers share what they have.[24]

Xenophon: A particularly telling example of 'giving and receiving' is found in *Oeconomicus*. Ischomachus reports that the gods made male and female different to perform different tasks within the family. Nevertheless, because it would be necessary for both to give and receive (διδόναι καὶ λαμβάνειν, 7.26), the gods impartially granted to both memory and diligence. Though these infinitives lack an object we can clearly see that the giving and receiving referred to here must be the reciprocal service the spouses grant to each other. Both spouses need good memories because

22 The LCL translator supplies this rendering.
23 A. S. F. Gow and D. L. Page, *The Greek Anthology. The Garland of Philip and Some Contemporary Epigrams*, 2 vols. (Cambridge: Cambridge University Press, 1968): 1.97. Gow and Page place the publication of *The Garland* during the principate of Gaius (*c.* AD 40; *Greek Anthology*, 1.xlix).
24 Gow and Page, *Greek Anthology*, 2.122.

memory plays an important role in social exchange. The one who is grateful remembers the good deeds done to him.[25]

An Egyptian Papyrus: Though late, a third to fourth century AD papyrus preserves an Egyptian school exercise which reflects the same social convention with these terms: Λαβὼν πάλιν δὸς ἵνα λάβῃς ὅταν θέλῃς.[26] This succinct statement is particularly telling since it demonstrates that there existed an awareness of this social convention, and that, in a sense, one could call others to account because of the social obligation caused by giving.

Acts 20.35: It seems particularly surprising that the only other use of the phrase 'giving and receiving' in the New Testament has not been brought into the discussion of δόσις καὶ λῆμψις in Philippians 4.[27] In Acts 20.17–35 the writer presents Paul's farewell speech to the Ephesian elders. Paul reminds them that he has coveted no one's gold, silver or clothing, rather, he has supplied his material needs through working with his own hands (vv. 33–4). His exemplary service is given to show that one should help the weak (v. 35a).[28] The general principle underpinning such an approach is ascribed to Jesus himself: 'It is more blessed to give than to receive' (μακάριόν ἐστιν μᾶλλον διδόναι ἢ λαμβάνειν, 20.35b).[29]

Commentators mention that this expression is probably a Greek aphorism that has been christianized.[30] Yet the social origins of such an expression are neglected. The mere existence of this saying shows that giving and receiving was a commonplace of daily society

---

[25] According to Seneca the memory of benefits ought not to grow old, 1.3.5; cf. 1.4.6, 3.1.3, 2.24.1: 'Nothing ought to be made more manifest than that services rendered to us linger in our memory.'

[26] Erich Ziebarth, *Aus der antiken Schule: Sammlung griechischer Texte auf papyrus holztafeln Ostraka* (Bonn: A. Marcus und E. Weber, 1910): 18.

[27] We know of no scholar treating Phil. 4.15 who refers to Acts 20.35.

[28] Even if this speech of Acts does not present an historical address by the apostle, the same concepts of exemplary work and giving are inherent in 1 Thess. 2.9–12 (cf. Eph. 4.28).

[29] For a helpful discussion on this Jesus logion see Joachim Jeremias, *Unknown Sayings of Jesus*, trans. Reginald H. Fuller (London: SPCK, 1958): 78.

[30] E.g., Hans Conzelmann, *The Acts of the Apostles*, trans. A. T. Kraabel and D. H. Juel (Philadelphia: Fortress Press, 1987): 176; I. Howard Marshall, *The Acts of the Apostles* (Leicester: Inter-Varsity Press, 1980): 336. Cf. Plut. *Mor.* 778C: 'Epicurus . . . says that it is not only nobler, but also pleasanter, to confer than to receive benefits' (τοῦ εὖ πάσχειν τὸ εὖ ποιεῖν οὐ μόνον κάλλιον καὶ ἥδιον εἶναι). Similarly, we saw above Aristotle's claim that virtue is displayed in doing good rather than receiving good (*Eth. Nic.* 4.1.7). For further parallels in Greek literature see J. J. Wetstein (*Novum Testamentum Graecum*, 2 vols. (Amsterdam, 1752): 2.600). Jeremias points out that in Greek literature the saying always occurs as a comparison, but in Judaism as an antithesis (*Unknown Sayings*, 79).

and that 'to give and receive' was a known referent for such interaction.

Bruce refers to the spirit of such a saying in Luke 6.38, 11.9; John 13.34.[31] Although Luke 6.38 does indeed refer to a situation of giving and receiving, there the emphasis is on the return which the giver is promised (δίδοτε, καὶ δοθήσεται ὑμῖν). On the other hand, Luke 14.12–14, not cited by Bruce, warns against receiving social repayment for one's generosity. Jesus asserts that if one gives a dinner, one should not invite friends lest the friends reciprocate the hospitality and one be repaid (γένηται ἀνταπόδομά σοι, 12b).[32]

Acts 20.35 is best understood against the social background seen in Luke 14. The concept of repayment seen there fits very well with the ideas of social reciprocity we have already seen in several writers. In addition, Luke 14 appears to be much closer to Acts 20.35 than is Luke 6.38 since in these first two receiving is being viewed in a negative light.[33]

Now to 20.35 itself. From the context we can see that 'giving and receiving' here refers to Paul's refusal of payment for his labour in preaching and teaching. Instead of receiving remuneration he has given help to the weak. This help may have come in the form of financial assistance: helping those who were socially weak and unable to support themselves,[34] though ἀντιλαμβάνω is certainly broad enough to include other types of aid.[35] The text presents only the general principle of helping the weak through labouring in this way (οὕτως κοπιῶντας), that is, supplying one's own needs rather than relying on the support of others.[36] Thus, this text certainly refers to giving and receiving in the social sphere.

---

[31] F. F. Bruce, *The Acts of the Apostles* (Grand Rapids: Eerdmans, 3rd rev. edn, 1990): 437.

[32] In a typically Jewish fashion, Jesus asserts that one's reward will come from God (v. 14b, cf. Matt. 6.2, 5, 16).

[33] We note that the strong ideas of social reciprocity found in Luke 14, commonly held to have the same author as Acts, have no parallel in Mark or Matthew.

[34] Rudolf Pesch, *Die Apostelgeschichte*, 2 vols. (Zürich: Neukirchener, 1986): 2.206; Bruce, *Acts*, 436; Jeremias, *Unknown Sayings*, 78.

[35] In 1 Tim. 6.2 it is unclear whether οἱ τῆς εὐεργεσίας ἀντιλαμβανόμενοι refers to the slaves (so J. N. D. Kelly, *A Commentary on the Pastoral Epistles* (London: Adam & Charles Black, 1963): 132) or masters (so Martin Dibelius and Hans Conzelmann, *The Pastoral Epistles*, trans. Philip Buttolph and Adela Yarbro (Philadelphia: Fortress Press, 1972): 82).

[36] And indeed in the close parallel of *Apost. Const.* 4.3.1 financial independence appears to be very important.

Plutarch *Moralia* 830A: Though not using δόσις καὶ λῆμψις, the same idea of a social exchange is referred to in *Moralia* 830A. Plutarch urges readers against borrowing. To those who ask how they shall then live, he responds that they have a body to do work and are capable of loving and being loved, of doing favours and being thankful for them (τὸ χαρίζεσθαι καὶ τὸ εὐχαριστεῖν).[37] At least three assumptions underlie the text. First, conveying favours will bring reciprocal favours. It is for reciprocal favours that the person gives thanks. Secondly, this social exchange helps one acquire the necessities of life. Thirdly, εὐχαριστεῖν is the normal response to χαρίζεσθαι.

We have reason to believe that here εὐχαριστεῖν does not simply denote a verbal response, but rather the active repayment of the favour or gift through a counter-favour or gift.[38] Thus the correspondence with δόσις καὶ λῆμψις is exact, with giving and receiving implied by both parties to the social transaction:

Person addressed by Plutarch χαρίζεσθαι (δόσις)	⟹ Favour Done	Implied Second Party (λῆμψις)
(λῆμψις)	⟸ Reciprocal Favour	(εὐχαριστεῖν = χαρίζεσθαι) (δόσις)
εὐχαριστεῖν (δόσις)	⟹ Thanks Given	(λῆμψις)

Cicero *De Amicitia*: In his treatise on friendship Cicero refers to the reciprocal character of such a relationship. The giving and receiving of favours is a part of friendship, indeed such mutual interchange is inseparable from it (8.26). Cicero rejects the view that friendship must be limited to an equal exchange of services. Indeed, that would be calling friendship to a very close and petty accounting (*ad calculos vocare*) to require it to keep an exact balance of credits and debits (*par ratio acceptorum et datorum*). True friendship does not seek to avoid paying out more than it has received (*plus reddat quam acceperit*, 16.58). Although the idea of calling friendship to a very close and petty accounting is being

---

[37] Compare the very similar thought in (Ps)-Plato's definition of friendship (*Def.* 413B1): κοινωνία τοῦ εὖ ποιῆσαι καὶ παθεῖν.
[38] See below, pp. 69–71.

rejected by Cicero, nevertheless his terminology shows that the concepts of balance, credit, debit and calculation may be properly applied to the giving and receiving that occurs within friendship. It is the demand for precise equality that is rejected, not the idea that the social exchange of friendship might be properly described in financial terms.[39]

Seneca *De Ira*: Seneca has a concern for similar issues as Cicero above. He urges his readers against the discontent that arises from feelings of imbalance in social exchange. To the one who feels that he should receive more for the favours he has shown Seneca retorts: 'Your book-keeping is wrong; what you have paid out, you rate high; what you have received, low.'[40] Here also giving and receiving refers to social reciprocity but is depicted with financial terminology.

Philo *De Cherubim* 122–3: This text is very close to Paul chronologically, linguistically and culturally. As we have already had recourse to it earlier,[41] we will only summarize here.

Philo asserts that those who are said to bestow benefits (χαρίζεσθαι) actually sell rather than give (πιπράσκοντας μᾶλλον ἢ δωρουμένους) while those who receive the benefits (λαμβάνειν χάριτας) actually buy (ὠνουμένους). This is true not only because the givers (διδόντες) look for repayment of the benefit (χάριτας ἀντίδοσιν), but also because the receivers of the gift (προσιέμενοι τὰς δωρεάς) endeavour to make a return (ἀποδοῦναι). Such givers in truth carry out a sale (πρᾶσιν ἐργάζονται), for it is the practice of those who sell (τοῖς πωλοῦσιν) to take something in exchange for what they offer.

The transactional character of Greco-Roman social reciprocity is very much like buying and selling. Here we see that the use of commercial terms (πιπράσκω, ὠνέομαι, πρᾶσις, πωλέω, ἀντίδοσις) does not mandate a commercial understanding of the relationship described. Paul has received a δόμα from the Philippians; for Philo the object is δωρεά. Paul uses the concept of giving and receiving to label his relationship with his congregation, along with other terms common in commercial transactions; Philo uses similar terms to

---

[39] Though Cicero rejects precise accounting, his statement encourages one to err on the side of excessive giving: True friendship does not seek to avoid *paying out more than it has received* (16.58). That is, it is nobler to give than to receive.

[40] *Falsas rationes conficis; data magno aestumas, accepta parvo*, 3.31.3; cf. *De Vita Beata* 4–5; Petron. *Satyr.* 45.

[41] See pp. 47–8.

describe a similar social relationship. If Philo is here plainly referring to a social transaction, then why cannot Paul be doing the same in Philippians 4.15?

Conclusion on δόσις καὶ λῆμψις

We conclude that δόσις καὶ λῆμψις is not a technical phrase referring invariably to commercial transactions.[42] The nature of friendship and social reciprocity in the first century allowed the use of financial language to refer to the mutual obligations of such relationships. These mutual obligations may have a financial character (as pointed out especially by Philo, *Cher*. 122–3) but they are essentially social obligations. On the other hand, δόσις καὶ λῆμψις is not a technical phrase restricted to the exchange of gifts or services (e.g., Plut. *Mor*. 11B; Xen. *Cyr*. 1.4.3; Sir. 42.7),[43] though it is well suited to label this exchange (e.g., Arist. *Eth. Nic.* 4.1.1; 4.1.30; Plato *Leg.* 774.C.3–D.2; Xen. *An.* 7.7.36; Plut. *Vit. Thes.* 10.3; perhaps Philo *De Specialibus Legibus* 1.340). The movement described may be one-way (Xen. *An.* 7.7.36) or two-way (Arist. *Eth. Nic.* 4.1.1; 4.1.15).[44]

Now although δόσις καὶ λῆμψις can be used in the social sphere, yet because in Phil. 4 it occurs in the context with other financial terms (εἰς λόγον, ἀπέχω), it might be asserted that it should be taken as a technical-financial phrase. Yet, it has already been seen that in the context of a discussion of social reciprocity terminology often occurs which also figures in commercial contexts (e.g., Arist. *Eth. Nic.* 4.1.1–29; Philo *Cher.* 122–3; Sen. *De Ira* 3.31.3; Cic. *Amic.* 8.26). These texts make it plain that financial language can appropriately be used when discussing social reciprocity. Therefore we have reason to believe that δόσις καὶ λῆμψις need not be taken as a technical-financial phrase even in Philippians. Further support for this assertion will be left to the exegesis of Philippians 4.

---

[42] *Contra* Hawthorne, *Philippians*, 204; Gnilka, *Philipperbrief*, 177; Moulton and Milligan, *Vocabulary*, 169.

[43] See the presentation of other uses of the phrase in Appendix B, pp. 205–7.

[44] Thus we have reason to question that the phrase must refer solely to the passing of money between Paul and the Philippians (*contra* Sampley, *Partnership*, 74 n. 20; J. B. Lightfoot, *Saint Paul's Epistle to the Philippians* (Grand Rapids: Zondervan, repr., 1953): 165).

Aspects of giving

Thus far we have looked at giving and receiving generally and have seen that the phrase δόσις καὶ λῆμψις (or cognates) was commonly used to refer to social reciprocity. Yet, there still remains the need to define some of the precise social expectations which attended giving and receiving. Below we will examine various aspects of social reciprocity with particular emphasis on the behaviour which was expected of the parties to the relationship.

Benefits as the foundation of friendship

Seneca makes very clear that beneficence wisely given establishes friendships.[45] This social practice can be seen as far back as Homer (*Od.* 21.31–41)[46] and other subsequent authors as well.[47] Horace asserts that wealth can buy all things, even friends (*Ep.* 1.6.36).[48]

According to Seneca the giving of a benefit should win the goodwill of the recipient (5.11.5). Consequently, we can make someone our friend by doing him a service (2.2.11; 2.18.5). It is kindness that establishes friendships (*Ep.* 19.11–12). Since only the wise man knows how to bestow a benefit properly (*Ep.* 81.10–11), the wise man is a master in the art of making friendships (*Ep.* 9.5).[49]

Since the offer of a benefit is an offer of goodwill and a social act, it is shameful to repudiate a benefit (1.1.3); not to accept a benefit when offered can be taken as an insult (Plut. *Phoc.* 18.1–4).[50] This is apparently true because the refusal of a benefit must reflect negatively on the social evaluation the potential receiver makes of the giver. Such negative reflections are assumed in the discussion at 2.18. Seneca asserts that one must be far more careful in selecting a creditor for a benefit than a creditor for a loan (2.18.5–6). For reception implies the establishment of a lasting

---

45   A. L. Motto, *Seneca Sourcebook: A Guide to the Thought of Lucius Annaeus Seneca* (Amsterdam: Adolf M. Hakkert, 1970): 34.

46   For a helpful summary of social reciprocity and friendship in Homer see Walter Donlan, 'Reciprocities in Homer', *Classical World* 75 (1981–2): 137–76.

47   E.g., Thuc. 2.40; Dio Cass. 48.16.3, Arr. *Epict. Diss.* 2.22.34; Plut. *Sull.* 3.1.

48   R. Bogaert, 'Geld', *RAC* 9 (1976): 839. Cf. Ar. *Vesp.* 606F; Soph. *Frag.* 85; Andoc. *Or.* 4.15; Men. *Sent.* 238). See also Marshall, *Enmity*, 1–9.

49   Motto, *Seneca Sourcebook*, 89.

50   This aspect of social convention is noticed and applied by Marshall (*Enmity*, esp. 13–18).

relationship and one will not wish to be under obligation to someone objectionable.

Discussing the subject more broadly, the mutual exchange of
goods and services is the very foundation on which society is based
(1.4.2). It is impossible to live in security apart from mutual aid
coming through an exchange of good offices. It is only through the
interchange of benefits that life becomes fortified against sudden
disasters (4.18.1–2).

Selecting the recipient of benefits

Because benefits establish friendships with others, Seneca warns
against the indiscriminate bestowal of gifts. Kindnesses do indeed
establish friendships if they are placed judiciously, for it is more
important who receives than what is given (*Ep*. 19.11–12). Therefore, the giver ought carefully to scrutinize potential receivers
(1.1.2). The proper recipient is one who will show gratitude
(1.10.4–5).[51] Seneca's direct statement here on the necessary quality
of the proper receiver is supported by several other indirect
comments made elsewhere. Only the wise man knows how to return
a favour (*Ep*. 81.11). Knowingly dispensing benefits to the ungrateful is a waste of one's benefaction (1.1.2, 1.10.4).[52]

That proper recipients must be selected is apparent also in Pliny
Letters 2.13. He asserts that a certain friend of his always receives
his benefactions with so much gratitude as to merit further. Thus
we see that a thankful recipient is more worthy. It is hinted at here
that gratitude is also a form of solicitation (we will see more on this
below).

How to bestow benefits

It is not enough that one select a worthy recipient of one's benefits.
In addition one must bestow benefits in the proper way. For Seneca
asserts that the giver is often the one to blame when a benefit fails
to evoke gratitude from the recipient (1.1.4, 2.17.5). This failure
occurs when the giver either draws undue attention to the gift or, in
contrast, denies the value of the gift by playing down its significance
when giving it (1.1.4). Those benefits win no thanks, which, though

---

[51] On the nature of gratitude see pp. 71–83 below. By gratitude is here meant a
material return or counter-gift as distinct from verbal thanks.

[52] Cf. Ps-Phocylides 152: 'Do no good to a bad man, it is like sowing in the sea.'

seeming great in substance and show, are either forced from the giver or are carelessly dropped (1.7.2–3).

In addition to the attitudes which are expressed when a benefit is given, the giver should give attention to the gift itself. Expensive or unique gifts are better in that they draw a greater sense of gratitude from the recipient (1.14.1). Likewise, every receiver likes to think that he is receiving a unique show of goodwill from the giver (1.14.4).

The expected result of benefits

It has already been seen that goodwill is the expected response to benefits (5.11.5). We saw this aspect of social practice arise in connection with other aspects. Here attention is drawn to it directly.

Seneca states that the giver of a benefit really hopes for the goodwill of the recipient. Goodwill is really the only return the giver seeks (2.33.1–2, *Ep*. 36.5–6). But, nevertheless, Seneca defines goodwill in such a way as to make obvious that goodwill without a return is dead, it must be seen in gratitude (2.35.1; 2.35.4). If the system operates properly, benefits will establish friendships by gaining the goodwill of the recipient (*Ep*. 19.11–12). On the one hand, Seneca asserts repeatedly that the giver should not bestow a benefit in order to get a return, or, in other words that he ought not to enter his benefactions in an account book (1.2.3; 1.4.3). Such would be acting like a creditor and not a friend. On the other hand, Seneca also contends that all men everywhere agree that thanks should be returned for benefits (3.1.1; *Ep*. 81.31). When a giver has someone grateful to him he gains an advantage (2.33.1–2). The fact that goodwill which leads to a return can be the expected result of benefits is also seen in Seneca's instruction concerning verbalized gratitude. One should assert, 'You have laid more people under obligation than you think' (for everyone rejoices to know that a benefit of his extends farther than he thought, 2.24.4). Thus the giver expects feelings of debt to result and is glad to hear that many people may need to be involved in the discharge of this debt.[53]

---

[53] If the giving and expected results Seneca describes here smack of bribery to modern readers, we must bear in mind the cultural chasm between twentieth and first-century social conventions. On the distinction between gifts and bribery see Herman, *Ritualized Friendship*, 75–81.

Aspects of receiving

From looking at the bestowal of benefits, we now move to Seneca's discussion of how benefits are to be received. The whole matter may be summed up here with one word: gratitude. At the beginning, however, we should be careful to derive our understanding of gratitude from the sources in the Greco-Roman world. There, if one is grateful, one makes a return for the goodwill or gift which has been received. The issue is not primarily, as it often is in the twentieth-century west, a matter of verbalized gratitude.

Though gratitude has been touched on several times and we have clearly seen that gratitude, especially in the form of a return, was an integral part of social reciprocity, yet this point needs special attention here for three reasons: first, Paul is on the receiving end of the social transaction referred to in Philippians. He is the one expected to express gratitude. Secondly, the letter to the Philippians contains a *verbal* response to the gift. Yet, thirdly, the scholarly consensus asserts, in various ways and degrees, that Paul actually gives the Philippians a thankless thanks.[54] Thus the discussion here will be helpful regarding the exegesis of Philippians 4.

The necessity of gratitude

'Not to return gratitude for benefits is a disgrace and the whole world counts it as such' (3.1.1). This citation sums up the ancient world's attitude toward gratitude.[55] Seneca asserts that men will always be wicked. There will always be homicide, theft, adultery and sacrilege, but the greatest crime of all is ingratitude (1.10.3–4). Ingratitude is to be avoided because nothing else so effectively disrupts the harmony of the human race (4.18.1).

Thus, it naturally follows that when one receives a benefit it is considered a social obligation to show gratitude[56] (2.31.1, 2.32.4, 2.33.1–2, 2.35.1). But what is this gratitude that is demanded? On the one hand, this gratitude may include a verbal display of

---

[54] For example, Ernst Lohmeyer (*Der Brief an die Philipper, an die Kolosser und an Philemon* (Göttingen: Vandenhoeck & Ruprecht, 1930): 178), asserts that Phil. 4.10–20 should give thanks for the Philippians' gift. Yet, every direct word of thanks is absent (cf. 183 and Gnilka, *Philipperbrief*, 173; Hawthorne, *Philippians*, 195).

[55] On the concept of gratitude see Peter Kraft, 'Gratus Animus (Dankbarkeit)', *RAC* 12 (1983): 733–52.

[56] Conzelmann, 'εὐχαριστέω', *TDNT*, 9: 407.

appreciation. Thus, Seneca urges that if one has received a great favour, one should express one's feelings of debt. One might say, 'You have laid more people under obligation than you think.' This response is appropriate because everyone rejoices to know that his benefit extends farther than he thought (2.24.4). Here we see that a verbal expression of gratitude is an expression of debt.[57]

On the other hand, the debt of gratitude is not primarily discharged with a verbal expression. First, goodwill ought to be displayed in response to the goodwill received. The exchange of goodwill is the crux Seneca sees underlying social reciprocity. Yet there is a paradox here (2.31.1). Friendly goodwill is really the only social response expected from a benefit, and in a sense the entire repayment for the benefit is accomplished merely in the proper acceptance of it (1.34.1). Yet, nevertheless, after goodwill has been shown in response to goodwill, an object is still owed for an object (2.35.1). The giver's further use of the receiver and the advantage he derives from having a person grateful are still expected. But these are additional consequences of the goodwill gained (3.33.1–2). Simply put, gratitude must be ultimately expressed in a return. He who does not return a benefit sins (1.1.13).

In other authors we see the same assumptions that gratitude must ultimately be expressed in repayment. An analysis of the relationship between goodwill and the return, however, is typically absent. Xenophon says he supposes that all men consider it necessary to repay goodwill to the one from whom a gift has been received (ἐγὼ μὲν οἶμαι πάντας ἀνθρώπους νομίζειν εὔνοιαν δεῖν ἀποδείκνυσθαι τούτῳ παρ' οὗ ἂν δῶρά τις λαμβάνῃ, *An.* 7.7.46).

In a discourse to the people of Rhodes Dio Chrysostom condemns their lapse into the practice of changing the inscription on older statues in order to honour newer benefactors. This practice is an outrage since 'to let the memory of the noblest men be forgotten and to deprive them of the rewards of virtue cannot find any plausible excuse, but must be ascribed to ingratitude, envy, meanness and all the basest motives' (*Or.* 31.25; cf. 31.27, 37). The honour granted to benefactors in the form of a statue was repayment for their benefaction. Dio asserts that by taking away these honours the Rhodians were bringing such shame on their benefactors that they more than cancelled the original honour paid

---

[57] Verbal expressions of gratitude will be covered at length below, pp. 73–83.

to them (cf. 31.29).[58] In short, they are taking away their gratitude. Ingratitude toward benefactors is a serious offence.[59]

According to Cicero, all men detest ingratitude (*Off*. 2.83; cf. *Planc*. 81). In several other passages we see that when one wants to slander another, one only needs to point out that the person is ungrateful.[60]

Though the elements of the discussion overlap quite a bit here, we have seen in the section above that gratitude for benefits received is an expected social convention. Ingratitude is seen as a heinous social evil. These observations only take us as far as the demand for gratitude. They do not tell us how gratitude must be expressed specifically.

The form of gratitude

The chief issue with gratitude is the return. Man is the most grateful (εὐχαριστότατος) of creatures because when he is benefited (χαριζομένος) he seeks to do a benefit in return (ἀντιχαρίζεσθαι, Xen. *Cyr*. 8.3.49). If one has been benefited one is under a debt to repay a benefit when the opportunity arises (*Ben*. 1.1.13; 2.24.4; 4.40.5; 5.11.5; Cic. *Off*. 1.48).[61] If one is able and fails to repay a benefit, one is ungrateful (this is the definition of ἀχαριστία offered by Xen. *Mem*. 2.2.1; cf. *Cyr*. 1.2.7). According to Seneca this obligation even exists if one has been benefited by an objectionable or hateful person (2.18.3; 3.12.3).[62] We see that in terms of the form gratitude takes, it is primarily displayed in the return.

We should also notice the importance of equity and the role of 'interest' in social reciprocity. First, as we noted regarding Arrian *Epictetio Dissertationes* 2.9.12, a balance of 'givings and receivings' is optimum in exchange relationships. The one who receives more is

58 C. P. Jones, *The Roman World of Dio Chrysostom* (Cambridge: Harvard University Press, 1978): 29.

59 S. C. Mott, 'The Power of Giving and Receiving: Reciprocity in Hellenistic Benevolence', *Current Issues in Biblical and Patristic Interpretation*, ed. G. F. Hawthorne (Grand Rapids: Eerdmans, 1975): 62.

60 Cf. Polyb. 2.6.9–11; 3.16.2–3; 6.6.6; Diod. Sic. 8.12.10–11; Dio Chrys. *Or*. 31.5; Plut. *Frag*. 160; Arr. *Epict. Diss*. 1.4.32; 2.23.23.

61 We should also mention that according to Seneca once a return has been made the relationship does not end, for the second gift puts the original giver under obligation and the process goes on (*Ben*. 2.18.5–6; cf. Arist. *Eth. Nic*. 8.13.9).

62 Indeed, Seneca says 'it is grievous torture to be under obligation to someone whom you object to' (*Ben*. 2.18.3).

greedy, not virtuous. Parity maintains not only the *status quo* of the relationship but also the *status* of each individual. In the event one member is able to out-give another, the relationship is threatened to move from one of friendship, that is equality, to one of patronage. In such a case the superior giver gains in social status and as a result the inferior giver must return all that he can, namely, honour and verbal thanks.[63] Along with this new respect the new benefactor can expect the devotion and love of his beneficiary.[64]

Secondly, because of these social dynamics, Seneca can speak of giving and receiving as a contest where the parties vie to outdo one another in conferring greater benefits (1.4.4; cf. Arist. *Eth. Nic.* 8.13.2).[65] When money is owed to a creditor one needs only to repay the same amount back, but when one is in debt for a benefit one must not only repay the benefit but also make an additional payment (2.18.5–6; cf. Diod. Sic. 1.70.6). A man is ungrateful if he repays a benefit without interest (Sen. *Ep.* 81.18). According to Aristotle the Great-souled man will return a service done to him with interest (καὶ ἀντευεργετικὸς πλειόνων), since this will reverse the tables and put the original benefactor in debt to him (*Eth. Nic.* 4.3.24; cf. Ps-Phocylides 80).

Thirdly, in light of our discussion of equity and 'interest' there arises a question: what expectations regarding material gratitude existed in the case of unequal exchange relationships? When one party is obviously socially inferior, how can a semblance of parity be maintained? The solution lies in the inferior offering praise and honour to the superior.

A clear example comes from Aristotle. He asserts that honour (τιμή) is the due reward for virtue and beneficence (ἀρετὴ καὶ εὐεργεσία, *Eth. Nic.* 8.14.2). Therefore, the principle that should

---

63 See the comments offered below on P.Mert. 12 and P.Oxy. 3057, pp. 74–7, 80–2. This point will be seen to be especially important in our exegesis of texts in Philippians. For there Paul implies that by receiving the Philippians' gifts he has not lost social standing, rather they have been elevated to the praiseworthy position of partners with him in the gospel (cf. κοινωνία εἰς τὸ εὐαγγελιον, Phil. 1.5 and συγκοινωνήσαντές μου τῇ θλίψει, 4.14).

64 Compare the statement made by Jesus: the kings of the Gentiles lord it over them and those who exercise authority over them are called benefactors (οἱ ἐξουσιά-ζοντες αὐτῶν εὐεργέται καλοῦνται, Luke 22.25). Likewise the good man for who one would die (Rom. 5.7) is doubtless the benefactor (see the treatment of Rom. 5.7 on pp. 193–4 and Andrew Clarke, 'The Good and the Just in Romans 5', *TynBul* 41 (1990): 128–42; cf. Ps-Demetrius' thankful letter, pp. 82–3).

65 Mott, 'Giving and Receiving', 61.

regulate interaction between unequal friends is that the one benefited must repay what he can, namely honour (8.14.3–4). Similarly, Plutarch urges rulers to share their benefaction (φιλανθρωπία) with their friends. These friends should praise and love them (ἐπαινεῖν καὶ ἀγαπᾶν) as the author of the favours (*Mor.* 808D). Though this is not a recurrent theme in *De Beneficiis*, Seneca apparently recognizes the problem of disparity at 6.29.2. He asserts that we can repay whatever we owe, even to the well-to-do. This is done through loyal advice, pleasing conversation, friendly intimacy and attentive ears. This general approach to the problem is confirmed by the gratitude seen in honorary inscriptions below.

A very common example of an unequal relationship of giving and receiving is found with parents in relation to their children.[66] Seneca asserts that the greatest of all benefits are those which parents give their children (*Ben.* 2.11.5; 5.5.2; 6.24.2), and his view is common in the sources.[67] Because a parent gives the child life and all that is needed from infancy to adulthood, the child is a great debtor to the parent. The adult is characterized as the giver, the benefactor, in the relationship. The child is the receiver, the socially inferior, the one obligated to show love and honour.[68]

There remains a question, however, regarding the form of verbalized gratitude in the first century. Was a verbal expression of gratitude expected at all? If so, what form did it take? In our attempt to answer these questions, our study will refer to the directions given by Seneca. We shall also examine actual examples of verbalized gratitude in the literary and non-literary sources. These examples will act as a check with regard to the didactic material in Seneca.

(i) Verbal gratitude [69]

We have seen that Seneca recommends expressing one's feelings of debt upon receiving a benefit. The greater the benefit, the greater

---

[66] We have mentioned this relationship briefly above. See the treatment of Josephus *Ap.* 2.206 and Philo *LA.* 3.10 on pp. 45 and 48.

[67] E.g., Philo *Spec.* 2.229; *Decal.* 112; Xen. *Mem.* 2.2.3; Arist. *Eth. Nic.* 8.11.1–4; SelPap. 1.121.27–8 (2nd AD); Sir. 7.28 (LXX); 1 Tim. 5.4.

[68] Seneca *Ben.* 3.1.5. These observations will be very helpful for understanding Paul's financial relationship with the Corinthians below (pp. 162–74).

[69] The following section is a revised and expanded version of the author's '"Thankless Thanks"', 261–70.

one should emphasize these expressions of debt (2.24.4). Such expressions correspond well to what we have seen elsewhere. When one receives a benefit one is under obligation to make a return. The making of a return may be called the discharge of a debt. Thus, an expression of debt acknowledges this obligation.

However, it is only at 2.24.4 that Seneca offers any advice on verbal gratitude. This text in itself does not allow us to make broad conclusions concerning verbal gratitude, but it does allow us to propose a theory. Since in the matrix of social reciprocity the return is primary, it is easy to see how verbal gratitude could be seen to consist most appropriately of a profession of debt: when material gratitude is owed, one can declare one's willingness to abide by the social conventions with a profession of debt. We assert that an expression of the receiver's feelings of debt is the most common element of verbalized gratitude in the ancient world. A verbal expression was not considered necessary, however, since the primary issue in gratitude was the return. Both to verify and to fill out this theory, we present some other texts below.

We begin with a statement concerning thanks made by a certain Chairas (P.Mert. 12; 29 August AD 58).[70] He writes in response to a letter received from a friend:

Χαιρᾶς Διονυσίωι τῶι φιλτάτωι ²πλεῖστα χαίρειν καὶ διὰ
πάντο(ς) ³ὑγιαίνειν. Κομισάμενός σου ἐπι(στολ(ὴν))
⁴οὕτως περιχαρὴς ἐγενόμη(ν ὡς εἰ) ⁵ὄντως ἐν τῇ ἰδίᾳ
ἐγεγόνειν, ἄ(νευ) ⁶γὰρ ταύτης οὐθέν ἐστι. Γράφειν δὲ
⁷σοι μεγάλας εὐχαριστίας παρετέο(ν)· ⁸δεῖ γὰρ τοῖς μὴ
φίλοις οὖσι διὰ λόγων ⁹εὐχαριστεῖν. Πείθομαι δὲ ὅτι ἐν
¹⁰γαληνείᾳ τινὶ ἐνεισχύω, καὶ εἰ μὴ ¹¹τὰ ἴσα σοι παρασχεῖν, βραχεια τινὰ ¹²παρέξομαι τῇ εἰς ἐμὲ φιλοστοργίᾳ.

Chairas to his dearest Dionysius, many greetings and continued health. I was as much delighted at receiving a letter from you as if I had been in my native place; for apart from that we have nothing. I may dispense with writing to you with a great show of thanks; for it is to those who are not friends that we must give thanks in words. I trust that I may maintain myself in some degree of

---

[70] Since private letters rarely bear a date (P. W. Pestman, *The New Papyrological Primer* (Leiden: E. J. Brill, 1990): 35; John L. White, *Light from Ancient Letters* (Philadelphia: Fortress Press, 1986): 8), this papyrus is particularly relevant for our present purpose.

serenity and be able, if not to give you an equivalent, at least to show some small return for your affection towards me.[71]

This text supplies us with a strikingly significant example, one in which a literate writer reflects on the nature of friendship and gratitude.[72] The correspondents here are apparently physicians.[73] Chairas receives from Dionysius a prescription for plasters (lines 13ff)[74] and for this favour, as well as the pleasure of receiving word from a friend, he expresses his joy.[75] This joy is readily understandable, not only because of the separation of the friends, but also because it is Chairas who is away (line 5), and the letter has brought him all that is truly desirable: the comfort of home (line 6a). Lines 6b–12 are the crux, and on them the following observations are made.

On 6b–9a the editor comments: 'The thought is that since verbal thanks are given to perfectly indifferent people they are misplaced between intimate friends: deeds (see the next sentence) are the medium there.'[76] Assuming the truth of this analysis we need to ask how the statement functions in the letter. Further, if deeds are the proper medium of thanks among friends, why does Chairas even need to mention verbal thanks?

Obviously Chairas' comment is not intended to be an almost didactic pronouncement on the social appropriateness of verbal gratitude. For if it were so, it would be at best superfluous and at worst an insult. Rather, his statement is made to rehearse social convention in order to assert the existence of friendship. Chairas in effect declares that their relationship has reached a point of parity,

---

[71] Text and translation from H. Idris Bell and C. H. Roberts, *A Descriptive Catalogue of the Greek Papyri in the Collection of Wilfred Merton, F.S.A.* (London: Emery Walker Limited, 1948): 50–2, lines 1–12. The provenance of P.Mert. 12 is uncertain (Oxyrhynchus or Hermopolis).

[72] Cited also by S. K. Stowers (*Letter Writing in Greco-Roman Antiquity* (Philadelphia: Westminster Press, 1986): 61–2) as an example of a friendly type letter. White (*Light*, 145) comments: 'This letter is striking because of its literate, almost philosophical expression of cordiality and friendship.'

[73] Bell/Roberts, *Greek Papyri of Wilfred Merton*, 50.

[74] It appears that a request had first been sent by Chairas. First, because it seems more likely that details of specialized prescriptions would only be given on request. Secondly, Chairas refers to two types of dry plaster mentioned, without recourse to their precise formulation, by Dionysius. This appears best understood as a response of Dionysius to a general or ambiguous request made by Chairas.

[75] An expression of joy at the reception of a letter is cited as an epistolary commonplace by Stowers, *Letter Writing*, 186; cf. P.Oxy. 3069, Phil. 4.10.

[76] Bell/Roberts, *Greek Papyri of Wilfred Merton*, 52.

a point at which verbal gratitude would be inappropriate if not socially awkward. When Chairas states that written verbal gratitude is necessary only to those who are not friends,[77] he in effect says, 'We *are* friends', though these words are omitted from his syllogism. We may reconstruct the logic this way:

> Premise 1:
> Verbal thanks are given to those who are not friends (lines 8–9a).
>
> Premise 2 (omitted):
> (We are friends).
>
> Conclusion:
> I need not give you verbal thanks (lines 6b–7).

Though Chairas' statement asserts friendship, it is not without its own truth. For his declaration of friendship to be valid he must assume Dionysius will accept his judgment on verbal gratitude (Premise 1). In some real sense it is not necessary for one to offer verbal thanks to friends. Yet here the issue is only verbal gratitude. In line 6b γράφειν is probably emphatic. For not only does it begin the sentence, but Chairas draws an explicit distinction between written or verbal gratitude and material gratitude, and it is the *written* gratitude he may dispense with. Conversely, by implication from the contrast being drawn, material gratitude may not be dispensed with; rather, it is necessary (δεῖ, line 8) and Chairas pledges to make this gratitude known (παρασχεῖν, 9b–12a).

Despite Premise 1 and the Conclusion Chairas is in fact offering a form of verbal thanks. First, his reflections on the suitability of verbal thanks merely take the place of an actual expression of gratitude. Also, the thanks he does not need to write, μεγάλας εὐχαριστίας, hints that he in fact feels a great debt of gratitude. But moreover, secondly, Chairas' statement of intention to repay is an epistolary cliché which we will investigate more fully below. Suffice it to say here that this acknowledgment of debt confirms our assertion, based on the evidence of Seneca, that an expression of one's feelings of debt appears to be the most common element of verbal gratitude.

---

[77] δεῖ γὰρ τοῖς μὴ φίλοις οὖσι διὰ λόγων εὐχαριστεῖν (lines 8–9a). τοῖς μὴ φίλοις οὖσι are taken to be patrons, viz., those who are not one's social equals. The necessity here probably arises from the common understanding that benefactors must receive verbal gratitude (i.e., praise and honour) since material gratitude is impossible (see above, pp. 72–3).

At the close of the letter Chairas urges Dionysius to remember his words (μέμνησο τῶν εἰρημένων, line 26). We understand that he here refers to his comment regarding his promised material thanks. For not only are such statements of intention common to the closing of letters, but the main body of the letter contains requests for Dionysius to perform, not to remember. Also, Chairas' rehearsal of social convention cannot be the object of remembrance. Rather, he wishes Dionysius to remember his beliefs regarding their relationship.

In summary, several assumptions underlying Papyri Merton 12 are instructive. First, verbal gratitude might be thought appropriate in such a context (viz., the receipt of a favour). This comes as no surprise to the western mind. Yet, secondly, verbal gratitude is misplaced in friendships of equity. Thirdly, verbal and material gratitude are both labelled εὐχαριστία. The latter of these is the proper medium for friends. Fourthly, the material gratitude necessary in this social context is repayment for the favour. Such gratitude is a serious social obligation. Finally, the return ought to be equivalent (τὰ ἴσα, line 11) to the affection received (τῇ φιλοστοργίᾳ, line 12). Here the meaning is plainly that affection, and the gratitude which is appropriate to it, is seen in actions.[78]

Chairas asserts that although material gratitude is expected between friends, verbal gratitude is misplaced. Does the papyrological evidence bear out this assertion? We attempt a critical evaluation of Chairas' statement below.

We should note first the relative scarcity of parallel documents.[79] Despite the great number of letters which have survived from antiquity few can be of help for our purpose. In addition to Papyri Merton 12, twenty-five letters have been collected which mention the receipt of goods or favours.[80] If our hypothesis is correct, we

---

[78] I am indebted to Professor E. A. Judge for his insightful comments on P.Mert. 12 as well as on P.Oxy. 3057 below.

[79] We pass over expressions of gratitude offered to a third party. There are few with εὐχαριστέω although other constructions (e.g., P.Mich. 499.9 (2nd AD): ἀνθομολογοῦμ(α)ι πάσην χάριν σοι) are relevant. See P.Mich. 466.48 (AD 107): εὐχαριστῶ Οὐολυσσιῳ καὶ Λονγείνῳ τῷ Βαρβάρῳ; P.Oxy. 811 (c. 1st AD): ἔγρ(αψά σο)ι εὐχαριστῶν Ἑρμίππου ὅτι; P.Oxy. 3059 (2nd AD): εὐχαριστῶ δὲ Θεωνάτι τῷ ἀδελφῷ σου; Rom. 16.4.

[80] Documents dated later than the 3rd century AD have been excluded as well as those which mention goods or money received as payment for rents, taxes, loans or other goods. The assumption has been made that those letters which record

should detect a correlation between the friendship of the correspondents and the lack of verbal thanks. Friendship is not a relationship to be detected easily in most documents. But at least one criterion is the title given to the sender or receiver. Of the twenty-six letters gathered, at least twenty contain some term of endearment.[81] Yet, only four of the twenty-six documents contain a verbal expression of gratitude:

Papyrologica Lugdano-Batava 42: Taphes writes to her sister Heras: γράφο σοι ἕος ἀναβένο, εἵνα εὐχαριστήσο σοι περ(ε)ὶ τῶν εἱματίων.

Papyri Michigan 483: Julius Clemens writes to his most esteemed (τιμιωτάτωι) Socration: χάριν σοι ἔχω τῇ φιλαν(θ)ρωπίᾳ περὶ τοῦ ἐλαίου καθὼς ἔγραψέ μοι Πτολεμαῖος (π)αρειληφέναι αὐτο (lines 3–5a).

Papyri Michigan 498: Gemellus writes to brother[82] Apollinarius: χάρις σοι πλείστη, ἄδελφε, μεριμνήσαντί με· ἡ σύστασίς σου πολύ με ὠφέλησε (lines 4–7a).

Oxyrhynchus Papyri 963: Ophele writes to her mother: χάριν δὲ σοι οἶδα, μῆτερ, ἐπὶ τῇ σπουδῇ τοῦ καθεδραρίου, ἐκομισάμην γὰρ αὐτό.[83]

These expressions are much like what we would expect by western standards. There is mention of the good deed and its appreciation. With reference to our hypothesis there are significant observations to be made.

First, the terms used to address the receivers (τιμιωτάτωι,

---

private affairs will more closely parallel the Philippian letter than those recording commercial transactions. Operating with these guidelines the following documents have been found: CPR 7.54 (2nd AD), 8.10 (2nd–3rd AD); P.Haun. 18 (3rd AD); P.Lugd.Bat. 42 (2nd AD); P.Mert. 12 (AD 58); P.Mich. 281, 476, 477 (all early 2nd AD), 483 (time of Hadrian), 494, 496, 498 (all 2nd AD), 508 (2nd–3rd AD); P.Oslo 53 (2nd AD); P.Oxy. 113 (2nd AD), 531 (2nd AD), 963 (2nd–3rd AD), 1481 (early 2nd AD), 2190 (late 1st AD), 2983 (2nd–3rd AD), 3057 (1st–2nd AD), 3060 (early 2nd AD), 3063 (2nd AD), 3807 (AD 26–8); SB 6.9017.12, 6.9017.13 (both 1st–2nd AD).

81 Ἀδελφός, 8 times; μήτηρ, 4; πατήρ, 3; υἱός, 1; φιλτάτος, 3; τιμιώτατος, 1.

82 Though ἀδελφός is apparently used literally here, it often occurs figuratively as a mark of affection (White, Light, 106, 182; Stowers, Letter Writing, 72). In addition to White's examples see P.Oxy. 2783.

83 No line designations have been supplied by the editors (Bernard P. Grenfell and Arthur S. Hunt, The Oxyrhynchus Papyri, Part VI (London: Egypt Exploration Society, 1908): 318).

ἄδελφε, μῆτερ) would assume a degree of intimacy. Yet, in contradiction to our hypothesis, in these four letters we have a verbal expression of thanks.

Secondly, the absence of verbal gratitude in the other twenty-two examples is instructive. This absence would seem to confirm our hypothesis. For of these twenty-two examples at least fifteen contain some term of endearment, and the actual number may be higher since not all the texts are complete.

Thirdly, it should be noted that three of these four expressions of thanks are all given for a favour, not for the goods received. Julius Clemens acknowledges the good deed (τῇ φιλαν(θ)ρωπίᾳ περὶ τοῦ ἐλαίου) done on his behalf to Ptolemy. Gemellus refers to Apollinarius' concern (μεριμνάω) seen specifically in his recommendation (σύστασις). Although she has received a stool from her mother, Ophele's comment shows that the object of her thanks is her mother's eagerness (ἐπὶ τῇ σπουδῇ).[84] And indeed this is strengthened by the next line: οὐκ ἀλλότριο(ν γὰρ) τοῦ ἤθους ποιεῖς, φιλ(τάτη μῆτερ, σ)πουδάζουσα (. . .). These data neither support nor disprove our hypothesis. Moreover, they provide us with contrasting examples to Papyri Merton 12, where it appears that Chairas has received a favour from Dionysius, without giving thanks.

Fourthly, in Papyri Michigan 483 and 498 the thanks are not wholly restricted to the use of χάρις σοι. At the end of 483 we find: καὶ σὺ δὲ περὶ ὧν ἐὰν χρείαν ἔχῃς γράφε μοι (lines 5b–6a), and 498: γράφε μοι περὶ τῆς σωτηρίας σου καὶ ὧν θέλις (lines 22b–24a). The ending of Oxyrhynchus Papyri 963 has been lost. This phrase is another epistolary cliché common to papyri as late as the fourth century.[85] It displays a writer's willingness to repay through deeds and makes obvious that verbal gratitude was not seen as a replacement for the necessary material gratitude. In addition to the three examples cited above, such a phrase also occurs among our sample of twenty-six in Oxyrhynchus Papyri 113 and 531. This confirms the portion of our hypothesis which states that material gratitude is the necessary medium with friends.

---

[84] On this use of σπουδάζω see P.Jews 1 and Ps-Demetrius' thankful letter (quoted below, pp. 82–3).

[85] In addition to the examples of Henry A. Steen ('Les Clichés Épistolaires dans les Lettres sur Papyrus grecques', *Classica et Medievalia* 1 (1938): 128–30), see P.Tebt. 408 (AD 03): καὶ σὺ δὲ περὶ ὧν βούλε(ι) γράφε.

With regard to the other letters in our collection we can only speculate regarding the lack of verbal thanks because of the paucity of evidence. For example, in Oxyrhynchus Papyri 3060 Ptolemaeus catalogues the goods received from brother Horis. Only the bare acknowledgement (ἐκομι(σά)μην, line 2) is made with no personal reflection or word of thanks. Similarly in Papyri Michigan 281 Satornilos, without recourse to χάρις or cognates, acknowledges (ἐκομι(σά)μην, line 4) the monthly allowance sent by his mother Aphrodous.[86]

Slightly more instructive is Oxyrhynchus Papyri 1481 (early 2nd AD), in which Theonas, a young soldier, informs his mother of his welfare (lines 1-6a). Near the end he mentions receiving (ἐκομισάμεθα, line 7) gifts and a letter from her. Though εὐχαριστέω occurs immediately after this, the text has been lost. The editor supplies τοῖς θεοῖς as the object.[87] Of interest is the repeated request not to send anything (lines 6b-7a, and postscript). The text does not provide details to explain the acknowledgement the soldier puts forward. Here we will simply draw attention to three aspects of this acknowledgement which will be of use below. First, the soldier does not acknowledge receipt of the gifts at the beginning, secondly, there is no formal thanks given,[88] and thirdly, Theonas makes it obvious that he does not seek a gift.

Though not containing an expression of gratitude Oxyrhynchus Papyri 3057 (1st-2nd AD) is instructive because the same social conventions on debt are reflected:

> [1]Ἀμμώνιος Ἀπολλωνίωι τῶι [2]ἀδελφῶι χαίρειν. [3]ἐκο-
> μισάμην τὴν κεχιασμένην ἐπιστολὴν [4]καὶ τὴν ἱματο-
> φορίδα καὶ τοὺς φαινόλας καὶ τὰς [5]σύριγγας οὐ καλάς,
> τοὺς δὲ φαινόλας οὐχ ὡς [6]παλαιοὺς ἔλαβον ἀλλ᾽ εἴ τι
> μεῖζόν ἐστιν και – [7]νῶν διὰ προαίρεσιν· οὐ θέλω δέ σε,
> ἄδελφε, βα – [8]ρύνειν με ταῖς συνεχέσ{εσ}ι φιλανθρω-
> πίαις, [9]‘. . .’ οὐ δυνάμενον ἀμείψασθαι, αὐτὸ δὲ μόνον
> [10]ἡμεῖς προαίρεσιν φιλικῆς διαθέσεως νομί – [11]ζομεν
> παρεστακέναι σοι.

[86] J. G. Winter, 'In the Service of Rome: Letters from the Michigan Collection of Papyri', *Classical Philology* 22 (1927): 250.

[87] B. P. Grenfell and A. S. Hunt, *The Oxyrhynchus Papyri: Part XII* (London: The Egypt Exploration Fund, 1916): 240. In view of (τοῖς θεοῖς) πάντοτε we may conjecture that this is the beginning of a salutation and prayer to the gods for the health of the recipient (White, *Light*, 158).

[88] Alexander, 'Structure', 97.

> Ammonius to Apollonius his brother, greetings. I received the crossed letter and the portmanteau and the cloaks and the reeds, not good ones – the cloaks I received not as old ones, but as better than new if that's possible, because of the spirit (in which they were given). But I don't want you, brother, to load me with these continual kindnesses, since I can't repay them – the only thing we supposed ourselves to have offered you is (our) feelings of friendship.[89]

The historical situation, at least as far as it concerns us, is not difficult to reconstruct. Ammonius has received a gift, probably unsolicited.[90] The response gives every impression of being unforced and sincere, reflecting a good relationship. The writer asserts his confidence in Apollonius (lines 26–7) and is free to mention the current distress he experiences (οὐχ ἔθος ἐχούσης ἠρεμεῖν διὰ τὰ ἐπερχόμενα, lines 27–8). If we can assume that this letter reflects a positive and fairly intimate social relationship,[91] then, at least by twentieth-century standards, the absence of 'thank-you' is notable. But should this letter be labelled 'thankless thanks'? If these papyri permit a generalization, we should say that in private letters one should acknowledge debt and assert one's intention to repay. This document is conspicuous for its use of βαρύνειν.[92] That is, not only do we see the system of exchange working here, but also the apparent feeling that it was a burden for some to operate under these social expectations.[93] Ammonius acknowledges receipt and the *obligation to repay*, but asserts his inability to meet this social expectation. As a result, Ammonius appears to be struggling with a challenge to his social status. Because he is unable to repay, and

---

[89] Text and translation are taken from P. J. Parsons, *The Oxyrhynchus Papyri XLII* (London: The Egypt Exploration Society, 1974): 144–5.

[90] Since the writer asserts his reluctance to receive future favours owing to his inability to repay, it seems more likely that this gift was unsolicited.

[91] On a possible Christian context for this papyrus see C. J. Hemer, 'Ammonius to Apollonius, Greeting', *Buried History* 12 (1976): 84–91; P. J. Parsons, 'The Earliest Christian Letter?' *Miscellanea Papyrologica*, ed. R. Pintaudi (Firenze: Gonnelli, 1980): 289; G. R. Stanton, 'The Proposed Earliest Christian Letter on Papyrus and the Origin of the Term *Philallelia*', *ZPE 54 (1984): 49–63*.

[92] This text may have relevance to Paul's desire not to be a burden to the Corinthians (2 Cor. 11.9) and thus his refusal to receive their support. Marshall, *Enmity*, does not mention P.Oxy. 3057. See our discussion of βαρύνειν below, pp. 168–71.

[93] E. A. Judge, *Rank and Status in the World of the Caesars and of St. Paul* (Canterbury: University of Canterbury Press, 1982): 23; cf. Tac. *Hist.* 4.3; Thuc. 2.40.4.

asserts that these gifts are out of keeping with his mere offers of friendship, it may well be that the kindnesses[94] here shown are becoming gifts which put him below Apollonius in social standing.

Finally, the thankful letter found its way into Ps-Demetrius' list of epistolary types (2nd BC–3rd AD). Since the epistolary types listed in Ps-Demetrius' work are distillations of the conventions suitable for each type, this letter is especially relevant in our attempt to define the basic characteristics of verbal gratitude. We cite his example in full:

'Απευχαριστικός ἐστιν τὸ μνημονεύειν ὀφείλειν χάριν.
οἷον·
    'Εφ' οἷς εὐεργέτησάς με διὰ λόγων, σπουδάσω ἔργῳ δεῖξαι τὴν ἐμαυτοῦ προαίρεσιν, ἣν ἔχω πρὸς σέ. ἔλαττον γὰρ τοῦ καθήκοντος ὑπείληφα τὸ δι' ἐμοῦ σοι γινόμενον, οὐδὲ γὰρ τὸν βίον ὑπὲρ σοῦ προέμενος ἀξίαν ἀποδώσειν χάριν ὧν εὖ πέπονθα. τῶν κατ' ἐμὲ δὲ ὅ τι βούλει, μὴ γράφε παρακαλῶν, ἀλλ' ἀπαιτῶν χάριν. ὀφείλω γάρ.

The thankful type calls to mind the gratitude that is due (the reader). For example:

I hasten to show in my actions how grateful I am to you for the kindness you showed me in your words. For I know that what I am doing for you is less than I should, for even if I gave my life for you, I should still not be giving adequate thanks for the benefits I have received. If you wish anything that is mine, do not write and request it, but demand a return. For I am in your debt.[95]

We point out the absence of εὐχαριστέω (or ἔχειν χάριν, etc.) in an epistolary pattern given as a thankful letter. If a verbal expression of gratitude is to be found, this expression consists, not in the use of εὐχαριστέω, but in acknowledging the affection and goodwill received, professing debt, and promising to repay. Notice the words chosen in this paradigm which we see in other non-

---

[94] Φιλανθρωπία (line 8b) is wide enough in its meaning to denote aid or help as well as benevolent condescension. If the later of these is preferable it shows Ammonius views Apollonius' gifts as given from a spirit of benefaction rather than of friendship.

[95] Text and translation are taken from Abraham J. Malherbe, *Ancient Epistolary Theorists* (Atlanta: Scholars Press, 1988): 40–1. For a modern catalogue of epistolary types see Harold E. Meyer, *Lifetime Encyclopedia of Letters* (Englewood Cliffs: Prentice Hall, Inc., 1983). Under the thankful letter category Meyer supplies 26 sub-types (*Encyclopedia of Letters*, 297–315).

literary letters: προαίρεσις, χάρις (and cognates), ἀποδίδωμι. In addition καθήκω and ἀξίος are common in honorary inscriptions to speak of the appropriate and worthy return made for benefactions.[96]

To conclude this discussion of verbal gratitude, we see that the sparse comments of Seneca encourage a receiver to acknowledge debt verbally. In actual papyrus examples of written gratitude phrases such as σὺ δὲ περὶ ὧν ἐὰν χρείαν ἔχῃς γράφε μοι (Papyri Michigan 483) seem to perform this function. But these phrases are not common in our collection. Likewise, expressions of gratitude employing εὐχαριστέω (or cognates) are uncommon. It appears from our papyrus examples that verbal gratitude in written form was not a social expectation, except when writing to someone who was socially superior.

(ii) Material gratitude

Seneca's comments on the return for benefits has stressed the place of the material return in social reciprocity. Even after goodwill has been shown in response to goodwill, an object (the material gratitude) is still owed for an object (the benefit; see 2.35.1). What this object might be will vary with the persons, the context and the social standing. Nevertheless, we have seen clearly that a counter-gift or favour was understood to be the item that discharged the debt of obligation.

There is one form of verbal (written) gratitude which, for the sake of discussion, we will call material gratitude: the honorary inscription given in response to the goodwill of a benefactor.[97] Since, by definition, such honorary inscriptions are given out of gratitude, it is not surprising that εὐχαριστία occurs often.[98] The social conventions we see operating with regard to inscriptions are the same as those we have seen repeatedly in the literary authors and in papyri. The goodwill of a benefactor is requited with the

---

[96] See below pp. 84–6 and *SIG*[2] 324.33; 326.14, 47; 330.6; 732.29.

[97] We label such gratitude 'material' because of its lasting, physical character. Recall Dio Chrysostom's protestation that the people who changed the inscriptions on statues took away the rewards due to those honoured (*Or.* 31.25, 27, 29; see above, pp. 70–1).

[98] It is unfortunate that, despite the large number of uses of the word group, Conzelmann's treatment of εὐχαριστέω and cognates has little reference to the use in inscriptions ('εὐχαριστέω', *TDNT*, 9.407–9).

show of goodwill the people offer in the inscription.[99] The wording
of these honorary inscriptions typically follows a set pattern. This
pattern seldom varies, and is found to have prevailed in honorary
inscriptions for the 500 years preceding the reign of Caesar
Augustus.[100] Therefore we do not consider it advantageous to
multiply examples. We will simply provide a few texts which
demonstrate the social expectations and practice.[101]

The pattern followed was this: 'Whereas (ἐπειδή) our benefactor
is a good man, be it resolved (δεδόχθαι) by the city to praise our
benefactor and honour him with the following honours.' Less
often, yet still common, a final clause appears: 'in order that (ὅπως
or ἵνα) all may see our gratitude'. This final clause is most
instructive for our purpose. Here gratitude obviously is displayed in
the public praising of the benefactor and the physical monument
raised to his honour. That is, *the praise and the monument are the
gratitude*. Below we present a few examples.

A certain Apollonios from Kalindoia is hailed as ἀνὴρ ἀγαθὸς
καὶ πάσης τειμῆς ἄξιος (lines 8–9).[102] After a description of his
virtue and accomplishments (lines 10–39), it is resolved (δεδόχθαι)
to praise him on account of the brilliance of his soul and of his
virtue displayed toward his land (ἐπαινέσαι αὐτὸν ἐπὶ τῆ<ι>
λανπρότητι τῆς ψυχῆς καὶ τῆς εἰς τὴν πατρίδα φιλοδοξίας, lines
39b–43a). These honorary measures are proposed in order that all
the rest of the citizens may see the gratitude of the city (ἵνα καὶ οἱ
λοιποὶ τῶν πολειτῶν ἀποθεωροῦντες εἰς τὴν εὐχαριστίαν τῆς
πόλεως) and may become eager to seek glory and the benefit of
their country (πρόθυμοι γείνωνται φιλοδοξεῖν καὶ τῆι πατρίδι
προσφέρεσθαι φιλανθρώπως, lines 46b–48). This last clause is
especially telling for our understanding of gratitude and the role it
plays in the social convention. The assertion is that viewers will see
the gratitude of the people as they view the monument (ἄγαλμα,

---

[99] We refer to indiscriminate euergetism offered by the benefactor and the group
   return given by the city. On such euergetism see Paul Veynre, *Bread and Circuses.
   Historical Sociology and Political Pluralism*, trans. Brian Pearce (London: The
   Penguin Press, 1990).

[100] F. W. Danker, *Benefactor: Epigraphic Study of a Graeco-Roman and New
   Testament Semantic Field* (St Louis: Clayton Publishing House, 1982): 27; Bruce
   W. Winter, 'The Public Honouring of Christian Benefactors: Romans 13.3–4 and
   1 Peter 2.14–15', *JSNT* 34 (1988): 88.

[101] See further Wilhelm Larfeld, *Handbuch der griechischen Epigraphik*, 2 vols.
   (Leipzig: O. R. Reisland, 1902–7): 2.763–7, and Ernst Nachmanson, 'Zu den
   Motivformeln der griechischen Ehrenschriften', *Eranos* 11 (1911): 180–96.

[102] *SEG* 35.744 (1 AD).

lines 44, 45). The appropriate thanks are contained in the recognition and praise which the monument displays. Also this demonstration of gratitude should incite others to pursue the same honours through benefaction. Consequently, this award, in addition to discharging the debt of gratitude the city owes Apollonius, actually solicits further benefaction.[103] Although the wording varies, such final clauses occur frequently and reflect the same conventions of gratitude.

A tablet from Chersonesus memorializes the virtuous Diophantes of Asklapiodoros.[104] He is called the φίλος (καὶ εὐεργέτας) of the city (lines 2b–3a). On account of (ἐφ᾿ οἷς)[105] his good deeds in the past the people gave thanks and honoured him with the appropriate honours (εὐχαριστῶν ἐτίμασε ταῖς καθηκούσαις αὐτὸν τιμαῖς, line 14). However, in light of his continuing aid to the city further honours are conveyed, in order that the city may be seen to return the appropriate thanks to benefactors (ὁ δᾶμος τοῖς εὐεργέταις ἑαυτοῦ τ(ὰς) καθηκούσας φαίνηται χάριτας ἀποδιδούς, line 46). Here again the presentation of praise and the conveyance of honours are viewed as the expressions of thanks. Particularly in this case the construction with the participle (εὐχαριστῶν ἐτίμασε) shows that the medium of thanks is praise. Moreover, these honours are appropriate (καθηκούσαις, line 14, καθηκούσας, line 47), the implication being their suitability to the benefactions received. The city should award these suitable honours in order to be seen by others as doing so, thus discharging their social obligation to give back thanks. Here ὅπως ὁ δᾶμος φαίνηται χάριτας ἀποδιδούς is the structural equivalent of ἵνα οἱ λοιποὶ ἀποθεωροῦντες εἰς τὴν εὐχαριστίαν τῆς πόλεως in SEG 35.744 above and shows that εὐχαριστεῖν and χάριν ἀποδιδόναι can be synonymous.[106]

Here we summarize the findings from our cursory treatment of inscriptions. First, the ideology assumed in the texts shows gratitude to be a serious social obligation. Sufficient proof are the

---

[103] We will have recourse to this aspect of the social convention below (pp. 86–8). Also see Mott, 'Giving and Receiving', 63–4.

[104] *SIG*² 326 (Roman period).

[105] We note the use of ἐπί with the dative to give the grounds for thanks, a significant factor when we come to examine Phil. 1.3.

[106] Helmut Engelmann, Dieter Knibbe and Reinhold Merkelbach, *Die Inschriften von Ephesus. Teil IV*. (Bonn: Rudolf Habelt, 1980): 1440.11b–12a. For further examples of the final clause see *SEG* 546.22–25; *SIG*² 192.44, 330.6, 365.6, 465.10, 529.43, 928.14; *IE* I.5.43–6, IV.1412.7–8, V.1447.14–15.

numerous clauses which are concerned to *show* the people giving the appropriate response to benefaction as well as the statements that these honours conveyed are the appropriate response to the benefactors. Secondly, although εὐχαριστία occurs frequently in these texts, it does not appear as an address to an individual or group in the second person. Rather, εὐχαριστία is a label used to describe the *actions* of the grateful. Thanks consist in the public praise the benefactor receives. Thirdly, not infrequently the final ἵνα or ὅπως clause purposes to incite others to benefaction. The thanksgiving which these dedications present is an honour that other potential benefactors are encouraged to strive after. In this sense then εὐχαριστία is used to solicit goodwill and not merely repay it.

Gratitude as solicitation

Thus far in our consideration of aspects of receiving we have seen the necessity of gratitude. Material gratitude, that is, gratitude in the form of a return, was a social obligation. Also, we have seen that verbal gratitude, when given, consisted of an expression of debt. This expression acknowledged one's willingness to abide by the social convention. Yet to be considered is gratitude as a form of solicitation, to which we have already referred briefly.[107]

In our section on the gratitude mentioned in inscriptions we noticed that these sometimes contain a final ὅπως or ἵνα clause which gives a further purpose for the gratitude of the inscription. Those who see the public praise and honour paid to benefactors should be stirred to display the same virtue which brought the original benefactor such recognition. Although examples of gratitude as solicitation are scarce in the literary texts, there is some evidence. A clear example comes from Pliny. In *Letters* 2.13 he writes to Priscus on behalf of a certain Voconius Romanus, desiring that the latter be promoted. Pliny states that there is no one besides Priscus to whom he would rather be under an obligation. This reference is a before-the-fact allusion to the return Pliny will owe to Priscus as a result of this favour. The patronizing language is obviously being used as a form of solicitation. Further, at the end of Pliny's description of Romanus' good character he asserts that the best way to maintain the obligation that Romanus feels toward

---

[107] See above, p. 85. See also Mott, 'Giving and Receiving', 63–4.

Pliny is by adding to it, especially since Romanus always receives Pliny's good offices with so much gratitude as to merit further benefaction.

Very similar to Pliny *Letters* 2.13, we saw above that papyri which make requests sometimes contain promises to do a favour in return.[108] We take these statements as references to the social convention used as a way to encourage the desired behaviour from the addressee.[109]

In Acts 24.3 Tertullus begins his speech to Felix with praise for the procurator. After reference to his past wisdom and foresight, Tertullus reminds Felix that the people have always received the procurator's many benefactions with all gratitude (πάσης εὐχαριστίας).[110] With these comments Tertullus is obviously trying to gain yet another benefit: the condemnation of Paul.

Dio Chrysostom, upon honours being proposed for him, delivers *Oration* 44 to the people of Prusa.[111] He mentions the honours already paid him in the past, as well as those given to his ancestors and relatives (44.3–5). He asserts that he himself even feels the obligation to give back thanks for these honours, since the people, in giving honour and praise, more than requited his relatives for their benefaction (44.4). Here we see the response from the side of the socially superior who has received the public recognition. There is a feeling of the need to respond further (cf. Polyb. 18.16).[112]

In conclusion we refer to the comments of Mott:

> Receiving a benefit thus was a source of power, not only from the boon of the initial gift, but also because it gave the recipient the fortunate opportunity of placing a person from a more advantageous position in society under obligation.[113]

From the above we have seen that gratitude was an important and expected social convention. The subject arises surprisingly often in

---

[108] E.g., P.Tebt. 408; P.Mich. 483, 498. For further examples see Steen, 'Les Clichés', 128–30.

[109] White, *Light*, 205; cf. Pliny *Letters* 3.2.

[110] On the function of such introductory praise in legal proceedings see Bruce W. Winter, 'The Importance of the *Captatio Benevolentiae* in the Speeches of Tertullus and Paul in Acts 24: 1–21', *JTS* 42 (1991): 505–31.

[111] On the benefactions which evoked this proposal of honours see Jones, *Dio Chrysostom*, 106–12.

[112] See also our collection of texts on gratitude as solicitation taken from Seneca (Appendix A, pp. 201–4).

[113] Mott, 'Giving and Receiving', 63.

ancient literature. Indeed, as far back as Hesiod and Homer and right into the first century with Seneca, one sees the assumption reflected that kindness or favours bring with them the obligation to make a return.[114] Further, gratitude is primarily considered to take the form of a material return, viz., a counter-gift or favour as opposed to a merely verbal response.

Conclusion

This chapter has demonstrated that in the Greco-Roman world social reciprocity played an integral part in the conventions that dominated inter-personal relationships. Gifts and favours were not to be taken for granted and carried serious obligations.[115] The sources show this to be true, not only for the wealthy such as Seneca, but also for those at all levels of society.

What were the social expectations with which the Philippians operated? We are constrained to assume that they adopted the prevailing view with regard to the giving and receiving of gifts as reflected in the literature we have studied above. We shall need strong evidence to assume otherwise. Thus, as we approach the response of the apostle in the next chapter, we need to keep in mind these social conventions.

Here we offer a brief summary of the conventions we have uncovered: (1) One may establish a social relationship by giving a gift or favour. If this gift is accepted and repaid, a lasting relationship is formed. If it is rejected, enmity can result, for the refusal reflects negatively on the social status of the giver. (2) Such reciprocal relationships and obligations can obtain between individuals, between groups, and between individuals and groups. (3) The receipt of a gift or favour places the recipient under obligation to respond with a counter-gift or favour. This counter-gift is the expected expression of gratitude. (4) The giver is the socially superior member of the relationship. If parity in giving and receiving can be maintained, the parties will retain their relative

---

[114] E.g., Hes. *Erga* 349; Lys. 3.5; 15.10; Ps-Plato *Def.* 413A.10; Xen. *Mem.* 2.1.28; 4.4.24; *Oec.* 5.12, 7.37; Arist. *Eth. Nic.* 4.1.29–30, 5.5.6–7, 8.7.2. In Hellenistic Jewish literature the same conventions appear, e.g., 1 Macc. 10.26–11.53; 2 Macc. 12.29–31; Sir. 12.1–2; Philo *Virt.* 82–84; Joseph. *AJ* 4.266, 8.300, 19.184.

[115] This convention also appears in primitive societies of the 19th and 20th centuries. For older literature see Hamilton-Grierson, 'Gifts (Primitive and Savage)', 197–209. More recently see Mauss, *The Gift*; Foster, 'Peasant Society', 293–315; Gregory, 'Image of Limited Good', 73–92.

statuses. If, on the other hand, one party gains the advantage in giving, that party will likewise gain greater social status. (5) Praise and honour (i.e., verbal thanks) is one part of the expected return from the inferior party in an exchange relationship. Such a verbal response is considered the appropriate repayment to be offered by the inferior member who cannot offer a material equivalent to his benefactor. (6) Words and phrases which often figure in commercial contexts are sometimes used to describe social relationships of giving and receiving. Because of the transactional character of social relationships in the Greco-Roman world, this use is quite comprehensible. (7) Divine reward does not enter into Greco-Roman social reciprocity.[116] Although social reciprocity was found to operate in the social world of the Old Testament,[117] didactic sections of the Old Testament made clear that Yahweh rewards benefactors. Comparable statements are completely lacking in the Greco-Roman sources.

[116] Herman, *Ritualized Friendship*, 49.
[117] See our conclusions to chapter 2, pp. 49–50.

4

PARTNERSHIP IN PHILIPPIANS 1–2

After our presentation of background material to illustrate the reciprocal character of gift and service relationships in the Greco-Roman world, we now come to the Pauline texts. A complete understanding of Paul's response to the Philippians' gifts will require exegesis of several texts in the letter which mention their financial support and their missionary partnership.[1] We begin with Philippians 1–2. Study begins here because these chapters prepare the readers for the direct response Paul makes to the Philippians' gift in 4.10–20.

We undertake study of texts from chapters 1–2 in order to gain a fuller understanding of the meaning and significance of the giving and receiving the apostle experienced with this congregation. We shall focus our attention on two issues. First, those sections which demonstrate that the apostle's relationship with the Philippians was unique amongst his congregations. The primary theme for us to notice is that of the gospel and its advance.[2] Secondly, we shall devote attention to those texts which help us to discern the particular epistolary situation which produced this letter. We shall do this in order to evaluate the assertion of scholars that response to the Philippians' gift could not have been one of the primary reasons for the letter.[3]

---

[1] Phil. 4.10–20 will receive study below, pp. 121–61.

[2] Significantly, the other prison letters (Eph., Col., Phlm.) contain no reference to the advance of the gospel despite the apostle's chains.

[3] If indeed a reason for 'the letter' can be spoken of at all in light of the partition theories which are so widespread. The theory of redaction has been so well accepted that some scholars even approach study of the text with the view that compilation is the 'firm discovery' of scholarship, feeling no need to defend the hypothesis; e.g., Pheme Perkins, 'Christology, Friendship and Status: Rhetoric in Philippians', *Society of Biblical Literature 1987 Seminar Papers*, ed. Kent Harold Richards (Atlanta: Scholars Press, 1987): 509–20. See our discussion in chapter 1, pp. 17–19.

We shall attempt to show presently that the gospel is a significant theme in Philippians.[4] It is no coincidence that the gospel plays such a significant role, for the Philippian 'giving and receiving' is based on a certain attitude toward that gospel. The Philippians are partners in the advance of the gospel message.

Partnership in the Gospel: 1.3–11

We begin with Paul's introductory thanksgiving. Since, next to 4.10–20, Philippians 1.3–11 contains the clearest data to help us define the financial relationship which Paul enjoyed with the Philippians, we shall discuss this passage in some detail. In addition, this passage has similarities with 4.10–20 which are particularly helpful in understanding the context from which Paul's direct response to the Philippians' gifts is to be understood.

We should assume that the letter's introduction will present the main themes the apostle wishes to cover.[5] We will see this assumption borne out in our treatment of several texts. First, we see it verified, at least in part, by the considerable verbal and conceptual similarity between 1.3–11 and 4.10–20. The following chart makes this clear:[6]

Phil. 1	Phil. 4
v. 3 εὐχαριστῶ τῷ θεῷ	Ἐχάρην δὲ ἐν κυρίῳ, v. 10a.
v. 3 μνείᾳ ὑμῶν	ἀνεθάλετε, v. 10a.
v. 4 χάρα	ἐχάρην, v. 10a.
v. 4 δεήσει μου ὑπὲρ ὑμῶν	ἐφ᾽ ᾧ καὶ ἐφρονεῖτε, v. 10c.
(understood of past habit)	
v. 5 κοινωνία	ἐκοινώνησεν, v. 15.
v. 5 εὐαγγέλιον	εὐαγγέλιον, v. 15.
v. 5b ἀπὸ . . . ἄχρι τοῦ νῦν	ἐν ἀρχῇ, v. 15.

---

[4] This has already been noticed by Peter T. O'Brien, 'The Importance of the Gospel in Philippians', *God Who is Rich in Mercy*, ed. Peter T. O'Brien and David G. Peterson (Homebush West, Australia: Lancer Books, 1986): 213–33; Robert C. Swift, 'The Theme and Structure of Philippians', *BSac* 141 (1984): 237.

[5] That Paul's introductory thanksgivings perform this function, amongst others, is recognized by P. T. O'Brien, *Introductory Thanksgivings in the Letters of Paul* (Leiden: E. J. Brill, 1977): 262–3, Paul Schubert, *Form and Function of Pauline Thanksgivings* (Berlin: Töpelmann, 1939): 24, and Lohmeyer, *Philipper*, 13.

[6] Several other scholars have referred to the similarity between these texts (e.g., Schubert, *Form and Function*, 77; Jewett, 'Epistolary Thanksgiving', 53; O'Brien, *Philippians*, 514; William J. Dalton, 'The Integrity of Philippians', *Bib* 60 (1979): 101). It appears, however, that a detailed comparison has never been undertaken.

v. 6 ὁ ἐναρξάμενος	ἐν τῷ ἐνδυναμοῦντι
ἐν ὑμῖν ἔργον	με, v. 13.
v. 7a φρονεῖν ὑπὲρ ὑμῶν	τὸ ὑπὲρ ἐμοῦ φρονεῖν, v. 10b.
(understood of current action)	
v. 7b συγκοινωνούς	συγκοινωνήσαντες, v. 14.
v. 7b δεσμοῖς	θλῖψις, v. 14.
v. 9 περισσεύῃ	περισσεύω, vv. 12, 18.
v. 11 πεπληρωμένοι	πεπλήρωμαι, vv. 18, 19.
v. 11a καρπός	καρπός, v. 17.
v. 11b Ἰησοῦς	Ἰησοῦς, v. 19.
v. 11c δόξαν θεοῦ	τῷ θεῷ ἡ δόξα, v. 20.

This close similarity demonstrates three points. First, it shows that Paul's response to the Philippians' gift is not an afterthought. Though the message of 4.10–20 is more concrete and specific, that message is basically a reiteration of the thought found in 1.3–11. Thus, Paul's reflections on the personal and theological meaning of the gift begin early. The Philippians will desire a social response to their gift and these reflections provide it. That is, these early reflections answer the question, 'How does Paul feel about receiving our gift?' Likewise they provide the theological response the Philippians need in order to understand properly the gift in their social context. That is, they answer the question, 'What is the real Christian meaning and significance of our gift?'

Secondly, and more significantly, this similarity demonstrates the importance of κοινωνία εἰς τὸ εὐαγγέλιον as that which is primary in the apostle's evaluation of the meaning and significance of the gift. The Philippians' partnership in the early days of their acquaintance with the gospel (4.15, cf. 1.5) is that for which Paul gives thanks to God in an early part of the letter. As an unmistakable glance back to 1.5, 4.15 stresses the unique place of the Philippians as workers who forward the gospel not only through their own witness and life in Philippi (1.27–8, 2.15), but also through their financial sharing with the apostle to the Gentiles.

Thirdly, as a matter of structure, we see that the letter opens and closes with a reference to the Philippians' support. Others have noticed the extensive use of inclusion in Philippians,[7] and we will have recourse to further discussion of structure below. Here it should be said that the large-scale inclusion forces us to view the

---

[7]   E.g., Garland, 'Composition', 141–73, esp. 159–60.

thought of the letter as more concerned with providing a response to the Philippians' support than has commonly been recognized.

Now we come to the actual content of 1.3–11. This section is arranged in three parts: Thanksgiving (vv. 3–6), Statement of Affection (vv. 7–8) and Prayer (vv. 9–11).

Thanksgiving, 1.3–6

Here, the apostle begins his letter, as is his habit, with thanksgiving. This is the most lengthy of Paul's εὐχαριστέω-periods.[8] Since the thanksgiving section will introduce the main themes of the letter, we are particularly concerned to notice what is unique to this thanksgiving period. Further, we should remember that the Pauline thanksgivings are an indirect compliment to the addressees.[9] Though they are certainly thanksgivings to God, they likewise perform the function of encouraging the readers in the behaviour for which thanks are given. Further, as an encouragement to continue in a certain behaviour, these thanksgivings also serve to commend the readers for their past achievement.

Paul gives thanks for three things: (1) the Philippians' remembrance of Paul, (2) their partnership in the gospel, and (3) the good work which God has begun in them. We will arrange our comments in this same order.

(i) ἐπὶ πάσῃ τῇ μνείᾳ ὑμῶν (Phil. 1.3)

When we come to examine Philippians 1.3, we encounter two very significant questions. The first asks, who is the subject of the remembering in Philippians 1.3b, Paul or the Philippians? The second asks, is ἐπὶ πάσῃ τῇ μνείᾳ ὑμῶν to be taken as a causal or as a temporal phrase? That is, does thanks happen at the time of remembrance or because of remembrance?

Though these two questions actually give four interpretive possibilities, scholars conclude that there are actually two alternative renderings of 1.3. First, it could be rendered: 'I give thanks every time I remember you.' This alternative takes the prepositional phrase as temporal with the remembrance being Paul's. This is by far the majority view. Indeed the major versions and several

---

8 Schubert, *Form and Function*, 71; cf. Lightfoot, *Philippians*, 82.
9 Schubert, *Form and Function*, 148; O'Brien, *Introductory Thanksgivings*, 267.

commentators do not even mention the possibility that the reference may be to the Philippians' remembrance of Paul.[10] The second alternative takes the prepositional phrase as causal and renders verse three: 'I give thanks because of your every remembrance (of me).' This second position is defended strongly by Schubert and O'Brien. Because of the particular importance the choice of one of these two renderings will hold for our overall understanding of Philippians, we shall restate the arguments of Schubert and O'Brien here and add our own.

First, if taken as a temporal phrase, ἐπὶ πάσῃ τῇ μνείᾳ ὑμῶν would be the only major structural peculiarity of this thanksgiving period among the Pauline thanksgivings. The detailed work of Schubert demonstrates that the structure of Pauline thanksgiving periods is fairly well established.[11] For Schubert this is the 'decisive' factor in favour of the phrase being causal.[12]

Secondly, according to O'Brien, 'when ἐπί with the dative is used after εὐχαριστέω it *always* expresses the ground for thanks-

10 E.g., NIV, NASB, GNB, ASV, RV, NKJV and JB do not mention the possibility, and nor do the commentaries of Beare, Bruce (NIBC), Lightfoot, Motyer or Plummer. Similarly, R. L. Omanson ('A Note on the Translation of Philippians 1: 3–5', *BT* 29 (1978): 244–5) suggests that the ἐπί of Phil. 1.5 should be understood as grounds for thanksgiving (rather than joy), but does not mention that the ἐπί of 1.3 could be taken the same way.

11 See the table of syntactical elements in Schubert, *Form and Function*, 54–5. Included in Schubert's table are the thanksgiving periods of Eph. 1.15–16, Col. 1.3–4 and 2 Thess. 1.2–3 which are found to follow the same structure. We present the seven syntactical elements in their order of structural priority: first, there is the principal verb (εὐχαριστῶ or εὐχαριστοῦμεν). Second is the personal object (τῷ θεῷ). Third is the temporal adverb (typically πάντοτε). Fourth is the pronoun object phrase (typically ὑπὲρ ὑμῶν or περὶ ὑμῶν). Fifth is the temporal participial clause with a temporal adverbial phrase. This element presents the time when thanks are given. In Phlm. 4 this element is: μνείαν σου ποιούμενος ἐπὶ τῶν προσευχῶν μου (also Rom. 1.10; 1 Thess. 1.2; Eph. 1.15). (We should note that ἐπὶ τῶν προσευχῶν modifies ποιούμενος not εὐχαριστέω). In Philippians the same function is performed by the fuller element, ἐν πάσῃ δεήσει μου, μετὰ χαρᾶς τὴν δέησιν ποιούμενος. The addition of joy is explained by the epistolary situation. Joy is replete in the letter. Sixth is the causal participial phrase and/or adverbial phrase. This element gives the cause for thanks. In 1 Thess. 1.2–3 there are two participial clauses (introduced with μνημονεύοντες and εἰδότες respectively). In 1 Cor. 1.4 and 1 Thess. 3.9 this clause is introduced with ἐπί plus the dative. In Philippians, the same function is performed by the elements, ἐπὶ πάσῃ τῇ μνείᾳ ὑμῶν, ἐπὶ τῇ κοινωνίᾳ ὑμῶν and πεποιθὼς αὐτὸ τοῦτο. If, in Phil. 1.3 ἐπὶ πάσῃ τῇ μνείᾳ is a temporal clause, we are left with a structural peculiarity, unique to the Pauline thanksgivings. We would have two temporal phrases modifying εὐχαριστέω, both stating the same information. The seventh element is a final clause introduced with ἵνα, ὅτι or ὅπως.

12 Schubert, *Form and Function*, 74.

giving'.[13] In addition to texts cited by O'Brien and Schubert,[14] we can add several others.[15] Our list of examples is not exhaustive and thus we cannot make a definitive claim concerning the meaning of εὐχαριστέω ἐπί in extra-biblical literature. Nevertheless, it bears out O'Brien's assertion. As far as the extant literature reveals, in every other instance of εὐχαριστέω followed by ἐπί with the dative the preposition introduces the grounds for thanks. Therefore, we need strong evidence to the contrary before taking the construction in Philippians 1.3 as anything other than a statement of cause.

Thirdly, our detail of verbal and conceptual links between 1.3–11 and 4.10–20 suggests that the latter text does not contain the only reference to the Philippians' remembrance of Paul by means of their gifts. Owing to the character of the Pauline thanksgivings we have reason to believe that the apostle would introduce this topic in his introductory section.[16]

Fourthly, in the New Testament μνεία occurs only in letters claiming Pauline authorship.[17] Hawthorne is correct in pointing out that μνεία with the genitive elsewhere always refers to Paul's remembrance.[18] Nevertheless, in every instance except Philippians 1.3 μνεία is used with a verb (ποιέω or ἔχω)[19] which makes the

---

[13] O'Brien, *Introductory Thanksgivings*, 43, emphasis original. Silva also cites O'Brien here, claiming that O'Brien finds no instance where εὐχαριστέω + ἐπὶ has temporal force. Silva then proceeds to claim that his own interpretation does not precisely give the construction temporal force, but rather its local sense (Moisés Silva, *Philippians* (Chicago: Moody Press, 1988): 49 n. 14). Silva, however, misses O'Brien's point. O'Brien does not state negatively that the construction *never* has temporal force (and it is from this temporal force that Silva distances himself). Rather, O'Brien states positively that the construction *always* has causal force. Therefore, Silva's local sense does not help him escape from O'Brien's findings regarding εὐχαριστέω ἐπί with the dative.

[14] O'Brien, *Thanksgivings*, 43: Philo *Heres* 31; *Spec.* 1.67, 283–4, 2.185; Joseph. *AJ* 1.193; Perg. Inscr. 224A, 14; *UPZ* 59.10–11; *Herm. Sim.* 9.14.3. Schubert also presents: *OGIS* 323.13–14 (2nd BC); SB 7172.25 (217 BC); P.Vat. 2289.8 (168 BC); P.Lond. 42 (168 BC); Arr. *Epict. Diss.* 1.6.1–2; 1.16.6 (Schubert, *Form and Function*, 141, 148, 161, 163, 166).

[15] P.Oxy. 963 (2nd–3rd AD): χάριν δὲ σοι οἶδα, μῆτερ, ἐπὶ τῇ σπουδῇ; P.Haun. 18.8–10 (3rd AD); Polyb. 4.72; *SIG*² 326.44 (Roman period); *IE* I.22.23–24 (time of Antoninus Pius), *IE* IV.1390.4 (no date); Arr. *Epict. Diss.* 4.4.18, 4.72.7; Diogenes *Ep.* 162.3; Crates *Ep.* 84.19 (ref. to page and line in Malherbe, *Cynic Epistles*). Also see Larfeld, *Epigraphik*, 2.770 for examples of ἐπί with the dative used as a causal clause in honorary inscriptions.

[16] Schubert, *Form and Function*, 77; O'Brien, *Philippians*, 61.

[17] Rom. 1.9; Eph. 1.16; Phil. 1.3; 1 Thess. 1.2, 3.6; Phlm. 4; 2 Tim. 1.3.

[18] Hawthorne, *Philippians*, 17; cf. Silva, *Philippians*, 48; Rom. 1.9, Eph. 1.16, 1 Thess. 1.2, Phlm. 4.

[19] So also outside the New Testament it appears rarely without a verb, though it

subject of the remembering explicit. In those uses we have found where no verb occurs, μνεία may be used with a subjective or an objective genitive.[20] Further, in Philippians 1.4 we find the phrase δέησιν ποιούμενος, which performs the same function as μνείαν ποιούμενος in the other letters.

Fifthly, every other time ἐπί is used temporally in Paul's thanksgiving periods it is with the genitive (Rom. 1.10; 1 Thess. 1.2; Phlm. 4; cf. Eph. 1.16). Conversely in thanksgiving periods ἐπί occurs twice with the dative and it is causal (1 Cor. 1.4; Phil. 1.5). Further, Paul employs ἐπί with the dative to denote the ground for thanks in 2 Corinthians 9.15 and 1 Thessalonians 3.9.[21]

Two objections to the view that ἐπὶ πάσῃ τῇ μνείᾳ ὑμῶν is a reference to the Philippians' gift have been made. Hawthorne claims that the phrase ἐπὶ πάσῃ τῇ μνείᾳ ὑμῶν is a reference to set times of Jewish prayer which Paul continued to observe as a Christian. We have four points to make in response. First, Hawthorne supplies no evidence to support his assertion that Paul's terminology here should be understood as a reference to Jewish prayer times. The Old Testament texts he cites which refer to prayer offer no set vocabulary,[22] and, moreover, μνεία occurs in none of them. On the other hand, one New Testament text which certainly refers to a set time of prayer uses προσευχή (Acts 3.1).[23] Secondly, Hawthorne must assume that μνεία here functions, despite the absence of ποιέω (or another verb), in precisely the same way that it does with a verb; that is, it means 'to make mention'. He gives no evidence to support this assertion; as we have

may occur with ἔσται (Zach. 13.2; Barn. 21.7), γένηται (Isa. 23.16; Joseph. *BJ* 1.522) or μιμνήσκομαι (Deut. 7.18; Philo *Abel et Cain* 6.56).

20 Objective: Wis. 5.14 (μνεία καταλύπου μονοημέρου), Diod. Sic. 27.14 (ἐπὶ τῇ τούτων μνείᾳ); subjective: Bar. 5.5 (χαίροντας τῇ τοῦ θεοῦ μνείᾳ, cf. Bar. 4.27). Also helpful is Isa. 26.8, though it contains the verb ἐλπίζω: ἠλπίσαμεν ἐπὶ τῷ ὀνόματί σου καὶ τῇ μνείᾳ (σου). Note the Hebrew for μνείᾳ: *lzkrk*, 'your remembrance'.

21 Cf. the very similar ἐχάρησεν ἐπὶ τῇ χαρᾷ Τίτου in 2 Cor. 7.13b, δοξάζοντες τὸν θεὸν ἐπὶ τῇ ὑποταγῇ in 2 Cor. 9.13 and χαρὰν γὰρ πολλὴν ἔσχον καὶ παράκλησιν ἐπὶ τῇ ἀγάπῃ σου in Phlm. 7.

22 1 Chr. 23.30; Ezra 9.5; Ps. 5.3; 55.17; Dan. 6.10 (Hawthorne, *Philippians*, 16).

23 Cf. the language of 1 Thess. 1.2 (εὐχαριστοῦμεν τῷ θεῷ πάντοτε περὶ πάντων ὑμῶν μνείαν ποιούμενοι ἐπὶ τῶν προσευχῶν ἡμῶν) and Phlm 4 (εὐχαριστῶ τῷ θεῷ μου πάντοτε μνείαν σου ποιούμενος ἐπὶ τῶν προσευχῶν μου). We notice that both of these use ἐπί with the genitive plural of προσευχή. Perhaps this construction is a reference to set times of prayer (cf. Rom. 1.10 and Eduard A. von der Goltz, *Das Gebet in der ältesten Christenheit. Eine geschichtliche Untersuchung* (Leipzig: J. C. Hinrichs, 1901): 102–4).

seen above, μνεία without a verb can have the sense of remembrance (Bar. 5.5). Thirdly, in his explanation Hawthorne says, 'At every one (ἐπί πάσῃ) of these prayer times he (Paul) was compelled by love to mention his Philippian friends. This means, then, that Paul . . . gave thanks for them and mentioned them to God at set times of prayer.'[24] Yet, Hawthorne has destroyed the logic of the text. From the comments just quoted above we see that Hawthorne wishes to give μνεία two logically distinct referents. On the one hand, he wishes to take ἐπὶ πάσῃ τῇ μνείᾳ as a temporal expression with μνεία being a label for the apostle's regular prayer times. On the other hand, he wishes to say that μνεία is the specific mention Paul made (ἐποίησεν μνείαν?) of the Philippians during these times of prayer.[25] Fourthly, our interpretation does not deny that Paul engaged in regular times of prayer, nor does it deny that Paul gave thanks for the Philippians at such times. Indeed, a regular time of prayer could very well be referred to in v. 4 (πάντοτε ἐν πάσῃ δεήσει, κτλ). What our interpretation does is state positively that μνεία is one of the grounds for Paul's thanks. As one of the reasons for thanks, μνεία is most naturally taken as the Philippians' remembrance of Paul.

Hawthorne states further that the repetition of πᾶς in vv. 3–4 suggests there is a strong connection between these verses. Thus all the expressions speak of time.[26] Hawthorne, however, does not state the criteria by which he can conclude that the repetition of πᾶς is done for alliteration, nor by which he can conclude that such alliteration links the thought of vv. 3–4 and prevents v. 4 from being parenthetical.[27] We must 'distinguish between real rhetorical instances of paronomasia and structures where epistolary situation and convention, or Paul's own epistolary manner, produce a style which looks rhetorical without being so'.[28]

Vincent objects to taking ἐπὶ πάσῃ τῇ μνείᾳ as temporal by saying, 'the thought is quite unsuitable that Paul is moved to remembrance only by the exhibition of their care for him'.[29] This objection fails on two grounds. Our interpretation does not say

---

[24] Hawthorne, *Philippians*, 16–17.

[25] Thus, Hawthorne's explanation yields the following paraphrase: 'at every one of my prayer times I make mention of you'. But if the phrase ἐπὶ πάσῃ τῇ μνείᾳ were temporal, it would simply say 'every time I mention you (I give thanks)'.

[26] Hawthorne, *Philippians*, 17.

[27] Cf. the comments of Lightfoot, who, although he views the repetition of πᾶς as rhetorical, nevertheless also sees v. 4 as parenthetical (*Philippians*, 83).

[28] Schubert, *Form and Function*, 80.   [29] Vincent, *Philippians*, 6.

Paul is moved to thanksgiving *only* when the Philippians exhibit
their care for him, but rather that Paul is moved to thanksgiving
every time they do remember him.[30] And secondly, the issue is not
Paul's remembrance but Paul's thanks. The text does not say, as
Vincent's words plainly state, that Paul is *moved to remember them*
when they exhibit care. Rather the text says Paul is *moved to thank
God* when they exhibit care. Here the Philippians' μνεία is the care
which produces Paul's εὐχαριστία.

With regard to our study, the importance of the above conclusion
on the translation of Philippians 1.3b should be reiterated. The first
words to be penned beyond the introductory greeting are a
reference to Paul's thanks going to God for their financial support.
This early response provides us with two replies to the common
assertions of many exegetes. First, some believe that Paul strangely
saves his response to the gift for the end of the letter. We see here
that this view is incorrect. Paul's thanks, at least in part, are at the
very head of the letter.[31] Secondly, some assert that Paul's thanks
are thankless because of the absence of εὐχαριστέω.[32] This 'thankless thanks' view misreads Paul's response by applying twentieth-
century standards of the appropriate way to give thanks in a letter.
Our study of papyri in chapter 3 has shown that εὐχαριστέω, or
verbal gratitude, is not to be expected. Further, the 'thankless
thanks' view misreads the function of Philippians 1.3. Verbal
thanks are praise and honour. In 1.3 the apostle makes clear to his
readers where this praise goes, even while he commends the readers
for their actions.

Thus, the case is just to the contrary. Paul does give thanks for
the gift with εὐχαριστέω. There is a caveat, however. It is not the
Philippians whom Paul thanks for the gift at the very head of the
letter.[33] Indeed, he does not thank the Philippians at all. Instead he
thanks God.[34]

---

[30] A similar response to Vincent is made by O'Brien, *Philippians*, 60.

[31] Martin, *Philippians* (NCB), 64; Garland, 'Defense', 329.

[32] On the absence of εὐχαριστέω in 4.10–20 see Peterman, '"Thankless Thanks"',
261–70. Though εὐχαριστέω is absent from 4.10–20, it is an unfounded assertion
to say that its absence makes Paul's thanks thankless. The letter as a whole
provides a quite full expression of gratitude in keeping with the social response
the apostle seeks to give. See our exegesis of 4.10–20, pp. 121–61.

[33] Cf. the erroneous statement of Watson, who comments regarding 1.3: 'Paul
immediately begins to thank the Philippians' ('Rhetorical Analysis', 61).

[34] Lohmeyer, *Philipper*, 17.

This opening thanksgiving to God sets the agenda for the rest of the letter. If there is any uncertainty in the minds of the Philippians concerning their own part in Paul's life and ministry it is addressed directly here. What the Philippians do (viz., their supporting Paul) is meant to bring thanks and praise to God for their faithfulness to the gospel. We shall see money play this role again below. We shall notice that in 2 Corinthians 9.11–12 Paul says money given to the collection project would result in thanksgiving to God for the Corinthians' obedience to the gospel.[35] Thus we see the teaching given in 2 Corinthians 9 being worked out in practice in Philippians 1.3–5. Paul himself, as the recipient of a sort of collection, gives thanks to God for the Philippians' obedience.

(ii)   ἐπὶ τῇ κοινωνίᾳ ὑμῶν εἰς τὸ εὐαγγέλιον (Phil. 1.5)

The second motivation for Paul's thanks is the Philippians' partnership in the gospel, that is, for their participation in the advance of the gospel.[36] Paul's mention of the Philippians' partnership is not a reference to the gift only, though it includes it.[37] As we shall see, their partnership extends to various aspects of Christian service at different levels. Seesemann, however, objects to seeing κοινωνία as a reference to their gift. He asserts that in his introductory thanksgivings Paul never gives thanks for Christians' achievements but for God's work.[38] But he makes a false disjunction between these two activities. By contrast the biblical writers see no contradiction, for they put these two activities side by side.[39] For Paul the *work* of God is seen in the *achievement* of individual Christians. In addition, Seesemann finds it hard to believe that canonical Philippians should be the only letter the apostle opens with thanks for partnership, though he admits it would be easier to see if the letter

---

[35] See the conclusions to chapter 5, pp. 159–60, for parallels in thought between Philippians and 1 Cor. 9.8–13. See also pp. 180–1 for discussion of κοινωνία in 2 Cor. 9.13.

[36] Εὐαγγέλιον in Philippians is not simply a label for the message about Jesus, but is a '*nomen actionis*, describing the involvement of either Paul or the Philippians in the furtherance of the gospel' (O'Brien, *Philippians*, 24 n. 22). See also L.-M. Dewailly, 'La Part Prise a l'Évangile (Phil., I,5)', *RB* 80 (1973): 247–60.

[37] Lightfoot, *Philippians*, 83; Beare, *Philippians*, 53; Martin, *Philippians* (NCB), 65; Hawthorne, *Philippians*, 19; O'Brien, *Philippians*, 61; *contra* Heinrich Seesemann, *Der Begriff* KOINΩNIA *im Neuen Testament* (Gießen: Töpelmann, 1933): 74; Lohmeyer, *Philipper*, 17 n. 3.

[38] Seesemann, KOINΩNIA, 74, following Lohmeyer, *Philipper*, 17.

[39] Cf. Phil. 1.6, 2.12–13; see also Acts 4.27–8, 13.48.

clearly had thanks for financial support as its goal.[40] Our chart of parallels between 1.3–11 and 4.10–20, as well as the exegesis undertaken in chapter 5 and the present chapter, should make it quite clear that response to the Philippians' financial support is more important to the letter than is commonly realized.

Κοινωνία is a significant theme in Paul's letters and especially in Philippians.[41] We will have further recourse to defining the Philippians' κοινωνία as our study continues. Here we offer a few comments on the significance of κοινωνία in Philippians 1.5.

First, if ἐπὶ τῇ κοινωνίᾳ is taken as a second ground of thanks we see a natural progression in which Paul moves from a narrow to a broader reason for his gratitude. At first he mentions the actual demonstration of the Philippians' concern in their gifts (ἐπὶ πάσῃ τῇ μνείᾳ). Then he gives thanks more generally for their partnership in the gospel (ἐπὶ τῇ κοινωνίᾳ), which includes their support but also takes into account their prayers for him (1.19), their own witness in Philippi (1.27–8, 2.15), their suffering with him (1.30) and their taking part in his affliction (4.14).[42]

Secondly, in the New Testament the phrase κοινωνία εἰς τὸ εὐαγγέλιον is unique to Philippians and its occurrence here is very indicative of the apostle's distinctive relationship with the Philippian believers. After the reference to the tangible expression of the Philippians' care in their gifts (μνεία) Paul adds that he is also thankful for the relationship he has with them which is implied by the gifts, viz., their κοινωνία. Yet, immediately following is the critical qualifying phrase εἰς τὸ εὐαγγέλιον. The real meaning of the apostle's special relationship with them is partnership of a

---

40 Seesemann, ΚΟΙΝΩΝΙΑ, 74. Thus we see again how false assumptions regarding Paul's response to the Philippians' gift have led to conclusions about the intention of the letter and consequently have influenced the exegesis of individual texts.

41 Our comments on κοινωνία must of necessity be cursory as the concept is in itself the subject of several monographs (e.g., Seesemann, ΚΟΙΝΩΝΙΑ; P. C. Bori, *L'idea della communione nell'ecclesiologia recente e nel Nuovo Testamento* (Brescia: Paideia Editrice, 1972); Josef Hainz, *KOINONIA. 'Kirche' als Gemeinschaft bei Paulus* (Regensburg: Friedrich Pustet, 1982)) and articles (e.g., J. Y. Campbell, 'Κοινωνία and its cognates in the New Testament', *JBL* (1932): 352–80; H. H. Ford, 'The New Testament Concept of Fellowship', *Shane Quarterly* 6 (1945): 188–215. Michael McDermott, 'The Biblical Doctrine of ΚΟΙΝΩΝΙΑ', *BZ* 19 (1975): 64–77, 219–33). On κοινωνία in Philippians see P. T. O'Brien, 'The Fellowship Theme in Philippians', *Reformed Theological Review* 37 (1978): 9–18.

42 For a fuller description of various aspects of their partnership see pp. 119–20 below.

certain kind. A partnership which he probably would have desired for all the congregations, but which is unique to this one. It is a partnership in the gospel's advance.[43] By use of this phrase, Paul defines the relationship early on and removes all doubt as to the character of the partnership they have.

Thirdly, though the exact phrase κοινωνία εἰς τὸ εὐαγγέλιον is unique to Philippians, we might compare similar thoughts found in Romans 15.26, 2 Corinthians 8.4 and 9.13. Christian κοινωνία and money are closely linked.[44] In Romans 15.26 and 2 Corinthians 9.13 a relationship (κοινωνία) is carried on toward or established with (εἰς) someone through the giving of money. We must guard against reading this meaning from Romans or Corinthians into Philippians, especially since the object of εἰς in the latter is the abstract εὐαγγέλιον. Nevertheless, the occurrence of κοινωνία εἰς in the context of giving and receiving should alert us to the possibility of a similar understanding in Philippians.

Fourthly, this reference to partnership in 1.5 definitely finds a counterpart in 4.15 with the mention of sharing in giving and receiving.[45] These two phrases, κοινωνία εἰς τὸ εὐαγγέλιον and ἐκοινώνησεν εἰς λόγον δόσεως καὶ λήμψεως open and close the main ideas around which the themes of the letter are structured. Further, both of these phrases are qualified by very similar temporal phrases: ἀπὸ τῆς πρώτης ἡμέρας in 1.5 and ἐν ἀρχῇ τοῦ εὐαγγελίου in 4.15. Between these two references to partnership, the apostle takes the opportunity to delineate what are the characteristics of this partnership: they are fellow-partakers of grace in the defence of the gospel (1.7), the Philippians struggle together for the gospel just as the apostle is doing (1.27, cf. 4.3), they hold onto the word of life (2.16).[46] These texts show that the partnership involves active participation.[47]

Fifthly, a reference to κοινωνία, especially in the context of

---

[43] John Reumann, 'Contributions of the Philippian Community to Paul and to Earliest Christianity', *NTS* 39 (1993): 441.

[44] Yet it is questionable whether κοινωνία ever has an exclusively financial sense, meaning 'alms' (*contra* O'Brien, *Introductory Thanksgivings*, 24 n. 24). See our treatment of Romans 15.25–31, pp. 175–85.

[45] Martin, *Philippians* (NCB), 65; Schubert, *Form and Function*, 77.

[46] In this context ἐπέχοντες could entail *holding fast* to the word in light of Paul's fear of the Philippians' falling away (v. 16b) or *holding forth* the word (i.e., evangelizing) in light of Paul's statement that the Philippians shine as lights (v. 15b).

[47] Dewailly, 'La Part Prise a l'Évangile', 249.

mentioning their gift (1.3), might be thought to bring up ideas of
Greco-Roman reciprocity. Κοινωνία is certainly a term which is
used in very different senses in the Greco-Roman world.[48] In
secular usage the κοινων- group is applied to many different areas,
such as business associations or marriage,[49] but for the Greek
world friendship is a supreme expression of fellowship.[50] Chapter 3
demonstrated that friendships were established and maintained
through the exchange of gifts or favours.[51] That is, the basis for
κοινωνία was ἀλλαγή.[52] But is the Philippian κοινωνία mere social
reciprocity? No. It is partnership in the gospel. At a very basic level,
this partnership can be understood using vocabulary which so often
figures in the semantic complex of friendship,[53] but in the final
analysis will require its own definition in order to instruct the
Philippians properly as to the real Christian meaning of the gift and
its reception by the apostle. This definition Paul gives throughout
the letter and will only complete in 4.10–20 with his direct response
to the gift.

In light of our discussion above and in chapter 3 we can see the
importance of κοινωνία here at such an early point in the letter and
the importance of it being specifically defined with εἰς τὸ εὐαγγέλιον. The Philippians, as financial supporters, actively participate
in the advance of the gospel. This active participation (working to
propagate the gospel message) presupposes static participation
(receiving the gospel message). In this sense then, v. 5 is explicated
by v. 7. The Philippians are partners in grace as they are partners in
the defence and confirmation of the gospel. Their partnership in
giving and receiving finds its ground in the gospel and is not to be
confused with the giving and receiving of Greco-Roman social

---

[48] See W. Popkes, 'Gemeinschaft', *RAC* 9 (1976): 797–907.

[49] For the latter of these see the examples in Moulton and Milligan, *Vocabulary*,
351.

[50] Hauck, 'κοινωνός', *TDNT*, 3.798. The *Definitiones* attributed to Plato offer us
the following definitions for φιλία and κοινωνία (413A10–12): Φιλία ὁμόνοια
ὑπὲρ καλῶν καὶ δικαίων· προαίρεσις βίου τοῦ αὐτοῦ· ὁμοδοξία περὶ προαιρ-
έσεως καὶ πράξεως· ὁμόνοια περὶ βίον· κοινωνία μετ᾽ εὐνοίας· κοινωνία τοῦ εὖ
ποιῆσαι καὶ παθεῖν.

[51] See esp. aspects of giving, pp. 66–8.

[52] Cf. Aristotle, who, in the context of discussion on relationships of giving and
receiving, says that if there were no reciprocity there would be no fellowship
(οὔτε γὰρ ἂν μὴ οὔσης ἀλλαγῆς κοινωνία ἦν, *Eth. Nic.* 5.5.14; cf. 5.5.6).

[53] As is noted by White, 'Morality,' 206; Stanley K. Stowers, 'Friends and Enemies
in the Politics of Heaven: Reading Theology in Philippians', *Pauline Theology I:
Thessalonians, Philippians, Galatians, Philemon*, ed. Jouette M. Bassler (Minneapolis: Augsburg Fortress, 1991): 112.

reciprocity. To avoid such confusion the apostle starts immediately to define the true meaning of this exchange. It has not merely established a special, reciprocal relationship between them, though that is included. It has created a working partnership which has the advance of the gospel as its purpose and goal.[54]

Similarly, the apostle's presentation of the theological meaning of their giving and receiving at the very head of the letter allows us to discern a certain method in his presentation. Paul provides first an abstract theological definition and undergirding for his response to the Philippian gift (1.5–11). This theological definition is partnership in the gospel. There follows teaching about personal sacrifice for the gospel (1.12–26), life as a citizen that is worthy of the gospel (1.27–2.18), and examples of servants who live lives worthy of imitation (2.19–30). Yet, his direct response to the gift, along with his personal reflections, comes at the end (4.10–20).[55] Paul does not delay his thanks for the gift to the end of the letter because of his embarrassment about money matters.[56] Rather, if we should speak of a delay at all, we should say it arises from a certain method in his instruction. The specific response (4.10–20), by its location, must be read in light of the theological undergirding, with examples and application, which has already paved the way. In a sense, 1.1–4.9 are prolegomena to the response of 4.10–20. In our discussion of the letter body (1.27–4.3) we shall see Paul employ this same method to the conflicts at Philippi.

(iii) πεποιθὼς αὐτὸ τοῦτο κτλ *(Phil. 1.6)*

In this verse Paul's grounds for thanks broaden further. After thanks for the Philippians' specific gifts of financial support and for the partnership in the gospel seen in their gifts and in other ways, he also gives thanks for confidence that the good work being performed in them will be perfected.[57] Πεποιθὼς here should be

---

54 Garland, 'Defense', 330, is correct in seeing κοινωνία as a reference to money partnership, but there is no reason to conclude that the apostle's description uses 'delicate euphemisms'.

55 This A–B–A structure in Philippians, as well as in 1 Cor. 8–10, 12–14, has also been noticed by William S. Kurz, 'Kenotic Imitation of Paul and of Christ in Philippians 2 and 3', *Discipleship in the New Testament*, ed. F. F. Segovia (Philadelphia: Fortress Press, 1985): 106.

56 *Contra* Garland, 'Composition', 153; cf. Hawthorne, *Philippians*, 194; Silva, *Philippians*, 230; Dodd, 'The Mind of Paul: I', 71–2.

57 O'Brien, *Introductory Thanksgivings*, 26; Schubert, *Form and Function*, 78. Lohmeyer sees in v. 6b a formulaic reference to 'the beginning and the end',

taken as a causal participle.[58] Paul has this (αὐτὸ τοῦτο) confidence, the content of which is introduced by a recitative ὅτι.[59] The apostle is confident that God will complete the good work which he has started.

This good work the apostle refers to is not specified. In the context it might be thought to refer to their partnership in the gospel.[60] That is, the Philippians are doing a good work in supporting the apostle and entering partnership with him. There are convincing arguments against this view, however.[61] First, ἔργον ἀγαθόν is the object of both ὁ ἐναρξάμενος and ἐπιτελέσει, and these two have God as their subject. It is God who begins and ends the good work. This in itself, however, does not preclude human activity.[62] Secondly, the good work is to be carried out ἄχρι ἡμέρας Χριστοῦ Ἰησοῦ, i.e., until the parousia. This statement does preclude the Philippians from being the subject of the good work in terms of gospel partnership. Thirdly, ἐν ὑμῖν is most naturally taken as 'among you', not 'by means of you'.[63]

We notice here that it is not the Philippians who are being praised for the good work which they have done, as Paul in Romans 13.3 says those who do good will be praised by the state.[64] Although on one level it is the Philippians who have done the good work of supporting Paul, *God* is the benefactor who has begun in them the good work of partnership in the gospel.[65] This good work,

---

citing such NT examples as Gal. 3.3; 2 Cor. 8.6, 10; Rev. 21.6, 22.13; Heb. 12.2. See his discussion, *Philipper*, 20–1.

58   O'Brien, *Philippians*, 63; Lightfoot, *Philippians*, 83–4; *contra* Vincent, *Philippians*, 7, Beare, *Philippians*, 52, and Hawthorne, *Philippians*, 20–1, who assert that πεποιθώς refers to attendant circumstances.

59   Lohmeyer, *Philipper*, 19. But as Schubert notes, it is not Paul's mere confidence that causes thanks, but his confidence *that* God will complete the work. Thus 'the grammatically recitative ὅτι is logically a causal ὅτι' (*Form and Function*, 45). BDF entertain both possibilities that αὐτὸ τοῦτο refers forward or back (*Grammar*, 290/4). Here αὐτὸ τοῦτο certainly looks forward to ὅτι and not back to the content of vv. 3–5. First, every other occurrence of the construction πείθομαι . . . ὅτι in the New Testament looks forward (Rom. 8.38, 14.14, 15.14; 2 Tim. 1.5, 12; Heb. 13.18). Secondly, it is more logical that confidence should have the future as its object rather than the past. Thirdly, if πεποιθὼς αὐτὸ τοῦτο refers back to the content of vv. 3–5, then ὅτι must be taken as causal.

60   So Lightfoot, *Philippians*, 84; Hawthorne, *Philippians*, 21.

61   Here we follow the discussion by Judith M. Gundry Volf, *Paul and Perseverance: Staying in and Falling Away* (Tübingen: J. C. B. Mohr, 1990): 33–47.

62   Cf. Paul's statement in 2.12–13.

63   O'Brien, *Philippians*, 64 n. 42; *contra* Hawthorne, *Philippians*, 21.

64   See Bruce W. Winter, 'The Public Praising of Christian Benefactors: Romans 13.3–4 and 1 Peter 2.14–15', *JSNT* 34 (1988): 87–103.

65   That ἔργον ἀγαθόν can refer to a specific act of generosity appears clear from 2

however, cannot refer solely to gospel partnership in terms of financial support, but also to sharing in salvation. For the apostle asserts that it will not be completed until (εἰς) the day of Jesus Christ.[66]

This shifting of the praise for benefaction from the human agents to the divine agent is consistent with the response we see Paul has offered by thanking God for the Philippians' gifts (1.3) and which we shall continue to see him offer. The apostle drops the familiar social categories for the sake of giving a Christian interpretation and meaning to the Philippians' financial sharing.

Statement of affection, 1.7–8

After revealing the grounds for his thanks Paul moves on to a two-fold expression of affection which is unique to Philippians.

The opinions Paul has expressed regarding the Philippians' partnership in the gospel (1.5) and that partnership's lasting character (1.7) are justified because he has the Philippians in his heart (διὰ τὸ ἔχειν με ἐν τῇ καρδίᾳ ὑμᾶς).[67] In other words, there is a direct link between partnership and affection.[68] Then, the subject being changed once again, there is a further link between affection and the Philippians' status as Paul's partners[69] in grace both in his imprisonment and in the defence and confirmation of the gospel. How to understand the precise function of ὄντας is difficult, though the general sense is clear. Christians in Philippi have a special solidarity with the apostle; they are not just those who share with Paul in receiving the grace of God, but they also share in the affliction of Paul's chains (cf. 4.14) and in the task of

Tim. 2.21 and Tit. 3.1. The writer does not exhort the readers to do good works (a general activity) but to be ready to do good works (i.e., to be prepared to display generosity when the situation arises). Compare Paul's words in 2 Cor. 9.8: God is able to make all grace abound to the Corinthians so that they will always have the means (αὐτάρκεια) for every good work (πᾶν ἔργον ἀγαθόν). That is, though they give to the collection, God will cause them to have all the financial resources they need to show generosity.

[66] Thus Paul has included the spectrum of time: from the first day, now, and until the day of Christ (Lohmeyer, *Philipper*, 17).

[67] This construction may be taken differently, with the subject of the infinitive ἔχειν being not με but ὑμᾶς (Hawthorne, *Philippians*, 23). Yet the following declaration of affection (v. 8), introduced with γάρ, is best taken as a reiteration of the thought in v. 7 (O'Brien, *Philippians*, 68).

[68] Cf. the assertion of holding in the heart in the strained discussion of 2 Cor. 7.3.

[69] Though συγκοινωνός figures in Rom. 11.17 and 1 Cor. 9.23, here it is uniquely given as a title to the Philippians (cf. συγκοινωνέω in 4.14).

defending and confirming the gospel.[70] This solidarity has resulted in a unique affection on the apostle's part.

Paul follows up this proclamation of affection with an oath of longing for them (1.8). Σπλάγχνον figures in Paul several times,[71] but only here does he employ it in a declaration of affection. We need not understand this declaration as arising from the idea that Paul's affection for them had been challenged.[72] Such a strong reiteration of his affection need only be taken as a fitting response in light of the continued displays of affection on the Philippians' part (cf. 4.10, 16). The reciprocal φρονεῖν of the apostle and this congregation evokes this singular statement of affection.

Prayer, 1.9–11

We should not think that, as a prayer, this section of text contributes nothing to the exegesis of the rest of Philippians. Rather, sensitivity to the issues addressed by the prayer should further alert us to the epistolary situation.[73]

We know of conflict between at least two members of the congregation (4.2). We may infer some rivalry between them from the way they are exhorted to agree (τὸ αὐτὸ φρονεῖν), which corresponds to Paul's general instruction to the congregation elsewhere (1.27–8). This rivalry will be excluded if their love overrides. Paul 'finds no need to describe love at this point, for as the letter unfolds its meaning will be fully illustrated'.[74]

The precise relationship of the clauses in Paul's prayer is hard to discover, yet fortunately for our purpose such a decision is not critical.[75] We see that the apostle prays for a love which grows in insight so that the Philippians may be able to discern those things that really matter (τὰ διαφέροντα, 1.10). It should become clear as we proceed that Paul sees a struggle in the congregation over things

---

[70] O'Brien, *Philippians*, 70.

[71] 2 Cor. 6.12, 7.15; Phlm. 7, 12, 20; cf. Phil. 2.1.

[72] *Contra* Hawthorne, *Philippians*, 24; Gordon P. Wiles, *Paul's Intercessory Prayers. The Significance of the Intercessory Prayers in the Letters of St. Paul* (Cambridge: Cambridge University Press, 1974): 190 n. 1. Compare the challenge to the apostle's affection in 2 Cor. 11.11, where the grounds for the challenge arise from the apostle's refusal of the Corinthians' gifts (see pp. 168–72 below).

[73] Wiles, *Paul's Intercessory Prayers*, 197.

[74] Ibid., 208.

[75] See the discussion in O'Brien, *Introductory Thanksgivings*, 29–37 and Schenk, *Philipperbriefe*, 110–23.

that do not really matter; an ambitious desire (ἐριθεία) to achieve glory, falsely so called (κενοδοξία, 2.3).

We should not miss the significance of the apostle's prayer ending with reference to God's glory. We have already seen that this reference has its counterpart in 4.20.[76] 'God's saving work among the Philippians, begun and continued in times of trial, will eventually redound to the divine glory. In this way he prefigures the climax of the great "Christ-hymn." '[77] Consequently, we see that the lessons of love result in glory. This observation allows us to say that the reference to Christ's glory in 2.9–11 is not out of place if Paul's use of the hymn intends to present Jesus as an example.[78] Glory, but of a kind that really matters, comes through following the example of Jesus. Glory, the kind that in the final analysis is irrelevant, springs from the ἐριθεία and κενοδοξία which motivate some of the Philippians (2.3).[79]

Report on the Gospel's advance: 1.12–26

Paul begins this section with a unique disclosure formula.[80] Whereas in Romans and 2 Corinthians the apostle begins the letter body after the introductory section with the negative formula οὐ θέλω (θέλομεν) ὑμᾶς ἀγνοεῖν (Rom. 1.13; 2 Cor. 1.8), this section begins with the positive γινώσκειν δὲ ὑμᾶς βούλομαι.

The section 1.12–26 is marked off by προκοπή in vv. 12 and 25, thus forming an *inclusio*.[81] The themes are the gospel, its advance and Paul's subordination of all his energies and desires to the accomplishment of this one goal.[82] This assertion is borne out also by the apostle's return to εὐαγγέλιον in 1.27: the gospel is advancing. Whether he will be able to have personal ministry among them is uncertain. Therefore they must make it their goal to live a life worthy of the gospel.

---

[76] See above our table of comparison between 1.3–11 and 4.10–20, pp. 91–2.

[77] Wiles, *Paul's Intercessory Prayers*, 213.

[78] *Contra* Ralph P. Martin, *Carmen Christi. Philippians ii.5–11 in Recent Interpretation and in the Setting of Early Christian Worship* (Grand Rapids: Eerdmans, rev. edn, 1983): 85.

[79] J. H. Michael, *The Epistle of Paul to the Philippians* (London: Hodder and Stoughton, repr., 1939): 23. See our discussion of ἐριθεία and κενοδοξία below, pp. 112–13.

[80] For papyrus examples of disclosure formulae see Terence Y. Mullins, 'Disclosure. A Literary Form in the New Testament', *NovT* 7 (1964): 44–50.

[81] O'Brien, *Philippians*, 88; Garland, 'Composition', 159–60.

[82] See O'Brien, 'The Importance of the Gospel in Philippians', 213–33.

Gospel advance and imprisonment: 1.12–14

Paul introduces this section with a reference to his personal situation (τὰ κατ᾿ ἐμέ), yet he never explains how he is doing personally,[83] but only mentions how the gospel has been affected owing to his circumstances. Moreover, this theme of personal subordination to the gospel continues throughout the sections that follow.

Unlike his other epistles, Paul in Philippians is concerned to let the church know of the advance of the gospel, and this despite his imprisonment. Knowing of his concern for the gospel elsewhere in the epistle, and the apostle's unique relationship with this church as partners in that gospel, this report by Paul is quite comprehensible. This church has been working for the advance of the Christian message. They have been doing so not only in giving to the apostle, but also through personal suffering and witness (e.g., 1.27–30, cf. 2.14–16).

Gospel preaching and false motives: 1.15–18a

Simply put, Paul makes it plain that he rejoices whenever Christ is preached. It makes no difference even if the preachers seek to harm him in their preaching.[84] The insistence that poorly motivated preachers seek to create affliction for Paul in his imprisonment is difficult to interpret.[85] Fortunately, it is not their precise goal, but the source of their motivations which concerns us.

As pointed out by others, we have here a carefully crafted section discussing the motivations of the Christian preachers.[86] We might present the structure in a diagram:

Introduction of	διὰ φθόνον καὶ ἔριν
differing	δι᾿ εὐδοκίαν
motives	τὸν Χριστὸν κηρύσσουσιν

---

[83] Cf. our discussion of 4.10–20 on pp. 121–61 below. There we see that the apostle only mentions his ὑστέρησις (4.11) in order to assert his αὐτάρκεια and only mentions his θλῖψις (4.14) in order to praise their κοινωνία with him in that affliction.

[84] We note here the different stance the apostle takes toward those preaching the (real) gospel with false motives and his stance toward those preaching a false gospel with whatever motives. The latter are anathema (Gal. 1.8–9).

[85] See T. Hawthorn, 'Philippians i.12–19. With Special Reference to vv. 15.16.17', *ExpTim* 62 (1950–1): 316–17; Robert Jewett, 'Conflicting Movements in the Early Church as Reflected in Philippians', *NovT* 12 (1970): 362–90.

[86] E.g., O'Brien, *Philippians*, 97–8; Martin, *Philippians* (NCB), 73.

Precise	ἐξ ἀγάπης
description	(τὸν Χριστὸν καταγγέλλουσιν)
of	εἰδότες κτλ.
motives	ἐξ ἐριθείας
and	τὸν Χριστὸν καταγγέλλουσιν
causes	οἰόμενοι κτλ.
Inclusio on	προφάσει
differing	ἀληθείᾳ
motives	Χριστὸς καταγγέλλεται

The repetition of the two motives in preaching Christ (v. 15, 18) serves as an *inclusio*. The central section (vv. 16–17) not only gives us the motives, but also explains how these motivations have come about. Significantly, the two motives are ascribed to love (ἀγάπη) and selfish ambition (ἐριθεία), the latter being that which the Philippians are warned against in 2.3. Note that in literature prior to the New Testament, ἐριθεία only occurs in Aristotle to refer to political ambition.[87] Love is the basis of Paul's prayer for the Philippians in 1.9–11. Thus, in Paul's report on the advance of the gospel in his own personal situation, the apostle is able to show that the basic motivations for the problems among the Philippians are the same as those which are causing the problems in his present context.[88] The difference is that these preachers are indeed proclaiming Christ.[89] The repetition of the phrase Χριστὸν καταγγέλλουσιν makes it obvious. Paul can rejoice in this because the gospel is being told. But in the Philippians' own case the gospel must be *told* and *lived* for their partnership in the gospel to have its fullest fruit. If there is ἐριθεία they cannot stand together in contending for the faith of the gospel. If there is ἐριθεία they cannot live as citizens (πολιτεύεσθε, 1.27) in a manner worthy of the gospel.[90]

---

[87] Arist. *Pol.* 1302B4; 1303A15; Bauer/Aland, *Wörterbuch*, 626. Compare Aristotle's description of party faction: 'The objects about which it is waged are gain and honour, and their opposites, for men carry on party faction in states in order to avoid dishonour and loss, either on their own behalf or on behalf of their friends' (περὶ ὧν δὲ στασιάζουσιν, ἐστὶ κέρδος καὶ τιμή, καὶ τἀναντία τούτοις, καὶ γὰρ ἀτιμίαν φεύγοντες καὶ ζημίαν ἢ ὑπὲρ αὑτῶν ἢ τῶν φίλων στασιάζουσιν ἐν ταῖς πόλεσιν, 1302A32–4). Notice the contrary position regarding gain and loss taken by Paul in 3.7–9.

[88] Garland, 'Defense', 333.

[89] *Contra* Watson, 'Rhetorical Analysis', 58; Lohmeyer, *Philipper*, 44–6.

[90] See our discussion of ἐριθεία and κενοδοξία below, pp. 112–13.

Gospel ministry and personal desires: 1.18b–26

The apostle makes it clear through his personal reflections on his present situation that glorifying Christ is his sole aim. In the final analysis it makes no difference for Paul whether this glorification comes about through his own life or death.

Paul's imprisonment will turn out for his deliverance through the Philippians' prayers (1.19). We see here one more element of the apostle's κοινωνία with this congregation: they pray for each other (cf. 1.4). Though Paul calls other churches to pray for him (e.g., Rom. 15.30, 1 Thess. 5.25), he here takes for granted the prayers of the Philippians.[91]

In 2 Corinthians 1.11 prayer plays a similar role as that which can secure Paul's rescue from trials. Yet, here we might add two observations. In 2 Corinthians 1.11 the prayers of the Corinthians do not seem to be assumed. The ambiguous genitive absolute only designates a cause for his rescue. It leaves uncertain whether these prayers actually occur. Also, the apostle sees the need to add that the thanks for the answer to the Corinthians' prayers, and indeed thanks for the prayers themselves, go to God. We might compare this statement with Paul's comment about giving to the collection in 2 Corinthians 9.11–12.[92] The Corinthians' giving to the collection project will yield thanksgiving to God for their obedience to the gospel. Paul implies that Christian works which might be thought worthy of praise should actually bring praise to God and not to the doer of the work.[93]

Further, this prisoner for Christ states that, though he would gladly depart to enjoy being with Christ,[94] staying to be with the Philippians again is more necessary. Yet once more personal desires are subordinated to the greater cause of the gospel. His presence will facilitate their advance in the gospel (v. 25).

---

[91] Wiles, *Paul's Intercessory Prayers*, 277, 281.

[92] See the conclusion to chapter 5, pp. 159–60, for a comparison of 2 Cor. 9.8–13 with elements from Philippians.

[93] We refer back to our comments on Seesemann's view of Phil. 1.5. If here in 2 Cor. 9.11–12 the prayers of Christians (their work) bring thanks to God, why cannot the work of the Philippians in partnership with Paul bring thanks to God as well? (See Seesemann, ΚΟΙΝΩΝΙΑ, 74.)

[94] Palmer cites several Greek authors, showing that it was a commonplace to consider death a gain if life was a burden. (D. W. Palmer, ' "To Die is Gain" (Philippians I 21)', *NovT* 17 (1975): 203–18.) Though these texts are illustrative, Palmer neglects the quite divergent religious viewpoints of Paul and pagan Greek authors on the significance of life and death (see O'Brien, *Philippians*, 123).

Conduct worthy of the Gospel: 1.27–2.18

Verse 27 opens the paraenetic section of the letter, which runs to 4.3. This letter body is an inclusion marked by the occurrence of πολιτεύεσθε, στήκετε and συναθλοῦντες (1.27) which have cognates in the same order in 2.30 (πολίτευμα), 4.1 (στήκετε) and 4.3 (συνήθλησαν).[95] These terms are linked to the thought that the Philippians are to be Christian witnesses in Philippi. As a mission-minded church, one that has the unique place as a financial partner with Paul (4.15), one that is apparently dedicated to the advance of the gospel (1.12), they too need to stand for the defence and confirmation of the gospel in their own context (1.27b–28). Living as citizens in a manner worthy of the gospel is the one (μόνον) thing toward which Paul exhorts them in the letter.

The grounds for Paul's exhortation are found in the assertion that suffering for Christ is a gift of God.[96] Note the ὅτι of 1.29. The Philippians must take steps to walk worthy *because* it has been granted them, not only to believe in Christ, but also to suffer for him (ὑπὲρ αὐτοῦ, v. 29b). They struggle under the same burden as Paul himself (v. 30), implying a partnership of struggle on behalf of the gospel.[97] If the apostle subordinates all his desires to the advance of the gospel, the Philippians should do the same as imitators of him (cf. 3.17). The Philippians, however, in their suffering for Christ, are apparently not experiencing a subordination of their desires to the one overarching goal of the gospel's advance. Otherwise, there would be harmony and not conflict among them.

Concord and discord in Philippi

The Philippians are exhorted to conduct themselves in a manner worthy of the gospel (1.27). Others point out that this section of text employs πολιτεύεσθε specifically, instead of περιπατεῖτε, to urge the Philippians to live as citizens in a manner worthy of the

---

[95] Garland, 'Composition', 160; cf. Watson, 'Rhetorical Analysis', 77.

[96] It has not been given them (ἐδόθη), it has been graciously bestowed on them (ἐχαρίσθη, 1.29a).

[97] Victor C. Pfitzner, *Paul and the Agon Motif* (Leiden: E. J. Brill, 1967): esp. 114–18: 'In v. 27 it is not merely a matter of standing on the defensive, or of protecting and guarding the faith, but rather of a positive offensive for the faith . . . A unity of fellowship and suffering does find clear expression in v. 30' (118).

gospel for which they shine as lights.[98] The section 1.27–2.18 opens
and closes with a reference to proper conduct in the view of
outsiders and doing so whether the apostle is present or absent
(1.27, cf. 2.12, 15–16).[99] This lifestyle is a proclamation of the
gospel. Their life as citizens, however, will not be worthy of the
gospel if they are motivated by ἐριθεία or κενοδοξία, 2.3. These
terms belong to the semantic complex of socio-political concord
and discord and suggest a struggle for primacy within the Philippian congregation.[100] The evidence for this is as follows.

First, Paul makes direct reference to disagreement in 4.2 where
he exhorts Euodia and Syntyche: τὸ αὐτὸ φρονεῖν. It should strike
us as significant that these two persons are named directly, for this
is not the apostle's common practice.[101] It is reasonable to assume
that Euodia and Syntyche were persons of some importance in the
congregation. The title and description of them supports this idea.
They are fellow workers (συνέργαι) who, in the past, have striven
together with Paul in the work of the gospel (ἐν τῷ εὐαγγελίῳ
συνήθλησαν, v. 3).[102] Now they are apparently parting company.[103] Further, their discord threatened the unity of the entire
church, which explained their being named in a letter for public
hearing.[104]

---

[98] Raymond R. Brewer ('The Meaning of *Politeuesthe* in Philippians 1.27', *JBL* 73
(1954): 76–83) asserts that πολιτεύεσθε here exhorts the Philippians to discharge
their obligations as citizens in the way Christians should. Bruce W. Winter goes
further and sees the whole of 1.27–2.18 as an extended exhortation which
instructs the Philippians how to live in the secular environment (see 'The Problem
with "Church" for the Early Church', *In the Fullness of Time: Biblical Studies in
Honour of Archbishop Donald Robinson*, ed D. Peterson and J. Pryor (Sydney:
Lancer Books, 1992): 203–17). If this view is correct it corresponds well with the
κοινωνία εἰς τὸ εὐαγγέλιον theme of the letter.

[99] Garland, 'Composition', 160.

[100] Winter, 'Church', 210. Jewett, however, goes too far in asserting that the
Philippians felt they had achieved perfection ('Conflicting Movements', 373–6).

[101] O'Brien, *Philippians*, 478. Note the nameless mention of an offender in 1 Cor. 5.1
and 2 Cor. 2.5–8.

[102] In any case, the persons, or perhaps parties, at dispute in Philippi could well have
been people of substance, though the evidence is too thin to ascertain precisely
the status of Euodia and Syntyche. See W. D. Thomas, 'The Place of Women in
the Church at Philippi', *ExpTim* 83 (1971–2): 117–20; Lilian Portefaix, *Sisters
Rejoice: Paul's Letter to the Philippians and Luke-Acts as Seen by First-century
Philippian Women* (Stockholm: Almquist & Wiksell, 1988): 137–8; Ben With-
erington, III, *Women and the Genesis of Christianity* (Cambridge: Cambridge
University Press, 1990): 185–6.

[103] We cannot agree with White, however, who conjectures that either Euodia or
Syntyche, as a house church patroness, had decided to support Paul no longer
('Morality,' 214 n. 59).

[104] O'Brien, *Philippians*, 478.

Secondly, the request Paul has for these two, τὸ αὐτὸ φρονεῖν, is language taken from 2.1–4, verses which intend to encourage unity, with their redundant use of τὸ αὐτὸ φρονεῖν and τὸ ἓν φρονοῦντες (v. 2, cf. 1.27).[105]

Thirdly, though in 2.1–4 the positive instruction is a call to unity, the negative instruction is a call to avoid ἐριθεία and κενοδοξία. We have already noted above that ἐριθεία is rare and occurs only in Aristotle's *Politics*. There, however, it clearly refers to political ambition. Similarly, κενοδοξία may be found in the context of political and social strife in Dio Chrysostom's discourse on concord (*Or.* 38). The Nicomedians and the Nicaeans are vying with one another for the title of primacy (38.24). But such a title is truly vainglory (τὸ κενοδοξεῖν), a title which makes no difference,[106] for it is no guarantee of true glory (38.29–30, 40). In addition to Dio's use of κενοδοξία, διαφέρει and δόξα, we note the occurrence of μέγα φρονεῖτε to label the Nicomedians' and Nicaeans' boasting (38.38, 42). Likewise in Philippians these terms suggest a form of socio-political competition.

Though we have no direct evidence for factionalism in Philippi, such a struggle for primacy by two people of power in the Philippian congregation would certainly yield factions taking sides with one or the other. This factionalism was the way leadership operated in the first century.[107] The repetition of τὸ αὐτὸ φρονεῖν, however, may at least allow us to assert that division existed.

Fourthly, in this context the Christ-hymn has the function of illustrating the behaviour the apostle calls for in 2.1–4.[108] This type of behaviour is clearly non-competitive, unselfish and is rewarded with the glory that really matters (2.9–11). But a fuller explanation of the function of 2.5–11 we leave for the following section.

---

[105] On the function of 2.1–4 in the letter see D. A. Black, 'Paul and Christian Unity: A Formal Analysis of Philippians 2: 1–4', *JETS* 28 (1985): 299–308.

[106] 38.29: 'We ourselves deride and loathe, and end by pitying, those persons above all who do not know wherein false glory differs from the genuine' (ἐλεοῦμεν τοὺς οὐκ ἐπισταμένους τίνι διαφέρει δόξα ψευδὴς ἀληθοῦς). Cf. our discussion above on the function of τὰ διαφέροντα in the epistolary prayer of 1.10, pp. 106–7.

[107] Cf. Dio Chrys. *Or.* 38.34: 'You are in the predicament of two men, both equally distinguished, when they become rivals over politics – of necessity they court the favour of everybody, even those who are ever so far beneath them.' See also A. D. Clarke, *Secular and Christian Leadership in Corinth. A Socio-Historical and Exegetical Study of 1 Corinthians 1–6* (Leiden: E. J. Brill, 1993).

[108] Black, 'Paul and Christian Unity', 305.

The Christ-hymn in context

With regard to the Philippians' own particular situation, the paradigm of Jesus put forward in 2.6–11 is crucial. It is debated, however, whether Philippians 2.5 (τοῦτο φρονεῖτε ἐν ὑμῖν ὃ καὶ ἐν Χριστῷ 'Ιησοῦ) should be understood as, 'Your attitude should be the same as that of Christ Jesus',[109] thus yielding a paradigmatic function for vv. 6–11. For several scholars prefer 2.5 be rendered as, 'Let your bearing towards one another arise out of your life in Christ Jesus.'[110]

Though the elliptical nature of 2.5 certainly makes its interpretation difficult, we must not lose sight of the broader *function* of 2.5–11 in the letter. If, as even Martin admits, Paul in this section of the letter's exhortation to the Philippians 'is setting a pattern of living before their eyes, and bidding them to conform to it',[111] then we see that at least part of the hymn's *function* must be to illustrate this pattern of living using the example of Jesus' humility. If this function is correct, then 2.5, as a transitional sentence, must introduce this function of vv. 6–11. Further, the τοῦτο of the phrase τοῦτο φρονεῖτε (v. 5) must have content, and this content must be found not only in 2.1–4 but also (ὃ καὶ ἐν) in or among vv. 6–11. Certainly at least vv. 6–8 depict the attitude and action of Jesus.[112]

We assert that the ethical exhortations of the letter take their focus from this hymn.[113] For unmistakably, φρονεῖτε in 2.5, and the content of it seen in 2.6–11, illustrate how the readers should receive Paul's extensive use of φρονεῖν in the letter.

---

[109] NIV; cf. O'Brien, *Philippians*, 205; Hawthorne, *Philippians*, 79; Stowers, 'Friends and Enemies', 115; C. F. D. Moule, 'Further Reflexions on Philippians 2: 5–11', *Apostolic History and the Gospel*, eds. W. W. Gasque and R. P. Martin (Exeter: Paternoster, 1970): 264–76.

[110] NEB; cf. Martin, *Carmen Christi*, 63–94; E. Käsemann, 'A Critical Analysis of Philippians 2.5–11', *JTC* 5 (1968): 45–88; Silva, *Philippians*, 107–8; Beare, *Philippians*, 75; Perkins, 'Politeuma', 92.

[111] Martin, *Philippians* (NCB), 90.

[112] For a similar view of the function of the hymn see, e.g., Reinhard Deichgräber, *Gotteshymnus und Christushymnus in der frühen Christenheit* (Göttingen: Vandenhoeck & Ruprecht, 1967): 189–96; G. N. Stanton, *Jesus of Nazareth in New Testament Preaching* (Cambridge: Cambridge University Press, 1974): 99–103; Georg Strecker, 'Redaktion und Tradition im Christushymnus', *ZNW* 55 (1964): 64; Watson, 'Rhetorical Analysis', 69–70.

[113] For current overviews of scholarship on the Christ-hymn of 2.6–11 see O'Brien, *Philippians*, 186–202, along with the bibliography, and Otfried Hofius, *Der Christushymnus Philipper 2, 6–11. Untersuchungen zu Gestalt und Aussage eines urchristliches Psalms*, 2., erweiterte Auflage (Tübingen: J. C. B. Mohr, 1991).

In basic agreement with this function of 2.6–11 is L. Michael White. He asserts that Paul adapts the ideal of friendship from the Hellenistic moralist tradition and uses it as the basis for his moral exhortations in the letter.[114] White believes that the technical vocabulary of the letter (e.g., κοινωνία, τὸ αὐτὸ φρονεῖν) is drawn from the broad semantic field of friendship. White asserts that in its present context, the hymn of Philippians 2.6–11 has been adapted to this moral paradigm of friendship.[115] 'The model of selflessness, the willingness to give up one's own status and share another's troubles, is the ultimate sign of true friendship. As Aristotle says, "To a noble man there applies the true saying that he does all for the sake of his friends . . . if need be, even to the point of death" (*Eth. Nic.* 1169a . . .).'[116] According to White, we should therefore see the apostle using the familiar concept of friendship as the basis for his ethical exhortation in Philippians.

Though White correctly asserts that friendship played an important role in Greco-Roman philosophical and ethical discussion, his citations are selective, are taken out of context, and as a result are rather misleading. For example, read in its context, *Ethica Nicomachea* 1169A does not demonstrate that Aristotle is talking about 'selfless love'.[117] Immediately after the sentence that White quotes, the text reads:

> For (the noble man) will surrender wealth and power and all the goods that men struggle to win, if he can secure nobility for himself (περιποιούμενος ἑαυτῷ τὸ καλόν); since he would prefer an hour of rapture to a long period of mild enjoyment . . . And this is doubtless the case with those who give their lives for others; thus they choose great nobility for themselves (αἱροῦνται δὴ μέγα καλὸν ἑαυτοῖς). Also the virtuous man is ready to forgo money if by that means his friends may gain more money; for thus, though his friends get money, he himself achieves nobility

---

[114] White, 'Morality', 201–15. A similar view is taken by Stowers, 'Friends and Enemies', 105–21.

[115] White, 'Morality', 210–11.

[116] Ibid., 212–13. In addition to Arist. *Eth. Nic.* 1169A, White cites support for his selfless love theory from Lucian *Tox.* 29–34 (cf. Stowers, 'Friends and Enemies', 119).

[117] White, 'Morality', 213. For the sake of clarity, we understand this term to refer to that display of concern for the welfare of others which has no regard for or thought of self (cf. 'Selfless', *The Oxford English Dictionary*, ed. James A. H. Murray, et al., 12 vols. (Oxford: Clarendon Press, 1933): 9.421).

(αὐτῷ δὲ τὸ καλόν), and so he assigns the greater good to his own share (τὸ δὴ μεῖζον ἀγαθὸν ἑαυτῷ ἀπονέμει).[118]

The love described in Aristotle, far from being selfless, is rather totally self-centred. The noble man does these noble deeds of help for others in order to display or cultivate his own virtuous self. As a result, though it is certainly true that he does good to others, nevertheless he is motivated by the desire to gain the greatest good for himself (τὸ δὴ μεῖζον ἀγαθὸν ἑαυτῷ ἀπονέμει, Arist. *Eth. Nic.* 9.8.9). Elsewhere in *Ethica Nicomachea* we see these same motivations for virtuous acts (e.g., 4.3.24; 8.1.1; 8.13.2).[119]

Although harder to detect, the selfless love which White finds in Lucan *Toxaris* actually arises from similar motives. For example, Toxaris says that great men among the dead are honoured for the purpose of getting the living to imitate them (*Tox.* 1). In this context we see that the living carry on honourable practices in friendship for the purpose of receiving honours; in short, for a selfish purpose (cf. 7). Mnesippus tells the story of Agathocles who followed friend Deinias into exile, being ashamed to desert him even after Deinias' death (12–18). In 37 Toxaris speaks of how the Scythians make friends: 'when we see a brave man, capable of great achievements, we all make after him, and we think fit to behave in forming friendships as you do in seeking brides, paying them protracted court'.

Besides being motivated by self interest and the desire for honour, the friendship of *Toxaris* is male dominated. Toxaris tells the story of Abauchos, who lodges a wounded friend Gyndanes. Abauchos should be praised, for when fire breaks out in his home, he abandons his children and pushes away his wife in order to rescue Gyndanes (*Tox.* 61). Thus, White is correct in his reading of Paul, who urges selfless love. But he is incorrect in his reading of Aristotle and other sources. As a result, we question his theory that the apostle takes up the Hellenistic moral paradigm of friendship.

Apart from White's inappropriate use of sources to support his friendship paradigm theory, we should remember that friendship was certainly not a merely personal relation in the Greco-Roman world. Every friendship had potential political elements,[120] and

---

[118] LCL translation, *Eth. Nic.* 9.8.9 (= 1169A20–29).

[119] See also A. D. M. Walker, 'Aristotle's Account of Friendship in the *Nicomachean Ethics*', *Phronesis* 24 (1979): 180–96.

[120] At least this is certainly true amongst the elite. See Seneca *Ben.* 1.4.2–3; 5.5.4; also P. A. Brunt, '"Amicitia" in the Late Republic', *PCPS* ns.11 (1965): 1–20;

also contained elements of competition. This aspect of friendship is referred to by Stowers, who relies on Peter Marshall. Stowers, however, misunderstands how competition operated.[121]

Friends competed with one another for honour.[122] The person in the relationship who gave more gained in status, the other party lost status. We saw this happening in Oxyrhynchus Papyri 3057 above.[123] We have likewise seen Seneca refer to giving and receiving benefits as honourable competition. His own work on giving and receiving (*De Beneficiis*) was written because people needed to be taught to give, to receive, and to return willingly, and to strive to outdo each other in deed and spirit (1.4.3).[124] Though friendship is by definition fellowship in the giving and receiving of benefits,[125] it is honour which is gained and displayed in the giving of benefits.[126] This type of competitive friendship is precisely what Paul combats with his appeal to the example of Jesus.[127] Instead of exploiting his status for his own advantage, Jesus relinquishes it in order to serve others (2.6).[128] Likewise Paul cares nothing for his own personal comfort, as long as Christ is preached (1.18).

To summarize, we see that in 1.27–2.18 Paul addresses the heart of the Philippians' problems: they are experiencing strife which is a

---

and T. P. Wiseman, 'Competition and Co-operation', *Roman Political Life 90 BC to AD 69*, ed. T. P. Wiseman (Exeter: Exeter University Publications, 1985): 3–19.

[121] Stowers, 'Friends and Enemies', 113; cf. Marshall, *Enmity*, 35–67.

[122] See, e.g., Arist. *Eth. Nic.* 8.13.2; *Magna Moralia* 2.1211A46. Glimpses of competition can be seen in the papyri. For example, in P.Flor. 332 (2nd AD) Eudaemonis writes to son Apollonius, reminding him that at his marriage Eudaemonis' sister-in-law gave a present of 100 drachmae. Now that the sister-in-law's son is about to marry, it is right to make a return gift, even though there are grievances still pending against them (δίκαιόν ἐστι καὶ ὑμᾶς ἀνταποδοῦναι, καὶ εἰ (ἐγκ)λημάτια ἐστι πρὸς αὐτοὺς ἐν μέσῳ, lines 24b–26).

[123] See our treatment of verbal gratitude on pp. 73–83. Note also our comments on P.Mert. 12 in the same section.

[124] Cf. Mauss' comment on 'a sort of amiable rivalry' which exists amongst the Andaman islanders (Mauss, *The Gift*, 18).

[125] Cf. (Ps)-Plato, *Def.* 413B1: κοινωνία τοῦ εὖ ποιῆσαι καὶ παθεῖν.

[126] Cf. again (Ps)-Plato, *Def.* 413E3: τιμὴ δόσις ἀγαθῶν ἐν ταῖς δι' ἀρετὴν πράξεσιν διδομένων· ἀξίωμα ἀπ' ἀρετῆς; cf. Dio. Hal. 11.16.2.

[127] Notice also Paul's appeal to a reversal of social practice in Rom. 12.10: τῇ τιμῇ ἀλλήλους προηγούμενοι, the readers should prefer one another in honour (Cranfield, *Romans*, 633), and 12.17: μηδενὶ κακὸν ἀντὶ κακοῦ ἀποδιδόντες, the readers should not seek to pay back evil for evil. Contrast the views of Arist. *Eth. Nic.* 5.5.6; Tac. *Hist.* 4.3; Dio Chrys. *Or.* 38.20.

[128] On this understanding of ἁρπαγμός see R. W. Hoover, 'The HARPAGMOS Enigma: A Philological Solution', *HTR* 64 (1971): 95–119.

hindrance to their reputation as a Christian community, which hinders the advance of the gospel, and is contrary to their status as partners in the gospel. The key elements of this strife are φθόνον, ἔρις, ἐριθεία, κενοδοξία and, by implication, a failure to be like-minded (τὸ αὐτὸ φρονεῖν). Such selfish ambition is directly contrary to the attitude of Jesus seen in 2.6–11. Thus, the Christ-hymn is the hub from which the ethical injunctions of the letter radiate.

Partnership in service: 2.19–30

In addition to the giving and receiving of Philippians 4.15, the apostle and this congregation also enjoyed reciprocal, sacrificial service.[129] This is a further unique aspect of the apostle's relationship with the Philippians.

The previous section (1.27–2.18) ended with a declaration of the apostle's willingness to be poured out on the sacrifice and service of the Philippians' faith (v. 17). The apostle's θυσία has its counterpart in 4.18, where the Philippians' gift is said to be a fragrant offering and sacrifice to God.[130] θυσία occurs rarely in Paul,[131] and we should not miss the significance of its unique sense in Philippians and its twofold appearance in the letter. Romans 12.1 urges believers to give themselves to God. Likewise in 1 Corinthians 10.18, sacrifice has been given to a god, though there θυσία refers to the body of the sacrificial animal. Only in Philippians do we find θυσία spiritualized.[132] Very similarly, λειτουργία, found elsewhere describing the collection in 2 Corinthians 9.12, occurs in Philippians twice and is spiritualized. Such personal abasement on Paul's part fits with the picture of Jesus painted in 2.6–11: a personal pouring out (σπένδομαι, 2.17) or a personal emptying (ἐκένωσεν, 2.7).

Also in 2.19–30 we learn of two further servants who are willing to give sacrificial service, and of Paul's interpretation of the errand of Epaphroditus: Epaphroditus' mission to Paul is an act of service on the part of the Philippians (v. 30).[133] This service is a reflection

---

[129] R. A. Culpepper, in labelling this section, rightfully entitles his article: 'Co-Workers in Suffering: Philippians 2: 19–30', *RevExp* 77 (1980): 349–58.

[130] See pp. 153–7 for treatment of 4.18.

[131] Phil. 2.17, 4.18; 1 Cor. 10.18; Rom. 12.1; cf. Eph. 5.2.

[132] Although compare Heb. 13.16; 1 Pet. 2.5.

[133] Epaphroditus' service to Paul while Paul was a prisoner was potentially dangerous. This could partially explain the commendation due him (2.30). On the risks for those associating with prisoners see Brian M. Rapske, 'The Importance of Helpers to the Imprisoned Paul in the Book of Acts', *TynBul* 42 (1991): 3–30, esp. 23–9.

of their partnership. Epaphroditus has come near to death for the work of Christ, i.e., for the work of the gospel. But what work is it that Epaphroditus has done? He has been the apostle (v. 25b) of the Philippian church in his mission to fill up what was lacking in the service of the church toward Paul.[134] That is, his work for the gospel was bringing cash to Paul. This act was service (λειτουργία, 2.30, cf., 25).[135] Paul on his part also is willing to be poured out for the sake of their service (λειτουργία, 2.17).

Further, Paul again employs the exhortation to imitation which he has used regarding Jesus (2.5) and will use regarding himself below (3.17). Timothy (2.20–2) and Epaphroditus (2.29–30) are examples of the kind of person who is more concerned for the good of others than for themselves (v. 21).[136] The Philippians know Timothy's proven character (v. 22): he does not seek his own selfish ends (τὰ ἑαυτῶν ζητοῦσιν) as all the others do.[137] The plural of 3.17b is likewise probably used to include Epaphroditus and Timothy with Paul as those worthy of imitation.

Conclusion

We have seen the apostle describe several ways in which his relationship with the Philippian church was unique. Not only did he engage in giving and receiving with no other church (4.15), but the Philippians also shared some of the same struggles that he had (1.30) and were participants with him in grace both in his imprisonment and in the defence and confirmation of the gospel (1.7). Paul and the Philippians engaged in reciprocal service for one another (2.17, 30), prayed for one another (1.3–4; cf. 1.19), and had affection for each other (1.7–8; cf. 4.10). It may well be that the Philippians' financial sharing was allowed because of the concern

---

[134] This phrase (ἵνα ἀναπληρώσῃ τὸ ὑμῶν ὑστέρημα τῆς πρός με λειτουργίας) need not imply that the Philippians had fallen behind in their financial support of the apostle, but only that Epaphroditus took the Philippians' place in the service they could not render while apart, cf. 1 Cor. 16.17.

[135] Notice also Paul's use of λειτουργία to label the collection (2 Cor. 9.12).

[136] Watson, 'Rhetorical Analysis', 71; Kurz, 'Kenotic Imitation', 118–19. This praise for Epaphroditus need not be taken as Paul's attempt to mediate in a conflict Epaphroditus was having with the Philippians (*contra* Bernhard Mayer, 'Paulus als Vermittler zwischen Epaphroditus und der Gemeinde von Philippi. Bemer- kungen zu Phil. 2,25–30', *BZ* 31 (1987): 176–88). Compare Paul's praise of Stephanus in 1 Cor. 16.16 and general exhortation in 1 Thess. 5.12.

[137] 2.21. Note here the return to the subject of ἐριθεία in order to contrast Timothy with the falsely motivated preachers of 1.17 (see Jewett, 'Conflicting Movements', 369).

they apparently had for the gospel's advance (1.12), rather than the situation arising the other way around. To be sure, the apostle puts the advance of the gospel, which happens despite his own confinement, at the beginning of the letter body and suggests thereby that the Philippians were very much a missionary church. He puts thanksgiving to God for their κοινωνία εἰς τὸ εὐαγγέλιον very early and also suggests thereby that one of the primary factors, if not the primary factor, accounting for their unique place in his heart (cf. 1.7–8) was their missionary attitude. Thus, the letter to the Philippians demonstrates for us a clear relationship between mission and money. The gospel and working/suffering for the gospel are themes which are integral to this letter because the recipients are financial partners in ministry with the apostle.

It should come as no surprise to us that the Philippians were the only church to engage in giving and receiving with the apostle. We have seen the role of gift and service relationships in the Greco-Roman world and though Paul employs the giving and receiving metaphor,[138] the social conventions regarding such relationships are not reflected in Paul's dealings with money in regard to his churches.[139] Paul mentions nothing of any debt which he owes to the Philippians because of the gifts he has received. Such a personal or individualistic response would be far too narrow and misleading. Instead Paul offers a theological response to the Philippians' financial sharing with him. Their giving and his reception has established a unique bond between them, a unique partnership in the gospel which looks far beyond the confines of mere social reciprocity.

[138] See the comments on ἐκοινώνησεν εἰς λόγον δόσεως καὶ λήμψεως on pp. 146–51.
[139] See further our reflections on this mission and money connection on pp. 157–60.

5

PHILIPPIANS 4.10–20: PAUL'S 'THANK-YOU' SECTION?[1]

In our previous chapter we observed that Paul describes his relationship with the Philippians as partnership in the gospel (1.5). We saw how the apostle subordinates all his activities and desires to the gospel and its advance (1.18, 21; 2.17) and urges the Philippians, as a missionary church, to do the same (1.27–2.18). These items which he stresses all come before his direct response to the Philippians' gift and must be seen as preparation for that response.

Now we come to the study of Paul's direct reply. Here we centre attention on 4.10–20 and the apostle's statements concerning their gift.[2] We hope to demonstrate that, in light of the information collected in chapter 3 and 4, this text should be understood as deliberately crafted to teach the Philippians the proper meaning and significance of their gift. In so doing Paul must confront and correct some of the accepted Greek and Roman social conventions regarding the exchange of gifts and favours. Paul's unique relationship with the Philippians is not merely a social one. He has received their financial aid because he sees that they have a partnership which advances the gospel.

There are a few items to note as we begin exegetical discussion of Philippians 4. They should alert us to issues for debate as we read the text.

As was mentioned in the Introduction, scholars divide on how to interpret Paul's response to the Philippians' gift in 4.10–20. The

---

[1] Most modern translations (e.g., NIV, NASB, NKJV) as well as most commentators (e.g., O'Brien, *Philippians*, 513; Martin, *Philippians* (NCB), 160; Beare, *Philippians*, 149; Hawthorne, *Philippians*, 193; Silva, *Philippians*, 230; Gnilka, *Philipperbrief*, 171) label this section of the letter as Paul's thanks for the Philippians' support.

[2] On this whole section see the author's, '"Thankless Thanks"', 261–70.

absence of εὐχαριστέω, the perceived discomfort of the apostle and the use of what are believed to be financial-technical terms has led to several theories.[3] Some assert that Paul's thanks are thankless.[4] On the other hand, some scholars see in Paul's words 'warm and affectionate thanks'.[5] This divergence arises because of twentieth-century assumptions scholars have about gratitude. If early in the letter he had said, 'I received the things you sent through Epaphroditus and give you many thanks for them',[6] then to our minds his gratitude would be less problematic. As we shall see in the discussion below, the reason Paul's response contains 169 words (4.10–20) instead of the eleven of our proposed alternative is that Paul took the opportunity, not only to respond personally to the gift, but to teach the Philippians the spiritual significance of their financial sharing.[7] This instruction required more than a single line.

Closely connected to the above, some scholars assert that the primary purpose for the Philippian letter cannot be to acknowledge receipt of their gift because the apostle's response comes only toward the end of the letter and is actually thankless.[8] Though it is not our purpose in this chapter to offer a precise reason for the writing of Philippians, we hope at least to show that the perceived lateness and thanklessness of Paul's written gratitude cannot be used to eliminate the possibility that response to the gift was one of the primary purposes of the letter.

We should remember the high degree of similarity between this

---

[3] See chapter 1, pp. 11–15 , for an overview of these theories.

[4] Lohmeyer, *Philipper*, 178; cf. Dodd, 'The Mind of Paul: I', 71; Beare, *Philippians*, 151; Collange, *Philippians*, 148–9; Brian J. Capper, 'Paul's Dispute with Philippi: Understanding Paul's Argument in Phil. 1–2 from his Thanks in 4.10–20', *TZ* 49 (1993): 207.

[5] C. J. Ellicott, *A Critical and Grammatical Commentary on St Paul's Epistles to the Philippians, Colossians and to Philemon* (London: Parker, Son and Bourn, 1886): xx. Similarly, Motyer says, 'Paul was glad to acknowledge his indebtedness' (*Philippians*, 215).

[6] Perhaps these words could have been used: ἐδεξάμην παρὰ 'Επαφροδίτου τὰ παρ' ὑμῶν καὶ πλεῖστην χάριν ὑμῖν ἔχω.

[7] *Contra* Lohmeyer, *Philipper*, 187, who suggests that the fullness of the words is explained by the temporal distance between his reception of the gift and the dispatch of the letter. Compare our conclusions offered at the end of this chapter.

[8] E.g., Silva, *Philippians*, 230; Hawthorne, *Philippians*, xlviii. This same argument is used to assert that canonical Philippians is not 'a' letter at all, but a redactional collection of three separate bits of correspondence; see Collange, *Philippians*, 5, 148; Beare, *Philippians*, 4; W. Marxsen, *Einleitung in das Neue Testament* (Gütersloh: Gerd Mohn, 1964): 63–4. See our discussion on the integrity of Philippians in chapter 1, pp. 17–19.

text and 1.3–11.[9] The subject matter which is common to these two texts alerts us to the meaning of Paul's relationship with the Philippians and to what is primary in his response to their gift.

J. Paul Sampley offers an in depth and comprehensive view of Paul's financial relationship with the Philippians.[10] At this point we offer a summary of Sampley's view, with a general response. Specific exegetical details will be left for discussion when they arise in our treatment of the text of Philippians 4.

Sampley contends that Paul's relationship with the Philippians is patterned after the Roman consensual *societas*; a verbal, legally binding, reciprocal partnership or association made between two or more people regarding a common goal. 'Consensual *societas* required neither witnesses nor written documents nor notification of authorities. Simple agreement was all that was required.'[11] In the primary literature which Sampley cites[12] *societas* has the following characteristics: each party contributes property, labour, skill or status, as the case may be, for the accomplishment of the goal; no partner can turn the *societas* to his own ends; the partnership lasts as long as the parties remain of the same mind; a partner is entitled to remuneration for expenses incurred on behalf of the *societas*;[13] death dissolves the association; the agreement is subject to enforcement by the courts; people of differing social strata, even slaves, may participate; and the Greek analog for *societas* is κοινωνία.[14]

With regard to Philippians, Sampley presents three arguments for seeing the relationship as a *societas*:

First, Paul's terms (e.g., ἀπέχω and εἰς λόγον, both used in their commercial sense) are consistent with the provision of *societas* that a partner is due reimbursement for expenses. Paul has preached the

---

9 See chapter 4, p. 91, for our chart of parallels.
10 J. Paul Sampley, *Pauline Partnership in Christ. Christian Community and Commitment in Light of Roman Law* (Philadelphia: Fortress Press, 1980).
11 Sampley, *Partnership*, 13.
12 Cicero *Pro Roscio Comoedo, Pro Quinctio*; Gaius, *Institutes*; *Digest* 17.2 *Pro Socio*.
13 The right to remuneration is particularly important for Sampley since, in Philippians 4, Paul receives a gift as a partner in the gospel.
14 *Partnership*, 12–17. Sampley draws these characteristics of *societas* from the following works: H. F. Jolowicz, *Historical Introduction to the Study of Roman Law* (Cambridge: Cambridge University Press, 1965); J. W. Jones, *The Law and the Legal Theory of the Greeks* (Oxford: Clarendon Press, 1956); Alan Watson, *The Law of Obligations in the Later Roman Republic* (Oxford: Clarendon Press, 1965); *The Law of the Ancient Romans* (Dallas: Southern Methodist University Press, 1970); Michael Wegner, *Untersuchungen zu den lateinischen Begriffen socius und societas* (Göttingen: Vandenhoeck & Ruprecht, 1969).

gospel on the Philippians' behalf and this gift can be seen as a request he made of them for support. Sampley refers only briefly to the phrase ἐκοινώνησεν εἰς λόγον δόσεως καὶ λήμψεως (Phil. 4.15) calling it 'the commercial terminology of bookkeeping'.[15] He follows Lightfoot in asserting that the phrase refers only to the passing of money between Paul and the Philippians.[16]

Secondly, κοινωνία appears in the letter with the meaning 'partnership', and partnership is the basic idea behind *societas*. 'The commercial technical terms associated with koinonia . . . leave it unmistakable that the partnership is *societas*.'[17]

Thirdly, there is a prominent place in the letter for other *societas* terminology. To be of the same mind (τὸ αὐτὸ φρονεῖν, Phil. 2.2; 4.2; cf. 1.7, 27; 2.5) is a characteristic of *societas* according to Gaius. The Philippians are fully aware of the significance of the phrase τὸ αὐτὸ φρονεῖν and are expected to understand it without explanation.[18]

After presenting these main arguments for his thesis, Sampley finds confirmation for his thesis in his understanding of χρεία. He asserts that χρεία (Phil. 2: 25, 4: 16, 19) may be understood as 'request'[19] and urges that we leave operative the full range of meaning of χρεία; it is a 'need-request'.[20] Since Paul is the Philippians' partner in *societas*, he has invoked his legal right to remuneration by requesting this payment from the Philippians.[21]

Sampley also asks why there was *societas* with the Philippians and not with other congregations. One answer he gives is that 'the church was apparently little marked by internal strife; it was early and enduringly a stable, unified Christian community'.[22]

Sampley's attempts to place Paul's epistle in a social context are welcomed. Nevertheless, there are difficulties with his conception of

---

[15] Sampley, *Partnership*, 57; cf. 74 n. 20.   [16] Lightfoot, *Philippians*, 165.

[17] Sampley, *Partnership*, 60–1.   [18] Ibid., 62–72, esp. 62–3.

[19] Sampley supplies no primary literature to support his assertion, but cites Liddell and Scott, *Lexicon*, 2002, and Fleury, 'Une Société de Fait', 53–4. The former offers Thuc. 1.37; Aeschylus *Pr.* 700, *Ch.* 481. These examples are no later than the fifth century BC. Unfortunately, in his treatment of χρεία Sampley makes no reference to Bauer's *Lexicon*.

[20] *Partnership*, 54–5. Sampley makes a similar appeal to a double meaning for δόμα (4.17). It is a 'gift-payment' (*Partnership*, 54).

[21] Contrast the situation at Corinth: there Paul insists that he will not make use of his right despite *offers* of gifts from the Corinthians (2 Cor. 11.9, 12.14). See our comments on these texts on pp. 168–71.

[22] Sampley, *Partnership*, 104.

Paul's special relationship with Philippians. We will begin with
responses to the specific arguments Sampley supplies before
moving to more general criticisms of his theory.

First, as we have seen, the words in Philippians 4.10–20 which
are commonly called technical financial terms need not be understood in a financial way. Rather, they can be taken in a social
way.[23] The transactional character of gift and service relationships
in the Greco-Roman world lends itself to such metaphors. Thus,
although ἀπέχω and εἰς λόγον are present, we need not label
Philippians 4.10–20 as Paul's 'receipt' for the Philippians' reimbursement. Further, the evidence collected in chapter 3, in this
chapter and by Marshall demonstrates that the phrase
ἐκοινώνησεν εἰς λόγον δόσεως καὶ λήμψεως (4.15) has a social
meaning in this context.[24]

Secondly, our preceding argument leads us to question Sampley's
bold assertion that, 'the commercial technical terms associated
with koinonia . . . leave it unmistakable that the partnership is
societas.[25] If such terms are not technical, then just what is the
κοινωνία which Paul has with the Philippians? Much of the force of
Sampley's argument rests on his claim that κοινωνία is equivalent
to *societas*.[26] Although the authors cited by Sampley supply us with
examples of κοινωνία used as 'partnership',[27] that in itself only
proves that κοινωνία is a possible *analog* for *societas*.[28] The fact
that κοινωνία *can* have the meaning 'partnership' does not demonstrate that κοινωνία *was used* by Greek speakers as a label for the
Roman association of *societas*,[29] nor does it demonstrate that Paul
employs κοινωνία in Philippians with the meaning *societas*. These
assertions must be demonstrated by harder evidence. Since
Sampley is attempting to attribute a specialized, technical meaning
to κοινωνία, the burden of proof must rest with him to demonstrate

---

[23] See chapter 3, pp. 56–65. In ancient texts see, e.g., Philo *Cher.* 122–3; Arist. *Eth. Nic.* 4.1; Cic. *Amic.* 16.58.

[24] Marshall, *Enmity*, 157–64.   [25] Sampley, *Partnership*, 60–1.

[26] A similar point is made in D. M. Sweetland's review of Sampley's work in *CBQ* 44 (1982): 690.

[27] Sampley, *Partnership*, 45 n. 26, citing Hauck, 'κοινός', *TDNT* 3: 789–809; Moulton and Milligan, *Vocabulary*, 351; Jones, *Legal Theory*, 163. Together, Hauck and Moulton provide BGU 586.11; P.Ryl. 117.16; *SIG²* 300.54. Support for Sampley's position is not found on the page he cites from Jones.

[28] Analog is the term Sampley himself uses (*Partnership*, 18 n. 7).

[29] The only text demonstrating this point is Theophilus' paraphrase of *The Institutes* by Justinian III.26 (6th AD) cited by Fleury, 'Une Société de Fait', 45 n. 23.

a connection between *societas* and κοινωνία. This he has failed to do.[30]

A text in which Seneca employs *societas* is telling against Sampley's view. Seneca asserts that an exchange of benefits fortifies one's life against sudden disasters, that man's safety lies in fellowship (*societas, Ben.* 4.18.1–2). Here *societas* is equivalent to a relationship of social reciprocity and such a relationship is built solely on the social exchange of goods and services and has no legal basis. No more needs to be found in Paul's use of κοινωνία than is found in Seneca's use of *societas* in *De Beneficiis* 4.18.1–2.

Thirdly, Sampley's statements on Philippian unity are exaggerated. Perhaps the Philippians suffered less in the way of strife than the Corinthians, but they certainly had internal strife (cf. 4.2).[31] It is conflict with the apostle which is absent at Philippi. We compare the Corinthians with whom Paul had great struggles concerning his own position and authority.

Fourthly, when Paul directly addresses his right to support (1 Cor. 9) the reasons he gives are not his *societas* with his churches. He has the right to support regardless of the nature or quality of his relationship with the church. To the Corinthians he stresses his right to receive support. Yet it is the Corinthians with whom he also has the greatest conflicts: certainly not a relationship based on the same mind.[32]

Fifthly, and closely related to the above, Paul says he has the right to support from a church while he is present and making that church the direct object of his ministry. He does not say he has the right to support while he is absent and working as the representative of that church. It is because of the spiritual blessings that the church receives from him, while he is present with them, that he has the right to expect material compensation (1 Cor. 9.11). Sampley speaks of Paul working to spread the gospel as the Philippians' *representative*.[33] Yet the concept of representation is not found in the letter. Indeed, in the Pauline corpus working as the representative of another is a concept foreign to Paul's presentation of himself. Further, although he can refer to Timothy as the child and himself as the father, nevertheless even in this relationship Timothy

[30] Reumann, 'Contributions', 441 n. 14. In addition, see our discussion of κοινωνία on pp. 146–51 below.
[31] See our discussion of concord and discord in Philippi on pp. 111–13.
[32] See our comments regarding the Corinthian conflict on pp. 162–75.
[33] Sampley, *Partnership*, 53.

serves *with him* in the work of the gospel (ὡς πατρὶ τέκνον σὺν ἐμοὶ ἐδούλευσεν εἰς τὸ εὐαγγέλιον, Phil. 2.22). Typically Paul prefers to use συνεργός of his *fellow-workers* in the gospel.[34] Instead of representation what we do find is Paul's assertion that he and the Philippians, despite being geographically distant, work alongside each other as they strive for the gospel in their respective contexts.[35]

Finally, Sampley's construction places the apostle's relationship with the Philippians in a very narrow framework.[36] There is a much broader one, not mentioned by Sampley, which is sufficient to explain Paul's terms, which appears to fit the epistle more easily and which is to be preferred because of its greater simplicity. This broad framework is the social practice of giving and receiving discussed in chapter 3.

With these observations in mind we begin exegetical discussion of Philippians 4.10–20.

Personal reflection: vv. 10–13, 18a[37]

The expression of joy: 4.10a

In 4.10 Paul asserts that the Philippians' gift, their remembering him (τὸ ὑπὲρ ἐμοῦ φρονεῖν), was a cause of great joy for him. With this statement Paul again strikes the keynote of the letter.[38] He says in 1.4 that his prayers for them are joyful and evidently even at that early stage in the letter his joy is linked to their concern for him. Here in 4.10 it is definitely the case that joy has resulted from the sharing which the Philippians undertook. Although this pleasant feeling is simple enough, we can consider profitably the various aspects of this joy as well as examine the Pauline causes of joy.

---

34 Rom. 16.3, 9, 21; 1 Cor. 3.9; 2 Cor. 1.24, 8.23; Phil. 2.25, 4.3; 1 Thess. 3.2; Phlm. 1, 24; cf. Col. 4.11. See E. Earle Ellis, 'Paul and His Co-Workers', *NTS* 17 (1971): 437–52.

35 See our treatment of ἐπὶ τῇ κοινωνίᾳ κτλ on pp. 99–103.

36 Other scholars have noted that Sampley's approach is too narrow and that the terms in Phil. actually refer to a broader semantic field (e.g., White, 'Morality', 210–11).

37 We include among the apostle's statements of personal reflection on the meaning of the gift the phrase ἀπέχω δὲ πάντα καὶ περισσεύω· πεπλήρωμαι found in v. 18a. Verse 18b is discussed on pp. 153–7.

38 Vincent, *Philippians*, 141.

The joy that Paul expresses in his letters is often called forth by his seeing or hearing of the faith and/or obedience of Christians. In this respect it is not far from expressions of joy seen in the papyri which often are based on the writer's hearing of a friend's good health.[39] Paul's converts ought to make him rejoice (2 Cor. 2.3) by their obedience to his teaching. In 2 Corinthians 7.5–7 he says that while in Macedonia he had grief. Yet his joy was greater than ever when he heard from Titus of the Corinthians' ardent concern for Paul. Because the Thessalonians stand firm in the Lord Paul has so much joy he cannot thank God enough in return for it (1 Thess. 3.9).[40]

In 4.10 we find the adverb μεγάλως, which in the New Testament appears only here. And indeed, though Paul seems never shy of expressing his feelings, this is the only place where he qualifies his own experience of joy.[41] Thus, the concern (φρονεῖν) of the Philippians is of special importance to the apostle. It is their concern for him which finds definite expression that draws from him the greatest joy. We should understand this joy as delight in the spiritual maturity of the Philippians.[42]

Schenk, however, asserts that Paul's joy is his expression of thanks because joy and thanks occupy the same semantic field.[43] But just what is the semantic field he has in mind? Schenk cannot make this assertion without establishing in advance the meaning and significance of an expression of thanks and the semantic field in which such an expression would lie.[44] Unfortunately, Schenk attempts neither of these tasks. We have already seen that an

---

[39] E.g., P.Petaus 29, P.Sarap. 95, P.Oxy. 3356, PSI 333.

[40] Note here the language of social reciprocity in 1 Thess. 3.9. Paul asks, τίνα γὰρ εὐχαριστίαν δυνάμεθα τῷ θεῷ ἀνταποδοῦναι περὶ ὑμῶν ἐπὶ πάσῃ τῇ χαρᾷ. Since a material return to God is impossible, one must resort to praise and thanksgiving (e.g., Philo *Spec.* 1.224–5, *Sob.* 58, *Plant.* 126; Arr. *Epict. Diss.* 1.16.15–21).

[41] Hawthorne, *Philippians*, 196.

[42] The concern (φρονεῖν) which the Philippians display in 4.10 is in keeping with the Christian mind set (φρονεῖν) which the apostle has delineated throughout the letter (esp. 2.2, 5, 4.2; cf. 4.14 where such thought, φρονεῖν, is called sharing in hardship).

[43] Schenk, *Philipperbriefe*, 43.

[44] The task is especially difficult since 'thanks is often expressed in highly idiomatic ways' (Johannes P. Louw and Eugene A Nida, *Greek English Lexicon of the New Testament Based on Semantic Domains*, 2 vols. (New York: United Bible Societies, 1988): 428–9). Louw and Nida, however, do not include expressions of joy in the semantic field of thanks.

expression of thanks using, for example, εὐχαριστέω σοι or χάρις σοι is not common in the papyri.[45] But, as Schenk apparently would have us believe, does an expression of joy perform the same function? It does not appear that it does. Schenk leans too heavily on the etymological connection between εὐχαριστέω and χαίρω,[46] and on the fact that thanks to God in the Old Testament often takes the form of an expression of joy.[47]

These exact words, to rejoice greatly, are found in several papyri.[48] Such expressions of joy serve to confirm the bond between the parties,[49] and are typically used at the receipt of a letter, not at the receipt of a gift.[50] We saw a similar expression of joy in the letter of Chairas, who received a delightful feeling of home upon receipt of Dionysius' letter.[51] Paul's expression of joy fits well with such expressions, for his joy is based on contact with and good news from the Philippians. Specifically, Paul's joy is neither linked to receipt of a letter nor to the Philippians' gift, but to their remembrance of him,[52] though this particular example of remembrance comes at least partially in the form of a gift.

We cannot, however, view Paul's joy solely against the background of papyrus letters. The difference is that Paul's joy is in the Lord (ἐν κυρίῳ). The joy arises because of their concern for him (τὸ ὑπὲρ ἐμοῦ φρονεῖν). In view of how this concern is described in the rest of the letter (viz, κοινωνία εἰς εὐαγγέλιον, 1.5, λειτουργία, 2.30, συγκοινωνήσαντές μου τῇ θλίψει, 4.14) we should define this as Christian concern. But all such Christian maturity and action has its grounds in Christ. For it is he who has begun this good work of partnership in them (1.6).[53] Therefore, Paul's joy is in the Lord because, in the final analysis, he will ascribe the cause to God.

---

[45] See the treatment of verbal gratitude in the papyri on pp. 73–83 above.

[46] This point is made by Silva, *Philippians*, 235, who nevertheless follows Schenk in his basic observation.

[47] Here Schenk follows Conzelmann ('χαίρω κτλ', *TDNT*, 9.363). See our comments on verbal thanks in the Old Testament (esp. Job 29.13 and 31.20) on pp. 35–6 above.

[48] E.g., P.Oxy. 1676 (3d AD), 3356 (76 AD).

[49] White, *Light*, 201.

[50] Koskenniemi, *Idee*, 77.

[51] See pp. 74–5 above.

[52] Compare the expressions of thanks cited above (pp. 78–80) which are not directly linked to goods received but favours (P.Mich. 483, 498; P.Oxy. 963).

[53] See the comments on this text on pp. 103–5 above.

The grounds for joy: 4.10b

The apostle's joy was caused by the Philippians' expression of concern for him. Apparently there had been an uncharacteristic gap since the last gift had been sent. He now rejoices at last, ἤδη ποτέ. The expression is found in several papyri and literary authors.[54] An undetermined length of time is referred to, but one which he had apparently not expected. That a length of time had elapsed is further implied by the use of ἀναθάλλω, which describes the Philippians' concern as 'springing to life' again.

Whether ἀναθάλλω is understood transitively or intransitively is a difficult decision, though fortunately not of great consequence for our purpose. There are so few examples from other authors that little help is offered in the decision. The presence of τό,[55] however, which must be taken as accusative, tips the scales in favour of the transitive understanding.

If τό in the phrase τὸ ὑπὲρ ἐμοῦ φρονεῖν is taken as anaphoric, as Blass and Debrunner suggest,[56] we have Paul rejoicing over this particular care of theirs, namely financial support. On the use of the neuter article in this way see also 1 Corinthians 4.6.[57]

The disproportionately high number of occurrences of φρονεῖν in this letter[58] signals to us the importance of the theme to Paul's mind.[59] Likewise the large number of examples help us to establish its particular significance here. We note the following observations on φρονεῖν in Philippians.

First, Paul's paraenesis centres on the example of Jesus (2.5–11). This pattern of humility and gracious condescension for the good of others is to be imitated (τοῦτο φρονεῖτε ἐν ὑμῖν ὃ καὶ ἐν Χριστῷ

---

54 E.g., P.Oxy. 237.7, 11, 19 (186 AD); P.Oxy. 2996.5 (2nd AD); cf. Josephus *AJ* 16.197; *BJ* 2.90, 4.159; Philo *Post.* 13.3, *Conf.* 196.6.

55 Apparently the scribe(s) of F and G had difficulty with this construction as well, substituting τοῦ for τό.

56 BDF, *Grammar*, 206 (para. 399): 'which you have previously done'; cf. Gnilka, *Philipperbrief*, 173 n. 112; Schenk, *Philipperbriefe*, 64.

57 The text as found in א² Cᵛⁱᵈ D² 𝔐 vgᵐˢ sy; cf. also τὸ ὑπὲρ αὐτοῦ πάσχειν, Phil. 1.29.

58 It appears nine times in four chapters, as opposed to ten times in Romans and once each in 1 and 2 Corinthians and Galatians.

59 Schenk (*Philipperbriefe*, 64) believes the high number of occurrences of φρονεῖν indicate that the phrase φρονεῖν ὑπέρ was the Philippians' own designation of their action in supporting Paul and Paul has taken over the word (cf. Reumann, 'Contributions', 440). Appealing though it is, evidence for this view is weak and the hermeneutical approach required is methodologically suspect.

'Ιησοῦ, 2.5).[60] In this context φρονεῖν has just been encountered twice (v. 2), and the conclusion is clear that if the Philippians imitate the mindset of Jesus as displayed in vv. 6–11, it will produce the concord that Paul urges in vv. 1–4.

Secondly, an actual instance of discord in the congregation can be solved if the parties will be like-minded (τὸ αὐτὸ φρονεῖν, 4.2). Here Paul dares to apply his teaching to a particular situation. The similarity of construction cannot be missed.[61] It may well be that the conflict between Euodia and Syntyche is in Paul's mind as he presents the status-lowering behaviour of Jesus in 2.5–11.[62]

Thirdly, when 1.7 is re-read in light of the comments in 4.10, we see that Paul and this congregation are displaying reciprocal concern (φρονεῖν).[63] This concern is just one of the elements of their κοινωνία.[64]

In Sampley's view the phrase τὸ αὐτὸ φρονεῖν plays a very important role: it is a necessary element of *societas*. If partners cease to be of the same mind, *societas* is dissolved.[65] He concludes that the repeated exhortation of Paul to be of the same mind is indication that the Philippians share a *societas*. But Sampley's logic here is not compelling. Though *societas* demands being of the same mind, being of the same mind does not demand *societas*. Being in harmony is a concern which we would expect to see, and do see, in a great variety of literature where *societas* is out of the question.[66] Restricting ourselves to the phrase τὸ αὐτὸ φρονεῖν[67] we can cite two examples.

In his description of the Essenes, Josephus refers to a splinter group which agrees in every way except for its view of marriage. These 'think that those who decline to marry cut off the chief function of life . . . and, what is more, that, were all to adopt the same view (εἰ πάντες τὸ αὐτὸ φρονήσειαν), the whole race would

---

[60] See our discussion of 2.5–11 on pp. 114–17 above.
[61] τοῦτο φρονεῖτε ἐν ὑμῖν ὃ καὶ ἐν Χριστῷ, 2.5.
    τὸ αὐτο φρονεῖν   ἐν κυριῷ,   4.2.
[62] See Concord and Discord in Philippi, pp. 111–13 above.
[63] Gnilka, *Philipperbrief*, 173.
[64] See P. T. O'Brien, 'The Fellowship Theme in Philippians', *Reformed Theological Review* 37 (1978): 9–18, and also our summary of reciprocities between Paul and the Philippians on pp. 119–20.
[65] Sampley, *Partnership*, 15.
[66] See, e.g., Arr. *Epict. Diss.* 2.16.42, 2.19.26   (ὁμογνωμονῶ); 2.22.24 (ὁμονοεῖν); Sen. *Ep.* 35.2 (*uno nos*).
[67] But cf. τὰ αὐτα φρονεῖν in Dio Cass. 42.10.2; Diod. Sic. 38/39.2.2; Plut. *Vit. Pyrrhus* 23.5; and also φρονεῖτε in Dio Chrys. *Or.* 38.38, 42.

very quickly die out' (*BJ* 2.160). Here the phrase apparently means only 'to agree on this particular issue'.

Dio Chrysostom warns the people of Tarsus about division in the city (*Or.* 34.16a). Even though concord was reached by the Council, Assembly and Elders a few days previously (34.16b), this is not to be trusted, for healing takes much time (34.18). He believes that in the entire list of citizens there are not even to be found two men who think alike (μηδ' ἂν δύο ἄνδρας εὑρεῖν ἐν τῇ πόλει τὸ αὐτὸ φρονοῦντας, 34.20). From this statement we can make no conclusions regarding *societas* in Tarsus, for, as in the text from Josephus, reference is being made only to general agreement.

Now, though Paul has expressed joy over the Philippians' concern (φρονεῖν), his reference to the delay since their last gift could be taken as a rebuke, as if he chided them for failure to help more quickly. This possible misunderstanding of Paul's words is noted by scholars,[68] but again they fail to draw out the significance of such a misunderstanding. With his reference to delay Paul could be taken as saying the Philippians were unwilling to give. Such a reference to their unwillingness might be thought to demean the gift.[69] Yet, in the next phrase, he sets out to correct this possible mis-understanding with the phrase ἐφ' ᾧ καὶ ἐφρονεῖτε. Whereas the Philippians had revived their concern (τὸ φρονεῖν), i.e., their support, nevertheless they had been experiencing concern for Paul all along, ἐφρονεῖτε. Thus the imperfect of the verb stresses the continuing nature of the concern even in the absence of tangible expression.[70]

Since this must be the function of 4.10b as a whole, we agree with Silva that the precise understanding of ἐφ' ᾧ must fit with such a corrective function.[71] The precise translation of ἐφ' ᾧ, however, is difficult to establish. The typical usage of ἐπί with the dative to denote grounds for an action, especially to denote the grounds for emotional or other reactions, as well as Paul's usage in Romans 5.12, 2 Corinthians 5.4 and Philippians 3.12 argue for a type of

---

[68] E.g., O'Brien, *Philippians*, 518; Silva, *Philippians*, 234; Beare, *Philippians*, 151; Gnilka, *Philipperbrief*, 173.

[69] Cf. Seneca *Ben.* 1.1.8: 'A benefit . . . should not be given tardily, since, seeing that in every service the willingness of the giver counts for much, he who acts tardily has for a long time been unwilling.'

[70] This is noted by several commentators: e.g., Hawthorne, *Philippians*, 197; Vincent, *Philippians*, 142; O'Brien, *Philippians*, 518.

[71] Silva, *Philippians*, 235.

causal understanding.[72] Perhaps some exegetes have been steered away from a causal understanding since the word 'because' appears awkward in the context. As in 3.12, so here, two clauses with the same verb, though in different tenses, are linked by ἐφ' ᾧ καί. In both cases the second clause enters unexpectedly giving the primary consideration and a ground for the action in the first clause. In Philippians 3.12a Paul seeks to take hold, whereas in reality the primary taking hold has already been accomplished (3.12b). In 4.10a the revival of concern in the present is actually an expression of concern that has been ongoing (4.10b).

The apostle asserts that the real cause for delay was that the Philippians were merely hindered in sending a gift (ἠκαιρεῖσθε δέ). Paul does not state what this hindrance was and thus we should be wary of attempts to define it precisely. Buchanan speculates in asserting that Paul's prohibition against receiving support had hindered them.[73] We have no evidence for such a prohibition. Capper, accepting the *societas* theory of Sampley, asserts that the temporary cessation of material support was deliberate. The Philippians' saw Paul's imprisonment as a breach of their initial contract with Paul to preach the gospel as their representative.[74] Since we have already seen several flaws in Sampley's theory, we should question constructions based on the theory.[75] Furthermore, if the Philippians had ceased support deliberately, Paul's choice of ἀκαιρέομαι is at least curious, if not misleading, for the middle/passive form does not lend itself to the idea of active withdrawal but to that of passive hindrance.

Unfortunately, the examples of ἀκαιρέομαι supplied by Bauer/Aland are little help in defining the exact nature of the hindrance.[76] In a further example from P.Enteux 45 (222 BC) the writer, whose name has been lost, petitions King Ptolemy for a redress of grievances against Apollonius and Philotida. They are refusing to repay a loan he made to them and even after his repeated demands they have not paid, claiming to be hindered (οὐκ ἀπεδ(ί)δουν μοι,

---

[72] BDF, par. 235. Maximilian Zerwick, *Biblical Greek* (Rome: Scripta Pontificii Instituti Biblici, 1963): 42–3; A. T. Robertson, *A Grammar of the Greek New Testament in the Light of Historical Research* (Nashville: Broadman Press, 1934): 963.

[73] Buchanan, 'Philippians', 157–66. Though following Buchanan to a large extent, Hawthorne wisely parts company with him here (Hawthorne, *Philippians*, 197).

[74] Capper, 'Paul's Dispute with Philippi', 207–9.

[75] See our discussion of Sampley above, pp. 123–7.

[76] Diod. Sic. 10.7.3; *Hermas Sim.* 9.10.5 (Bauer/Aland, *Wörterbuch*, 56).

φάμενοι ἀκαιρεῖν, line 5). The financial context leads us to understand this as inability to pay.

If an explanation for the Philippians' hindrance must be found, it
appears that a financial one should receive the most consideration.
We know that the Macedonian churches were poor in the eyes of
Paul (2 Cor. 8.1–3). Thus the slender evidence suggests that the
hindrance was the Philippians' own financial situation. In any case
it is certain that Paul views the hindrance as attaching no blame to
the Philippians.[77]

We conclude that Paul's expression of joy at the receipt of the
Philippians' gift should not be understood as performing the
function of an expression of thanks. Rather, it does just what it
appears to do at first sight: it displays Paul's personal reaction to
the meaning of the gift for him. The gift displays Christian
compassion. He on his part is made happy, in the midst of his
trouble (θλῖψις), because of their concern for him (φρονεῖν).

First qualification: the assertion of contentment, 4.11

Not only does the apostle's response to financial aid contain
positive statements, such as his expression of joy. It also contains
qualifying statements which must be added to keep the Philippians
from misinterpreting his words as fitting into their first-century
social assumptions about giving and receiving. Thus, at verse 11
Paul begins his first qualification. His expression of joy could be
misunderstood in two ways. It could be thought to arise from
feelings of relief. Anxiety is certainly a common reaction to material
shortage, in the first-century world as today.[78] Is it that he has now
finally had his anxiety assuaged by the receipt of financial support?
Paul asserts that this is quite to the contrary. He does not complain
because of need;[79] his expression of joy does not come about
because of the anxiety he felt prior to receiving.[80]

Further, Paul's joy, if it arises from feelings of relief from need,
might be misunderstood as a request. Seneca implies that merely

---

[77] Martin, *Philippians* (NCB), 162; Collange, *Philippians*, 150.
[78] E.g., Arr. *Epict. Diss.* 1.9.19–20. Note also the six-fold repetition of μεριμνάω in
Matt. 6.25–34. That Jesus attempts to assuage anxiety seems obvious.
[79] Lightfoot offers this paraphrase, *Philippians*, 159; cf. Martin, *Philippians* (NCB),
612; Beare, *Philippians*, 149.
[80] Wilckens, 'ὕστερος κτλ', *TDNT*, 8.599.

mentioning a need could be taken as a request (*Ben.* 2.2.1–2, 7.24.1–2). Sampley understands χρεία in a similar way. He finds confirmation for his *societas* theory in a particular definition of χρεία. Sampley asserts that the word may be understood as 'request' and urges that we leave operative the full range of meaning of χρεία: it is a 'need-request'.[81] Since Paul is the Philippians' partner in *societas*, he has invoked his legal right to remuneration by requesting this payment from the Philippians.[82]

Paul, however, denies speaking from need. Not that he was without need. He is quite candid that he has need (χρεία, 2.25, 4.16), that he is experiencing trouble (θλῖψις, 4.14). What he denies is that his need has given rise to his expression of joy.[83] Further, need has not evoked his expression of joy because he has learned to live at peace in all circumstances, to be content (αὐτάρκης εἶναι).

Several scholars correctly mention that αὐτάρκεια played an important role in Stoicism.[84] Some correctly notice one important difference between the apostle's contentment and that of the Stoics. The independence of the stoic wise man made it necessary to find contentment in virtue alone. Furthermore, virtue, as the only good which the Stoic needs, must be found within the self.[85] On the other hand, Paul declares that he is not content because of the strength that comes from within, but because of the strength that comes from without.[86] This contentment, empowered by the one who strengthens him, leads to an ability to cope with external circumstances.

There is, however, something lacking in this approach to αὐτάρκεια. Scholars are correct in seeing a different *source* for the strength of contentment, but fall short in describing the *scope* of

---

[81] Sampley makes a similar appeal to a double meaning for δόμα (Phil. 4.17). It is a 'gift-payment' (*Partnership*, 54).

[82] Contrast the situation at Corinth: there Paul insists that he will not make use of his right despite *offers* of gifts from the Corinthians (2 Cor. 11.9, 12.14). See our comments on these texts on pp. 168–71.

[83] Gnilka, *Philipperbrief*, 174.

[84] E.g., Vincent, *Philippians*, 143; Hawthorne, *Philippians*, 198; Collange, *Philippians*, 150; Lohmeyer, *Philipper*, 179–80; Gerhard Kittel, 'αὐτάρκεια, αὐτάρκης', *TDNT*, 1.466; Gnilka, *Philipperbrief*, 174.

[85] On the problems of 'the good', virtue, independence and αὐτάρκεια see John M. Rist, *Stoic Philosophy* (London: Cambridge University Press, 1969): esp. 7–10, 58–63.

[86] Sevenster, *Paul and Seneca*, 111. The NEB, however, incorrectly gives the Stoic sense to αὐτάρκεια, translating 4.11b as, 'I have learned to find resources in myself whatever my circumstances.'

contentment. For example, Vincent implies that, in terms of content, the αὐτάρκεια of Paul is essentially the same as that of the Stoic. First, Vincent states that πάντα ἰσχύω (v. 13) refers not only to all the things just mentioned in v. 12, but to everything.[87] Secondly, to illustrate his point, Vincent cites Seneca *De Vita Beata* 6.2: 'the happy man is content with his present lot, no matter what it is, and is reconciled to his circumstances'.[88] Just what reconciliation, contentment and circumstances mean in this citation from Seneca is not explained by Vincent. Seneca does make this clear, however, elsewhere in *De Vita Beata*. He states that the happy man is free from both fear and desire because of the gift of reason (5.1). When all fear and desire has been driven away there results an unbroken tranquillity, freedom, peace and harmony (3.4).[89] But the only means of procuring this state is through indifference to Fortune (4.5). That is, because the wise man knows certain things are outside his control, he realizes it is foolish to allow himself to be disturbed by circumstances.[90] Consequently, we see that for Seneca, the circumstances the wise man lives above are not just financial variations; rather, he lives above all of life's misfortunes. Further, in the midst of all these vicissitudes he maintains his emotional detachment.[91] The independence of the wise man must mean that his emotions remain a matter of his own rational choice. No matter what happens he is able to maintain his happiness since he is his own master. This emotional calm, or detachment (ἀπαθής) cannot be separated from αὐτάρκης.[92]

The concept of αὐτάρκεια as explained by Seneca appears in this

---

[87] Vincent, *Philippians*, 145. Likewise Kittel claims that 'πάντα ἰσχύω (v. 13) seems to be fully identical with the philosophical αὐτάρκης ἐν παντί, M. Aur. 1.16.11' (Kittel, 'αὐτάρκεια, αὐτάρκης', 467).

[88] LCL trans; Vincent, *Philippians*, 143. Hawthorne, *Philippians*, 198, following Vincent, claims that Paul borrowed αὐτάρκης from the Stoics 'to declare that he too has acquired the virtue of a spirit free from worry, untroubled by the vicissitudes of external events, independent of people and things. And Paul cherishes this self-sufficiency.'

[89] Cf. *Const.* 6.3, 8.2, 9.3, 19.2; *Ira* 2.12.6; *Ep.* 41.4, 59.16: 'The mind of the wise man is like the ultra-lunar firmament; eternal calm pervades that region. You have, then, a reason for wishing to be wise, if the wise man is never deprived of joy. This joy springs only from the knowledge that you possess the virtues.'

[90] Sevenster, *Paul and Seneca*, 117.

[91] The term 'detachment' is taken from John M. Rist, 'The Stoic Concept of Detachment', *The Stoics*, ed. J. M. Rist (Berkeley: University of California Press, 1978): 259–72. Our discussion here is indebted to Rist's work.

[92] Rist, *Stoic Philosophy*, 63. See further A. Mannzmann, 'Αὐταρκία', *Der kleine Pauly. Lexikon der Antike*, 5 vols., ed. Konrat Ziegler and Walther Sontheimer, Stuttgart: A. Druckmüller, 1964–75: 1.777–9.

same basic form in other Stoics.[93] Here is where we see two world views coming into conflict over the scope of contentment. Seneca asserts that contentment reaches to all areas, whereas in Philippians 4.11 contentment has to do with material (viz., financial) circumstances.[94] This is the contentment that Paul urges, solely one which is emotionally detached from material goods.

Regarding his response to life's other vicissitudes, Paul has a very different approach. For example, first, the body imagery of 1 Corinthians 12 is not consistent with Stoicism.[95] According to the apostle, Christians are interdependent in a very real way. Secondly, Paul admits – indeed boasts of – being in constant worry for the churches. If anyone from these churches is led into sin, he does not retain a tranquil mind, but burns inwardly (2 Cor. 11.28–9). Thirdly, Paul admits despairing of life (2 Cor. 1.8). This despair is something he does not want the Corinthians to be ignorant of, which is hardly the way one chooses to talk of moral failure. Fourthly, there is no Stoic calm on Paul's part when he tells the Philippians with tears of the sin of others (3.18). Fifthly, Plutarch asserts that it is good to help one's neighbours but not to share in their sorrows (*Mor.* 468D; cf. Arr. *Epict. Diss.* 3.25.1). Paul, on the other hand, urges Christians to rejoice with those who rejoice and weep with those who weep (Rom. 12.15). This can hardly be Stoic αὐτάρκεια.[96]

In light of the above we assert that the αὐτάρκεια of Paul has less in common with the Stoics than is commonly recognized. The contentment of the apostle is clearly related to material goods, the

---

[93] E.g., Cic. *Tusc. Disp.* 4.12; Arr. *Epict. Diss.* 1.9.7, 3.3.15, 3.8.2, 3.24.8. Similar are the views of the Platonist Plutarch (Plut. *Mor.* 101B–D, 523E, 468D, 475D–F). Epictetus describes the work of a philosopher: 'He should bring his own will into harmony with what happens, so that neither anything that happens happens against our will, nor anything that fails to happen fails to happen when we wish it to happen' (2.14.7). Cf. also Philo *Praemiis* 35. On the origins of αὐτάρκεια see Audrey N. M. Rich, 'The Cynic Conception of AYTAPKEIA', *Mnemosyne* series 4, 9 (1956): 23–9 and P. Wilpert, 'Autarkie', *RAC* 1 (1950): 1042.

[94] See further our discussion on 4.12, which is Paul's explanation of what αὐτάρκεια means.

[95] Despite Seneca's use of body language to describe the interaction of individuals in the human race it is clear that Seneca means something very different from Paul (Sevenster, *Paul and Seneca*, 171).

[96] In his excursus on Paul and Seneca, though not in his comments on Phil. 4.11, Lightfoot mentions that the Stoic detachment of Seneca is far from the thought of the apostle and draws attention to the basic theme we have presented here (*Philippians*, 297).

sort which he has received from the believers in Philippi. This conclusion is further supported by our discussion of 4.12 below.

The meaning of contentment: 4.12

Scholars are generally agreed that v. 12 is an explication of αὐτάρκης.[97] What Paul presents to us is not his ability to provide all his own needs through the skill he has developed as a philosopher. Rather, what he said he had learned in v. 11 he here refers to as what he now knows. He learned to be content in his circumstances. In v. 12 he describes what these circumstances are.

What strikes us immediately is the seven-fold repetition of καί. With the exception of one of these, the conjunction is used to stress the inclusion of two abilities in Paul's learning. He has learned to do two things which seem mutually exclusive. He knows *both* how to be humbled *and* how to abound. Likewise, the three-fold appearance of the contrast is not to be overlooked. The apostle is stressing that, when he learned contentment, he learned what was the appropriate behaviour for both of these circumstances.

To some commentators the need to learn contentment in the midst of shortage appears easy enough. On the other hand, they do not grasp what is to be learned in order for one to display contentment in the midst of plenty.[98] In contrast, others correctly assert that there is a need to learn contentment in the midst of plenty, yet they do not attempt to explain why this is so.[99]

Again, we can turn to the Greek and Roman sources to begin to gain a better understanding of what is meant by contentment in the midst of plenty. Plutarch reminds his readers that even the wealthy man will not be satisfied with riches unless he has cultivated contentment in his soul. Otherwise, he will only be harassed by the worry of losing his money and comfort and motivated by greed to amass an even larger store of goods (*Mor.* 101C). Having wealth does not indeed deliver one from the craving for it, but rather infects one with an inordinate desire for gold, silver and all the luxuries of life (*Mor.* 523E–F). Thus the call to contentment is a

---

[97] E.g., O'Brien, *Philippians*, 522; Vincent, *Philippians*, 143; Hawthorne, *Philippians*, 199. On the structure of vv. 12–13 see the detailed study by Schenk, *Philipperbriefe*, 30–8.

[98] As a result of this difficulty, Lohmeyer, *Philipper*, 181, concludes that the περισσεύω of 4.12 refers to spiritual goods.

[99] E.g., Gnilka, *Philipperbrief*, 175.

call to peaceful indifference to the amount of money one has. This peace does not typically characterize the rich.

Such a view toward the attitude of the rich is also found in the Old and New Testaments. In its most succinct form the proclamation is this: blessed are you who are poor, but woe to you who are rich (Luke 6.20, 24). In a sense, being poor is synonymous with piety.[100] It is easier for a camel to go through the eye of a needle than for a rich man to enter the kingdom of heaven (Matt. 19.23). The precise reason for the woes and the difficulty of entering the kingdom is not explained in these texts. The general thrust of the biblical tradition shows, however, that the deceitfulness of riches tempts the wealthy to become arrogant and to trust in riches (1 Tim. 6.17), to live in luxury and condemn the innocent (James 5.1, 5–6).[101] The rich man does not receive peace and comfort through riches, but rather anxiety which robs him of sleep (Eccles. 5.12).[102] While God has chosen the poor to be rich in faith (James 2.5), the actions of the wealthy are contrary to faith: they exploit others and drag them into court (v. 6).[103]

Therefore, Paul is not merely addressing the problem that people must learn to be content because they have so little and are therefore anxious. Rather they must learn to be content because, whether they have a little or have a lot, they will always experience some form of unhealthy anxiety concerning their material state.

Besides knowing how to abound, Paul says he knows how to be humbled (οἶδα καὶ ταπεινοῦσθαι). Bauer/Aland class this use amongst those in accordance with Old Testament usage, meaning something like humbling oneself in a religious sense, disciplining oneself, fasting.[104] For several reasons we prefer 'being made poor' or 'living on little'.[105] In this context, the financial sense is to be

---

[100] H. Bolkestein and A. Kalsbach, 'Armut I', *RAC* 1 (1950): 699.

[101] Cf. 2 Sam. 12.1–4; Prov. 18.23, 28.6, 11, 30.8–9.

[102] Plutarch asserts that, 'the owner of five couches goes looking for ten, and the owner of ten tables buys up as many again, and though he has lands and money in plenty is not satisfied but bent on more, losing sleep and never sated with any amount' (*Mor.* 524B; cf. Arr. *Epict. Diss.* 3.26.2).

[103] In the address of Eliphaz there is an implicit identification of the evil man and the rich man. He begins speaking of the evil man and what disasters will befall him because of his reprehensible behaviour (Job 15.20–8). Then, at v. 29, he suddenly adds, 'he will no longer be rich'. Zophar makes a similar equation (20.10b, 15, 19, 22).

[104] Bauer/Aland, *Wörterbuch*, 1605.

[105] So correctly B. Rolland, 'Saint Paul et la pauvreté: Phil. 4: 12–14, 19–20', *Assemblées du Seigneur* 59 (1974): 10–15.

preferred owing to Paul's general subject: the Philippians' gift. The parallel of ταπεινοῦσθαι with πεινᾶν and ὑστερεῖσθαι and its being contrasted with περισσεύειν suggests that financial humiliation is in view. In addition, although ταπεινοῦσθαι may be middle or passive, the reflexive idea prefers to take the pronoun.[106] Therefore it should here be taken as passive. Paul is not saying he humbles *himself* in a religious sense, but that he knows how to respond when *he is humbled* by circumstances beyond his control. And as a final consideration, when Paul tells the Corinthians that he humbled himself to exalt them (2 Cor. 11.7) the humiliation he speaks of is financial. It is his refusal to accept their support, and rather working with his own hands, which was humbling himself.[107] We might paraphrase it, 'I put myself in a financially weak position in order to exalt you.'

According to Greco-Roman standards, a virtuous man displays his virtue, at least to a great extent, in the beneficence he undertakes toward others. Since this giving establishes social power,[108] it follows that financial humiliation is shameful.[109] Indeed, for Dio Chrysostom and Plutarch the good man ought never to encounter any type of humiliation. Being humbled is for those of low birth and an abject spirit.[110]

On the other hand, Paul, with sharp irony, has claimed he will make it his practice to boast of his weaknesses (2 Cor. 11.30, 12.5). In so doing, he turns the social and financial expectations of the ancient world on their head.[111] Here in Philippians 4 he plainly

---

[106] Cf. Matt. 18.4, 23.12; Luke 14.11, 18.14; 2 Cor. 11.7; Phil. 2.8.

[107] This refusal, however, in keeping with the social conventions of the day, was interpreted as an insult by the Corinthians (see Marshall, *Enmity*, e.g., 165, 173).

[108] Arist. *Eth. Nic.* 4.1.7, 4.3.24; Seneca *Ben.* 2.33.1–2; 8.14.3–4; Plut. *Mor.* 808B; Luke 22.25; Rom. 5.7. For Jewish support see Job 29.7–13; Sirach 7.27–8; Jos. *AJ* 4.266; Philo *Decal.* 166–7. See also Bolkestein, *Wohltätigkeit*, 151.

[109] Similarly, according to the classic view, those who must earn wages through labour make themselves vulgar since such industries degrade and preoccupy the mind (ἄσχολον γὰρ ποιοῦσι τὴν διάνοιαν καὶ ταπεινήν) and make it unfit for the activities of virtue (Arist. *Pol.* 8.2.1). See the short discussion of working in Appendix C, pp. 213–14.

[110] Plut. *Mor.* 1B–C; Dio Chrys. *Or.* 4.118: 'the spirit who presides over men who love glory is always aspiring and never touches the earth or anything lowly' (ταπεινοῦ τινος); cf. *Or.* 2.49, 75; 34.33; *Mor.* 35D, 540D.

[111] Though Paul does not hesitate to mention his financially poor condition, he nevertheless makes clear that, though poor, he makes many rich (2 Cor. 6.10). This text provides evidence that Paul saw himself as a benefactor to his converts. See the treatment of 2 Cor. 6.13 and Phlm. 17–19 on pp. 172–4, 185–91.

asserts that learning how to be humbled and how to go hungry is a spiritually commendable activity. By contrast, we have seen evidence that in the Greco-Roman world hunger was dreaded.[112] Paul certainly reverses those categories. Rather than an experience to be loathed, he says that learning to go hungry and to be full is a spiritual experience; an initiation into the mystery of Christianity.[113]

Although the humiliation of Philippians 4.12 is financial hardship, the apostle's statement fits well into the portrait of humility being painted throughout the letter. Paul's obsession with the gospel causes him to die to self, to look beyond his imprisonment and to see the message about Jesus advancing (1.12). Jesus is the supreme example of humility in the hymn of 2.6–11. Those Christians are to be praised who (in imitation of Jesus) risk their lives for the sake of the gospel (2.29–30). This call to humility is in stark contrast to typical Greco-Roman thinking. For in that culture humility is not a virtue to be cultivated since it is an idea foreign to the Greco-Roman concept of virtue.[114] Rather, humility is a desirable virtue in Jewish ethics.[115] We see again that Paul operates with Jewish presuppositions rather than with Greco-Roman ones.

The source of contentment: 4.13

We have already referred to the significance of the phrase ἐν τῷ ἐνδυναμοῦντι με with regard to contentment and thus need only reiterate what has been said earlier. Though αὐτάρκεια was a crucial aspect of Stoic/Cynic ethics, Christian αὐτάρκεια means something fundamentally different for Paul. He claims that the strength he needs to encounter the vicissitudes of life does not come from his natural man but from his God in Christ.[116] This distinc-

---

[112] Arr. *Epict. Diss.* 1.9.19–20; Matt. 6.25–34.

[113] Lohmeyer (*Philipper*, 183) contends that one of the reasons Paul's thanks are thankless is that, as a martyr, Paul stands in a separated domain where no profane gifts (*profane Gaben*) can enter. Such gifts cannot alleviate his need, for it is much more deeply filled spiritually. Thus, Paul can acknowledge their concern, but can give no further thanks for the gift itself.

[114] Albrecht Dihle, 'Demut', *RAC* 3 (1957): 737; cf. Arr. *Epict. Diss.* 3.24.54–6; 4.1.54; 4.12.20.

[115] See W. Grundmann, 'ταπεινός κτλ', *TDNT*, 8.11–15.

[116] Whether we accept the variant reading of ℵ² D² F G Ψ and 𝔐 and add Χριστῷ is not significant.

tion has been noticed by several scholars,[117] but there are nuances which have yet to be pointed out.

Contentment is not something which the gods strengthen the philosopher to do, rather the gods have given man a certain mental capacity and with this capacity a man may learn to be content.[118] He must certainly learn the foolishness of anxiety over material goods.

The 'all things' which Paul is able to do certainly must be limited by the context.[119] The context, as we have said before, indicates that αὐτάρκεια is the proper response to life's varying financial circumstances which he refers to.

Thus, again, the apostle corrects in advance the Philippians' misunderstanding of the role of material possessions in their lives. These possessions would enhance their social standing and give them more power in relationships of giving and receiving. But for the Christian it is not the power of money but the power of Christ which is all that matters. They may learn of Christ's power both in poverty and in plenty.

Specific acknowledgement: 4.18a

As mentioned earlier, v. 18a is included in the discussion of Paul's personal reflections. For this phrase gives a personal response as opposed to theological interpretation on the meaning of the gift.

Though Paul has more than once referred to the Philippians' gift and the messenger who brought it (1.5, 2.25), he has never explicitly acknowledged full receipt of it. Therefore we should expect that at some point he would make things very precise. Because of the long distances and unsafe travel conditions to be overcome, it was customary for the receiver of goods to acknowledge that he had received all things (πάντα), and the person through whom he had received them (παρὰ Ἐπαφροδίτου). This Paul does here with ἀπέχω.

Scholars generally refer to the extensive use of ἀπέχω in papyrus receipts and in so doing largely follow the lead of Deissmann.[120] In

---

[117] E.g., Sevenster, *Paul and Seneca*, 111; O'Brien, *Philippians*, 521; Gnilka, *Philipperbrief*, 176.

[118] Arr. *Epict. Diss.* 1.1.27; 1.6.29, 40.

[119] Gnilka, *Philipperbrief*, 176; *contra* Vincent, *Philippians*, 145.

[120] Deissmann, *Light*, 110; Cf., Moulton/Milligan, *Vocabulary*, 57–8; O'Brien, *Philippians*, 539–40; Lohmeyer, *Philipper*, 186.

order to bring out this technical meaning some translate Paul's words with, 'Here then is my receipt for everything.'[121] Yet, a technical meaning for ἀπέχω should not be stressed for the following reasons.

First, what we call technical financial terms are able to occupy a different semantic field depending on the context in which they are used. This observation has relevance not only to ἀπέχω, but to δόσις καὶ λῆμψις and εἰς λόγον which are commonly referred to as technical financial terms. Some scholars have noted that these terms are used in commercial contexts to refer to debits and credits and to financial reckoning. But the question is: does Paul's letter to the Philippians constitute a commercial context? It clearly does not.

Secondly, we have already seen that terminology which figures in technical financial contexts was also used to describe the dynamics of exchange relationships in the Greco-Roman world.[122] We might refer to them as metaphors, but we should not thereby be led to conclude that real accounting and debt did not take place in the social world. We have seen from chapter 3 that they certainly did. If Philippians 4 is understood as a social context we have reason to believe these terms are being used socially.

Thirdly, the term 'receipt' has unwanted connotations in English and is misleading in this context. 'Receipt' often implies the acknowledgment that pre-arranged conditions have been met. Paul's so-called receipt does not perform this function, but merely informs the church that all which had been sent has been received, which leads to our next point.

Fourthly, ἀπέχω can also be used to refer to simple receipt with stress on the completeness of the reception. Philemon 15 is a significant example. Paul says that perhaps the reason Onesimus was separated from Philemon temporarily was that he might receive him back eternally (αἰώνιον αὐτὸν ἀπέχῃς). Here a clear contrast is being drawn between two types of receiving: one

---

[121] Hawthorne, *Philippians*, 206, and O'Brien, *Philippians*, 540, following the GNB; cf., Silva, *Philippians*, 238; Gnilka, *Philipperbrief*, 179. Deissmann says the apostle, in using this technical vocabulary, is being humorous (*Light*, 112) and Silva says the language reflects Paul's playfulness (238; cf. O'Brien, *Philippians*, 540). These assertions are not helpful. First, they are based on twentieth-century western definitions of humour and playfulness, and secondly, they make the unfounded assumption that the use of allegedly technical language in such a context constitutes humour.

[122] E.g., Philo *Cher.* 122–23; Cicero *Amic.* 16.58. See pp. 63–5 above.

temporary and one eternal. Likewise in Matt. 6.2–16, the Pharisees are said to receive *their entire reward* for their false piety when they are praised by men (cf. Luke 6.24). Here emphasis is on the fact that the hypocrites can expect no further reward from their religious displays.[123] The LCL translator of Plut. *Themistocles* 17.2 also correctly brings out this nuance of ἀπέχω. At a certain Olympic festival Themistocles receives the praise of the crowds. He was delighted 'and confessed to his friends that he was now reaping in full measure the harvest of his toils in behalf of Hellas'.[124] The nuance here is that Themistocles is receiving *all* the payment due him.

Moral commendation: vv. 14–17

Praise for sharing in affliction: 4.14

There is a theory that Paul's response to the Philippians' gift is strained because it is in actual fact a gentle rebuke to the Philippians and a reminder not to infringe again on his own self-reliance.[125] The commendation in this section is incongruous with such a theory. Indeed, Paul is quite pleased with their financial sharing. This is not to deny that there is discomfort on the apostle's part. Discomfort exists, however, not because he must stress his desire to be self supporting, but because he must make certain that an improper interpretation is not given to his acceptance of this gift.

What Paul has just said regarding contentment might be taken as degrading the gift, or worse yet, as tacitly rejecting it.[126] Both are potentially very insulting. So even though the apostle is strength-

---

123 Deissmann himself puts forward this understanding of Matt. 6.2–16 (*Light*, 111; cf. W. D. Davies and Dale C. Allison, Jr, *A Critical and Exegetical Commentary on the Gospel According to Saint Matthew* (Edinburgh: T & T Clark, 1980): 1.582). Mark 14.41, and its particularly difficult use of ἀπέχω, will not be discussed. See G. H. Boobyer, 'ἀπέχει in Mark xiv.41', *NTS* 2 (1955–6): 44–8.

124 ὥστε καὶ αὐτὸν ἡσθέντα πρὸς τοὺς φίλους ὁμολογῆσαι τὸν καρπὸν ἀπέχειν τῶν ὑπὲρ τῆς Ἑλλάδος αὐτῷ πονηθέντων. Note also the conventions of reciprocity in this text and that the return is called καρπός (cf. Phil. 4.17). For a similar use of ἀπέχειν, cf. Plut. *Alex.* 27.6; D.L. 7.100.

125 Hawthorne, *Philippians*, 195; cf. Buchanan, 'Philippians', 162.

126 Seneca warns that the proper method of accepting a gift is crucial. His description of one improper way reminds one of Paul, *Ben.* 2.24.2–3: 'One man receives (a benefit) disdainfully, as if to say: "I really do not need it, but since you so much wish it, I will surrender my will to yours."'

ened for both paucity and plenty, he does not remove merit from the Philippians' act of sharing. Thus, the use of πλήν, 'nevertheless', indicates that Paul wishes to interrupt the flow of thought and prevent misunderstanding. Though he has always been content, he praises the Philippians' behaviour: 'You did well' (καλῶς ἐποιήσατε). Martin says that this is perhaps the closest Paul gets to saying, 'Thank You'.[127] But καλῶς ἐποιήσατε does not perform the function of an expression of thanks, viz., it does not acknowledge social debt.[128] Rather, the phrase commends the Philippians for their demonstration of concern (φρονεῖν). It expresses praise which commends their Christian maturity (defined as sharing). It does not smack of servility, as a client praising a benefactor. But rather in light of the following verses it sounds more like a teacher congratulating a student. Specifically, the Philippians are approved for sharing in his hardship: συγκοινωνήσαντές μου τῇ θλίψει (cf. 2.30), and here the praise moves into theological categories.

The theological possibility of sharing in the suffering of others occurs elsewhere in Paul.[129] What is important for our purpose is this: Paul says that by giving him money they share the shame of his θλίψις, i.e., his imprisonment. Such service is potentially dangerous for Epaphroditus.[130] Because of their φρονεῖν on his behalf (4.10), they were willing to take this risk and this willingness demonstrates a certain solidarity with him. Because the Philippians are Paul's fellow-partakers of grace in his imprisonment and in the defence and confirmation of the gospel (1.7) they are willing to share in his suffering through a financial sacrifice.

---

[127] Martin, *Philippians* (NCB), 164, followed by Hawthorne, *Philippians*, 202. Compare Bruce's paraphrase of this verse: 'But I do thank you very much indeed for your fellowship in my tribulation' (F. F. Bruce, *An Expanded Paraphrase of the Epistles of Paul* (Exeter: Paternoster Press, 1965): 175).

[128] We must guard against making false semantic distinctions. Nevertheless, though καλῶς with the future or present of ποιέω often has the meaning of 'please' (e.g., P.Hib. 64.8; 82.9, 17, 25; 206.2 (all 3rd BC)) it does not appear that the past tense carries the meaning 'thank-you'. Rather it communicates moral commendation or praise (e.g., 1 Kgs. 8.18; Acts 10.32; Arr. *Epict. Diss.* 1.22.3; 2.11.4).

[129] E.g., Rom. 8.17, 2 Cor. 1.5–7, Gal. 6.17, Phil. 3.10; cf. Col. 1.24, Eph. 3.13, Heb. 10.33. See E. Best, *One Body in Christ* (London: SPCK, 1955): 131–2; E. Güttgemanns, *Der leidende Apostel und sein Herr: Studien zur paulinischen Christologie* (Göttingen: Vandenhoeck & Ruprecht, 1966): 323–8; O'Brien, *Introductory Thanksgivings*, 247–8.

[130] Service despite danger may in part explain the multiple titles Epaphroditus receives in 2.25: ἀδελφόν, συνεργόν, συστρατιώτην, ἀπόστολον and λειτουργόν. On the risks for Epaphroditus see Rapske, 'Helpers to the Imprisoned Paul', 3–30, esp. 23–9.

4.14 is not the first time Paul mentions the Philippians' fellowship with him in suffering. We have already discussed the significance of κοινωνία in Philippians.[131] Here we summarize some of our findings on Paul's suffering, i.e., his κοινωνία with the Philippians.

As is customary in his introductory thanksgivings, the apostle introduces this theme early in his letter (1.5). His mention of their being fellow-partakers of grace with him both in his *imprisonment* and in the defence of the gospel (1.7) hints at sharing in suffering. The first explicit mention of suffering comes in 1.29: it has been granted to the Philippians not only to believe but also to suffer for Christ,[132] and this struggle is the same one that Paul himself now experiences (1.30).[133] By implication as well, the Philippians share in the sufferings of the apostle through their apostle Epaphroditus (2.25–30). Though 3.10 is biographical, its inclusion is probably meant to exhort the Philippians in their suffering. Paul strives to experience the fellowship of Christ's sufferings and they should do the same. The συγκοινωνήσαντές μου τῇ θλίψει of 4.14 is very similar to the συγκοινωνούς μου τῆς χάριτος of 1.7.

Praise for financial partnership: 4.15–16

Having been commended for their sharing in his suffering through financial support, the Philippians are commended in 4.15 for being the only church to share in this way with the apostle.[134] The use of οἴδατε points up the particular importance of this issue in Paul's mind at this time[135] and the fact that the Philippians had been

---

[131] See the discussion of Philippians 1.3–11, pp. 93–107 above.

[132] On suffering for Christ in Philippians see Nickolaus Walter, 'Die Philipper und das Leiden: Aus den Anfängen einer heidenchristlichen Gemeinde', *Die Kirche des Anfangs*, ed. Rudolf Schnackenburg, Josef Ernst and Joachim Wanke (Freiberg: Herder, 1978): 417–33.

[133] Here the apostle strikes the note of participation which arises so often in the letter. See our discussion of reciprocity in Philippians, pp. 119–20 above.

[134] On the basis of the plural ἐκκλησίας in 2 Cor. 11.8, Reumann asserts that the 'you only' in 4.15 reflects the early days in Thessalonica and is *captatio benevolentiae*. Thus Corinth is the exception, Philippi and the other congregations are the rule (Reumann, 'Contributions', 442). The evidence is too sparse to provide for a clear decision. ἐκκλησίας in 2 Cor. 11.8 could refer to house congregations in Philippi. We cannot establish such a 'rule' for the other congregations since Paul does not mention receiving support in his letters to Galatia and Thessalonica.

[135] Compare the extensive use of οἴδατε to support the reiteration of crucial issues and doctrines in 1 Thess. 1.5; 2.1–2, 5, 11; 3.3–4; 4.2; 5.2. On the use of οἴδατε as a paraenetic device see Malherbe, *Paul and the Thessalonians*, 70–1.

previously informed of their unique status. The apostle will have informed them of their unique position in order to commend and encourage them, not in order to rebuke and discourage them.

We have already mentioned the variety of views taken on δόσεως καὶ λήμψεως.[136] Until recently, the scholarly consensus was that this phrase belonged to the 'commercial vocabulary of the ancient world'.[137] With the work of Marshall, however, there has begun a shift to see it as a social expression. Paul is not utilizing the terminology of the business world, but a metaphor common in discussion of social reciprocity.[138] Further, the evidence we have collected in chapter 3 should make clear that this phrase need not be understood in a technical sense.

Although Marshall's work is seminal, scholars have accepted his conclusions with too little critical evaluation.[139] On the one hand, Marshall correctly refers to the social practice of exchanging goods and services in the Greco-Roman world and understands the nature of gift and service relationships and what characterized them. He therefore sees the expression as 'an idiomatic expression indicating friendship'.[140] On the other hand, Marshall assumes too readily that Greco-Roman convention characterizes Paul's relationship with the Philippians. For example, he believes that these words (ἐκοινώνησεν εἰς λόγον δόσεως καὶ λήμψεως) imply mutual obligations between Paul and the Philippians.[141] We will refer to the idea of obligation below and see that obligation is not a concept found in this epistle.

The work of J. Hainz is helpful for our discussion of Philippians 4.15 because he sets this pericope within a complete study of κοινωνία in Paul.[142] His work suffers methodologically, however. After treating fellowship with Christ and fellowship with the Spirit

---

[136] See pp. 10–15 above.
[137] Hawthorne, *Philippians*, 204; cf. Lohmeyer, *Philipper*, 185; Gnilka, *Philipperbrief*, 177; Lightfoot, *Philippians*, 165; Dodd, 'Mind of Paul: I', 72; Bassler, *God & Mammon*, 79.
[138] For comments on δόσις καὶ λήμψις see pp. 53–65. Cf. Xen. *Oec.* 7.26, *Mem.* 2.6.2; Arist. *Eth. Nic.* 4.1.1–30; Men. *Monost.* 317, 322; Ps-Plato *Ax.* 366B-C; Arr. *Epict. Diss.* 2.9.12; Cic. *Amic.* 8.26; Sen. *Ep.* 81.10–11; Sir. 41.19; Acts 20.35.
[139] O'Brien, *Philippians*, 534–5, and Perkins simply accept Marshall's findings without further application nor referring to potential social problems which might be implied (Perkins, 'Heavenly Politeuma', 89–104).
[140] Marshall, *Enmity*, 163.   [141] Ibid., 173.
[142] Josef Hainz, *KOINONIA. 'Kirche' als Gemeinschaft bei Paulus* (Regensburg: Friedrich Pustet, 1982): esp. 112–15.

in his first two chapters,[143] Hainz begins his discussion of κοινωνία with Galatians 6.6. He finds here 'die paulinische Prinzip κοινωνία'. From Galatians 6.6 Hainz concludes that those who are taught are obligated to support financially those who teach them. This obligation is a form of thanks.[144] Therefore, having established this principle of κοινωνία, his discussion of all other texts presupposes this conclusion and is presented under the section labelled 'Die Anwendung des Prinzips κοινωνία bei Paulus'.[145]

Thus, Hainz's discussion of Philippians 4.15 is dependent on his conclusions regarding Galatians 6.6. For instance, while Hainz rightly stresses the reciprocal nature of Paul's relationship with the congregation at Philippi, an aspect underplayed by other scholars, yet he attempts to systematize the thought of the apostle and concludes that the Philippians' gift was an expression of their debt of gratitude for the preaching they received. It was an obligation on their part.[146] The text of Philippians, however, contains no mention of debt or obligation, neither on the Philippians' part nor on Paul's.

In agreement with Hainz, we may note that Paul certainly saw his preaching as worthy of repayment. The apostle's statements in 1 Corinthians 9 imply that support is a debt.[147] In Romans 15.27, the spiritual-material contrast (also found in Corinthians) as well as the actual use of ὀφείλω, makes it plain that the collection is a social debt.[148] If we attempt to integrate and generalize Paul's comments, we could say that debt is a legitimate category to apply to the Philippians.[149] But from the actual text we find no such language. Paul does not refer to the discharge of a social debt (ἀποδιδόναι χάριν) or to his obligation to repay the Philippians as our study of the papyri would lead us to expect.[150] Rather he refers

---

[143] Hainz, *KOINONIA*, 15–61.

[144] 'die geschuldete Dankbarkeit', Hainz, *KOINONIA*, 69.

[145] Hainz devotes 27 pages to his discussion of Gal. 6.6 (*KOINONIA*, 52–89) but only a total of 33 pages to all the other 14 texts he studies. Thus his study suffers in that the conclusions he reaches regarding Gal. 6.6 are too often imported into his discussion of other texts.

[146] Hainz, *KOINONIA*, 113.

[147] The word that Paul uses, however, constantly in reference to himself, is ἐξουσία (1 Cor. 9.6, 12, 18). The corresponding word with reference to the Corinthians (e.g., ὀφειλή) is not used.

[148] See further our comments on the collection, pp. 175–83 below.

[149] Lohmeyer, *Philipper*, 185, asserts that, because support was an obligation, Paul was not required to give the Philippians thanks for their gifts. Lohmeyer, however, confuses two categories, namely what Paul calls his right as an apostle (1 Cor. 9) with the social expectation of gratitude.

[150] See pp. 73–83 above.

to the creation and maintenance of a unique Christian relationship (κοινωνία εἰς τὸ εὐαγγέλιον). Paul's early reference to κοινωνία εἰς τὸ εὐαγγέλιον in Philippians 1.5 as well as the frequent recourse to this theme throughout the letter should lead us to conclude that for Paul the relationship is not best characterized as one of reciprocal debt.

In light of the broad social context of giving and receiving and the specific study of δόσις καὶ λῆμψις which we offered in chapter 3, we assert that with this phrase the apostle refers to the social practice of reciprocity in gifts and services. His relationship with the Philippians is unique in that there is reciprocity. That the nature of this relationship is not purely defined by Greco-Roman standards, however, is apparent from the way Paul chooses to describe the significance of the gift. First, all talk of debt is absent. Though an argument from silence, it surely must be significant that Paul does not express feelings of debt, neither for this particular gift nor the many that he has received in the past.[151] Secondly, and following from the above, all mention of repayment on his part is omitted. God is the one who repays. This is a Jewish idea as we shall see below.[152] Thirdly, the Philippians receive spiritual benefits from their giving (4.17), another Jewish idea. In the Greco-Roman world the only non-material return that givers could expect would be the honour the receiver(s) pay to the giver.[153] Fourthly, their giving is interpreted as sharing in his affliction, which is an idea not found in the Greco-Roman literature. Fifthly, their relationship is said to be one which furthers the gospel, again an idea untypical of Greco-Roman sharing.[154] Sixthly, Paul calls their gift a spiritual sacrifice pleasing to God (4.18). Again he draws on a Jewish idea

---

[151] Exactly how often this congregation sent support is impossible to establish. The phrase Paul uses to refer to their earlier giving (καὶ ἅπαξ καὶ δίς, v. 16) is difficult, but probably denotes that they sent help at least three times. See Leon Morris, 'Καὶ ἅπαξ καὶ δίς', *NTS* 1 (1956): 205–8.

[152] See pp. 155–6.

[153] See, e.g., Arist. *Eth. Nic.* 8.14.2–4; Plut. *Mor.* 808D. See also our discussion on pp. 72–3 above.

[154] Though Kiley claims to provide 'evidence of other people in the Greco-Roman period who . . . engaged in financial transactions on behalf of their mission' (Mark Kiley, *Colossians as Pseudepigraphy* (Sheffield: JSOT Press, 1986): 108), his examples are quite different. No text he cites makes an explicit link between money and mission (mission being the deliberate propagation of a religious or philosophical message). The closest texts to this subject are the Cynic epistles. But the authors of these do not link mission and money. They see money and its acceptance as related to their personal conduct, life, character or social relationships, but not directly related to the progress of their message (see Appendix C).

that mercy shown to one's fellow man is a praiseworthy religious act.[155] Such an act is pleasing to God and we can assume that it is therefore worthy of a reward. By contrast, divine reward does not enter into the discussion of giving in the Greco-Roman world; it was never considered meritorious.[156] Rather, one gives benefits to those who are worthy to receive; namely, to those who have the character and means to reciprocate.[157]

It is certainly significant that in v. 16 Paul refers to the support which they *sent* him while he was in Thessalonica. Here in Philippians 4 their support has again been *sent* while he is in prison.[158] The giving and receiving in 1 Corinthians refers to a spiritual-material exchange, a return of financial support for teaching received while the apostle is present making the Corinthians the direct object of his labours. The case with the Philippians, however, is quite different. It is giving and receiving while absent from the church geographically, yet working alongside the church to forward a common cause. Notice that *when Paul left* Macedonia no other church entered into this special relationship with him (v. 15). He need not remind them that while in Macedonia no church there entered into giving and receiving with him, for it was his settled policy not to accept support from a church while present with them.[159]

Our position is in contrast to Perkins. She believes that Paul did not set an example by working while in Philippi, but received supplies from Lydia upon his arrival there. She cites for support Acts 16.14–15.[160] The text of Philippians, however, implies that the apostle's partnership in giving and receiving began when he received supplies from them at Thessalonica (4.15). In addition, Acts 16.14–15 mentions only hospitality, and that in itself cannot preclude the possibility that Paul offered payment for his lodging and/or worked to support himself. Though at the end of his stay at

---

[155] E.g., Deut. 15.7; Prov. 19.7, 22.9; Isa. 58.7; Luke 12.33.

[156] Herman, *Ritualized Friendship*, 49; Bolkestein, 'Almosen', *RAC* 1 (1950): 302; W. Schwer, 'Armenpflege', *RAC* 1 (1950): 692.

[157] Seneca, *Ben.* 1.1.2; 1.10.4; 4.29.2; cf. Duncan Cloud, 'The Client-Patron Relationship: Emblem and Reality in Juvenal's First Book', *Patronage in Ancient Society*, ed. A. Wallace-Hadrill (London: Routledge, 1989): 210.

[158] This is a point not given enough weight by some scholars, that the support Paul received from the Philippians was always that which was *sent* (see our discussion of social obligations and the Corinthian conflict, pp. 162–74).

[159] See our discussion of Paul's support practices below, pp. 163–71.

[160] Perkins, 'Heavenly Politeuma', 103; see also 103 n. 70. A similar position is held by Fleury, 'Une Société de Fait', 7–8; and Register, *Giving and Receiving*, 109.

Philippi the apostle is still using Lydia's house as a base (16.40), this does not force us to conclude that he exhibited a fundamentally different practice from that which he reports in 1 Thessalonians 2.9 or 1 Corinthians 9.15. In the next chapter, Paul was apparently staying at Jason's house while in Thessalonica (Acts 17.7). Despite such hospitality, he claims to have worked at that time so as not to be a burden to anyone (1 Thess. 2.9). Further, in chapter 20 the writer of Acts has Paul saying that while in Ephesus he operated with the same policy: avoiding dependence on others by supplying his own needs through work (Acts 20.34).

Unlike the hospitality Paul enjoyed elsewhere, the Philippians are concerned for the apostle even in his absence. To their praise, they entered into a special partnership with the apostle (ἐκοινώνησεν εἰς λόγον δόσεως καὶ λήμψεως) when he left to preach elsewhere. Here we have a connection between mission and money. Though Paul's material-spiritual contrast implies debt and though he actually draws out this conclusion in Romans 15.27, this is not precisely the relationship in Philippians. They are not exactly giving back for his teaching but are partners with him to bring the teaching to others.[161]

Second qualification: rejection of solicitation, 4.17

Verses 15–16 are a clear commendation for the Philippians' support. By praising them for their good behaviour it may be thought that the apostle was personally interested in the monetary gain from it. This idea, this possible misunderstanding, he dispels with his second qualification (cf. the qualification of 4.11). Though the Philippians' gift was an expression of Christian compassion and fellowship in the gospel, Paul wants to make clear that it is not the gift itself that he seeks. Paul stresses that he does not seek the gift, he has not asked for it, nor is he anxious to have it given.[162] The

---

[161] Bassler, *God & Mammon*, 79. Note Paul's impassioned comment in 2 Cor. 11.8: 'I robbed other churches by receiving support from them so as to serve you.' The money from Macedonia (v. 9) made it possible for him to preach to the Corinthians.

[162] The apostle's profession that he does not seek the gift, besides giving insight into his personal contentment, could well be instructive for the Philippians. We noted above Jesus' words about anxiety (Matt. 6.25–34). Jesus asserts that food and clothing are items which the *Gentiles* eagerly seek (πάντα ταῦτα τὰ ἔθνη ἐπιζητοῦσιν, 6.32a). Why is seeking peculiar to the Gentiles? Davies/Allison assert that τὰ ἔθνη are the misguided and because they do not know the God of the Old Testament they do not trust God's providence (*Matthew*, 658).

apostle's comment plainly shows that the view of Sampley is faulty. Paul did not ask for support and χρείαν should not be translated as a need/request.[163] He has already said that he does not speak from need and here adds denial that the gift was sought in and for itself.[164]

But having made this negative assertion Paul follows it up closely with a positive assertion. His main concern is for the spiritual welfare of the Philippians. This welfare is enhanced, or shown to be enhanced, by their willingness to give and by actual giving. Thus the apostle can say that he in fact does seek something. He seeks the spiritual dividends that will accrue to the Philippians' account as a result of their Christian service (4.17).

Paul describes this enhancement of their spiritual welfare with a financial growth metaphor.[165] Though this particular phrase is unique in the New Testament, the idea certainly is not. We find elsewhere the concept that God will repay the giver who shows compassion for others by sharing material goods (Matt. 6.4, 19.21 = Mark 10.31, cf. Luke 6.38, 7.4–5, 12.33, 14.12–14, 18.22; Acts 10.4). We first saw this idea in the Old Testament.[166] The one who shares with his neighbour will be rewarded by Yahweh.[167] Here 'account' (λόγον) will be a metaphorical reference to a body of blessings received from the Lord. These blessings will increase as the Philippians give, as they continue their financial partnership for the advance of the Gospel.[168]

Thus, the idea of repayment for benefits, found extensively in the Greco-Roman literature, is also found in the canonical literature, but with a different nuance. In the canon, the Great Rewarder is the Lord God. The apostle here corrects the Philippians' possible misunderstanding by using the Old Testament understanding.

---

[163] Cf. Sampley, *Partnership*, 54–5. For our fuller treatment of Sampley see pp. 123–7.

[164] We should note, however, that the mere fact that the gift was unsolicited does not lessen Paul's obligation to gratitude (1 Sam. 25.1–17, 21; 2 Kings 4.8–17; Seneca, *Ben.* 2.18.3, 3.12.3).

[165] O'Brien, *Philippians*, 538; Martin, *Philippians* (NCB), 167; Kennedy, 'Financial Colouring', 43–4; Gnilka, *Philipperbrief*, 179; Lohmeyer, *Philipper*, 417.

[166] See above, pp. 23–7.

[167] We recall Prov. 19.17, which uses a financial metaphor to describe the transaction that occurs between the beneficent, the poor and God.

[168] For a different interpretation of τὸν καρπὸν τὸν πλεονάζοντα εἰς λόγον ὑμῶν see our discussion of Newton below.

Theological interpretation: vv. 18b-20

The apostle's language becomes sacrificial in 4.18 as he moves from describing his own response and view of the gift to describing God's view of the gift. Though the Philippians' financial aid is a gift given to a poor man, suffering as a criminal, and likely to produce no foreseeable return, yet in the eyes of God it is a most pleasing sacrifice, a sacrifice ultimately given to him it appears (ὀσμὴν εὐωδίας, θυσίαν δεκτήν).[169] With such sacrifices God is pleased (εὐάρεστον τῷ θεῷ, cf. Heb. 13.16; Hermas *Sim.* 5.3.8). Paul's powerful theological interpretation of their gift greatly enriches his response.[170] Such high praise for the Philippians' gift, namely that it is pleasing to God, must not only teach them the significance of such an act, but also commend them for it.

Michael Newton has suggested that the language of Philippians 4.17–18 is cultic, since it depicts Paul as the priest of the Christian cult.[171] He says, 'A temple requires a priest and for the Church which is the Temple Paul serves in this capacity.'[172] Paul depicts himself as a priest (Rom. 15.16) and expects to be supported as a priest (1 Cor. 9.13–14). Recognizing this theme, Newton asserts that the ideas of Philippians are decidedly cultic and contends that δόμα, καρπός and πλεονάζω have cultic ties to the Old Testament.[173] These alleged connections, in addition to the obvious sacrificial meaning of ὀσμὴν εὐωδίας, θυσίαν δεκτήν and εὐάρεστον τῷ θεῷ, lead Newton to conclude that the apostle views the gift from a cultic perspective. According to Newton, δόμα refers to those gifts offered in the Temple. Paul, however, in his adaptation of this cultic language has made converts his offering to God (Rom. 15.16) and these converts are referred to as first fruits in Romans 16.5 and 1 Corinthians 16.15. Thus καρπός in Philippians 4.17 refers to converts. Moreover, 'It is this gift, the Gentile

---

[169] Raymond Corriveau, *The Liturgy of Life* (Bruxelles: Desclée de Brouwer, 1970): 115; Gnilka, *Philipperbrief*, 179. There is a strong similarity here with the language of Eph. 5.2. Christ gave himself up for the church as προσφορὰν καὶ θυσίαν τῷ θεῷ εἰς ὀσμὴν εὐωδίας.

[170] Silva, *Philippians*, 232.

[171] Michael Newton, *The Concept of Purity at Qumran and in the Letters of Paul* (Cambridge: Cambridge University Press, 1985): 62–8.

[172] Newton, *Purity*, 60.

[173] See our discussion of δόμα, καρπός and πλεονάζω below, pp. 154–5.

converts to the church, which is the credit (λόγος) to those of the Philippian community.'[174]

It cannot be denied that Paul views his preaching of the gospel as a priestly activity in which he makes an offering of living souls to God (Rom. 15.16).[175] But that this concept applies so extensively to the terms of Philippians 4.17–18 is not so clear. Newton has over stated his case in the following ways.

First, the ties to Old Testament cultic language made with δόμα, καρπός and πλεονάζω are tenuous at best. Newton asserts that in the LXX δόμα 'sometimes' refers to secular gifts.[176] In fact, the use is fairly evenly divided.[177] Newton asserts that in the LXX of Leviticus 28.2, Numbers 18.11 and Deuteronomy 12.11 δόμα is linked with the offering of the first fruits (ἀπαρχή). These examples, however, cannot establish a necessary link between δόμα and καρπός, the very link Newton wishes to establish. Of more significance for his argument is Numbers 28.2, which he says parallels Philippians 4.17. The LXX text of Numbers 28.2 reads: τὰ δῶρα μου δόματά μου καρπώματά μου εἰς ὀσμὴν εὐωδίας. Though there is a similarity in terms here, there is little similarity in thought. Whereas in Numbers the Israelites bring their offerings to God, offerings which are described with three different terms, in Philippians three different terms are used to apply to three quite distinct elements in Paul's response to a single offering. There is no place for seeing an equation of δόμα and καρπός in Philippians. Furthermore, though πλεονάζω does occur four times in a cultic context (which Newton cites), with the exception of 2 Chronicles 31.5 the other fourteen uses have no cultic associations.

Secondly, Newton's case is confused in the logical connections which he attempts to make. For instance, if δόμα refers to the offering of the Gentiles as a gift to God, how then do we explain Paul's insistence that he does not seek the δόμα?[178] We have already mentioned in the preceding paragraphs that the equation of

---

[174] Newton, *Purity*, 65.

[175] On this text see Joseph Ponthot, 'L'Éxpression Culturelle du Ministère Paulinien selon Rm 15,16', *L'Apôtré Paul: Personnalité, Style et Conception du Ministère*, ed. A. Vanhoye (Leuven: University Press, 1986): 254–62.

[176] Newton, *Purity*, 62.

[177] Eighteen of these uses appear to be definitely cultic (e.g., Ex. 28.34; Lev. 7.20, 28.38; Num. 18.6, 7, 11, 29; Ps. 68.18), while sixteen are certainly secular (e.g., Gen. 25.6; Num. 27.6; 1 Sam. 18.25; Jud. 4.14, 16.18; Prov. 18.16; Eccles. 3.13, 5.18).

[178] This point is made by O'Brien as well (*Philippians*, 537 n. 163).

δόμα and καρπός is an equation which the apostle does not make. According to Paul, the δόμα comes to him, but the καρπός accrues to the Philippians. Newton says, 'Paul's rhetorical statement, "Not that I seek the gift", in addition to the material benefits accruing to him, refers also to what he considers to be the "fragrant offering" that he, as a priest, is presented in the form of converts to the faith.'[179] This statement gives δόμα a double meaning which the context will not tolerate.

Thus, Newton's understanding of the text is suspect because of its weak connections to the Old Testament and its strained association of divergent ideas. On the other hand, Paul's thought here does indeed have a precedent in the Old Testament. Our appeal, however, will be to more general concepts.

First, we have already seen that financial sharing was considered virtuous and worthy of reward in the Old Testament.[180] This background is sufficient to explain Paul's language in 4.17 and 19. One particular example is Proverbs 19.17: δανίζει θεῷ ὁ ἐλεῶν πτωχόν, κατὰ δὲ τὸ δόμα αὐτοῦ ἀνταποδώσει αὐτῷ. We should notice here that the author feels free to mix social, commercial and theological language. Further, there is a blurring of the ideas in reception, just as in Philippians 4: the mercy done to a second party, i.e., the poor, is considered as a loan to a third party, i.e., God. Likewise, not only is δόμα being used more closely to the way it is used in Philippians 4, viz., as help for the needy, but we also have the concept that God will repay which is found in Philippians 4.17, 19.

Secondly, the concept of spiritual sacrifice was certainly widespread in Paul's day.[181] We should notice specifically how the apostle seeks to define the deep religious significance of the act. The Philippians' gift of material goods is not simply a social transaction, nor indeed is it only a display of their concern for the apostle, though as such a display it reflects their Christian maturity. Rather Paul asserts that their contribution in this context is to be understood as an act of true spiritual worship and such descriptions are common in the literature. The true sacrifices of a pure worshipper to God were praise.[182] But that offerings of financial support to others was considered a sacrifice was relatively rare, and in any case

---

[179] Newton, *Purity*, 63.   [180] See pp. 23–7 above.
[181] Everett Ferguson, 'Spiritual Sacrifice in Early Christianity and Its Environment', *ANRW* 2.23.2, ed. Wolfgang Haase (1980): 1151–89.
[182] Johannes Behm, 'θύω κτλ', *TDNT*, 3.183.

a Jewish idea, as we noted above.[183] For example, Sirach asserts that, 'In works of charity one offers fine flour, and when he gives alms he presents his sacrifice of praise' (35.2–3).[184] Kindness done to a father will not be forgotten, it will serve as a sin offering (3.14–15; cf. 29.8–13); alms atone for sins (3.30; cf. Tobit 4.10–11, 12.9–12). This development already had its roots in Hosea 6.6 (cf. Matt. 9.13).[185] Further, and perhaps most significantly, the author of Hebrews sees financial sharing as a sacrifice pleasing to God: τῆς δὲ εὐποιΐας καὶ κοινωνίας μὴ ἐπιλανθάνεσθε· τοιαύταις γὰρ θυσίαις εὐαρεστεῖται ὁ θεός, 13.16. Unfortunately, reference is rarely made to this text in attempts to explain the thought of Philippians 4. In both texts we have financial sharing defined as a sacrifice pleasing (εὐάρεστος)[186] to God.

Generally speaking, however, in Greco-Roman society generosity toward the poor out of compassion for them in their state was not considered a virtuous act and therefore could expect no reward from God.[187] It was more blessed to give than to receive amongst the Greeks and Romans, not because of the display of compassion seen therein, but because giving displayed one's personal virtue and social power.[188] 'The most basic premise from which the Romans started was that honour and prestige derived from the power to give others what they needed or wanted.'[189] This view is confirmed by the presentation of giving and receiving which we saw in Seneca. He always places the significance of benefaction within the social realm. No mention is made of reward of any kind which will accrue to the giver from God; all return comes from the receiver.[190]

---

[183] See pp. 50, 89 above.

[184] Translation from Skehan/Di Lella, *Ben Sira*, 411. Cf. Philo (*Apol.* 7.6): 'If the poor or the cripple beg food of him he must give it as an offering of religion to God (πρὸς τὸν θεὸν εὐαγῶς ἀνέχειν)'.

[185] Benevolence is considered a sacrifice among the fathers as well, e.g., Polycarp *Ep. Phil.* 4.3; Hermas *Sim.* 5.3.3, 7–8; 2 Clement 16.4.

[186] Though Attridge asserts concerning εὐαρεστεῖται that 'The verb and related words appear in the NT only in Hebrews' (Harold W. Attridge, *The Epistle to the Hebrews* (Philadelphia: Fortress Press, 1989): 401 n. 153), nevertheless the adjective εὐάρεστος figures in Rom. 12.1–2, 14.18, 2 Cor. 5.9, Eph. 5.10, Col. 3.20 and Tit. 2.9.

[187] Bolkestein, 'Almosen', *RAC* 1 (1950): 302; cf. Schwer, 'Armenplege', *RAC* 1 (1950): 690–8; cf. Seneca *Ben.* 4.29.2.

[188] Bolkestein, *Wohltätigkeit*, 151; Hamilton-Grierson, 'Gifts', 197–209; Prov. 25.14; Arist. *Eth. Nic.* 4.1.7; Seneca, *Ben.* 2.33.1–2, 8.14.3–4; Plut. *Mor.* 808D; Sirach 7.27–8; Luke 22.25; Acts 5.1–10; 20.35; Rom. 5.7.

[189] R. P. Saller, *Personal Patronage under the Early Empire* (Cambridge: Cambridge University Press, 1982): 126.

[190] See above pp. 68, 89.

Thus we see again that in Philippians 4 what could and would easily be interpreted by the Philippians as an act of social significance is interpreted by the apostle as an act of religious significance. This gift of money is not the giving of a benefit to an individual but the offering of a sacrifice to God. Paul corrects the possible Greco-Roman interpretation with a Jewish interpretation, an interpretation which makes the Philippians' financial sharing a sacrifice pleasing to God. This sacrificial language helps complete the reciprocity of service found earlier in Philippians. The apostle had said that he would gladly be poured out on the sacrifice and service of their faith (2.17). This sacrificial act on his part corresponds to the sacrificial act on the part of the Philippians found in 4.18.[191]

At the end of this section, in 4.19, Paul does not state his intention to repay the Philippians, even though, as we saw from several papyri, this might have been expected. Nor does he solicit their requests so that he might do them a favour in return.[192] He has said that they supplied his need with their gift. Now in response God will supply their every need.[193] The Philippians do indeed get a return, but, in keeping with the Old Testament on this issue (cf. Prov. 19.17), they get their return from a far greater Benefactor. Lightfoot paraphrases Paul's words, 'You have supplied all my wants (vv. 16, 18), God *on my behalf* shall supply all *yours.*'[194]

Conclusion

We began by referring to the assertion of several scholars that Paul's so-called 'thank you' section of Philippians 4.10–20 is remarkable in its thanklessness. At this point we could respond by saying that if this pericope is indeed remarkable, it is so not owing to the absence of εὐχαριστέω, but to the omission of ὀφείλω or a similar expression of debt. In any case, Paul's response to the

---

[191] In addition, Paul and the Philippians are partners in the gospel (1.5), partners in grace (1.7), share the same φρονεῖν for each other (1.7, 4.10), have common struggles (1.30), share in tribulation (4.14, cf., 3.10) and have a unique relationship of giving and receiving (4.15). See our discussion of the reciprocity theme of Philippians on pp. 118–20.

[192] See p. 79 above.

[193] This third occurrence of χρεία argues against Sampley's assertion that it should be allowed to have its 'full range of meaning'. Such an appeal to a double meaning only obscures the otherwise clear message of the text. Clearly Paul does not assert that God will provide their every request as they have provided his request. χρεία must be the functional equivalent of ὑστέρησιν (v. 11).

[194] Lightfoot, *Philippians*, 167, emphasis original.

Philippians' gift should not be tagged a 'thankless thanks' simply because εὐχαριστέω is absent, for this would not be in accord with first-century social practice.

In view of the reciprocal character of gift and service relationships in the Greco-Roman world, perhaps we should now ask to what extent an expression of verbal gratitude would be consistent with Paul's purpose in Philippians. It is commonly asserted that Paul mixes his appreciation for the gift with statements of independence.[195] Must these statements be understood as displaying Paul's embarrassment over money matters, as some scholars contend?[196] Rather, should not these statements at least in part be understood as reflecting Paul's desire to avoid the assumption that he has contracted a personal social obligation by accepting this gift? Instead of an expression of debt or of his intention to repay, the apostle relates his personal reflection, gives moral commendation and offers a theological interpretation of the gift. From this it should be clear that the purpose of Philippians 4.10–20 is not simply to offer a personal response to financial support, but rather to offer instruction on the place of such sharing in the life of the Christian community.

Concerning Paul's personal reflection there are two issues: first, the gift displays a Christian mindset (φρονεῖν). In their giving to the apostle the Philippians have not so much displayed their virtue but their Christian mindset. The presence of this mindset brought the apostle great joy. Secondly, however, Paul's joy is mixed with contentment. In this context of receiving he feels that they must be made aware of his contentment. Further, the apostle's contentment is not Stoic αὐτάρκεια; it is not emotional detachment in the midst of all life's hardships. Rather, it is peace with one's financial conditions, whether they be paucity or plenty.

With regard to Paul's commendation, the chief issue is partnership. Paul and the Philippians are in a reciprocal relationship. Doubtless we are to understand that the apostle contributed spiritual things and they the material things (cf. Rom. 15.27; 1 Cor. 9.11). Yet the reciprocity is not restricted to this, as we have seen. Nor was their relationship seen only on the level with exchange. He says that by giving this gift they have been able to share in his

---

[195] See, e.g., Hawthorne, *Philippians*, 195; Martin, *Philippians* (TYN), 176; cf. Beare, *Philippians*, 157.

[196] E.g., Beare, *Philippians*, 152; Dodd, 'The Mind of Paul: I', 71; Collange, *Philippians*, 148–9.

trouble (4.14). This puts the partnership on a deep level. They are willing to associate with the lowly (Rom. 12.16).

Finally, regarding Paul's theological interpretation the issue is spiritual sacrifice. Such sharing as the Philippians have done is pleasing to God and is a true spiritual sacrifice. As such a sacrifice it is a type of praiseworthy behaviour and will receive reward from God.

In the light of Greco-Roman social expectations, Paul's response takes on fresh meaning. In each point of his response the apostle corrects a possible Greco-Roman understanding of the significance of the gift with a Jewish understanding of it. The Philippians stand alongside the apostle as those suffering and working for the defence and confirmation of the gospel (1.7).[197] Paul has not become socially obligated, and thereby in a sense inferior, by accepting their gifts. Rather, because he has accepted their gifts, they have been elevated to the place of partners in the gospel. Though Paul is in receipt of their gift and can mention his own benefit from it (4.18a), in 4.17b he rather makes it appear that they are actually the ones benefited.[198] Their gift does bring them a return. It is an investment that reaps spiritual dividends. But ultimately the responsibility to reward them rests not with Paul, but with God (4.19).

The position that Paul has taken with regard to the gift of money he has received may be surprising from a twentieth-century western standpoint. It should not be surprising, however, in light of Paul's overall teaching on the matter. In this regard we may note one particular text where the apostle mentions money: 2 Corinthians 9.8–13. The several points of correspondence between 2 Corinthians 9 and Philippians are by no means coincidental. In table form they are as follows:

2 Corinthians		Philippians
9.8	αὐτάρκεια, αὐτάρκης	4.11
9.10–11	God's reward	4.19
9.12	λειτουργία	2.25, 30
9.12	thanks to God	1.3
9.13	κοινωνία	1.5, 4.15
9.13	εὐαγγέλιον	1.5, 4.15

---

[197] See our comments on this text, pp. 105–6 above.
[198] Gnilka, *Philipperbrief*, 179.

With regard to the place of money in the behaviour and life of the Christian community, these issues keep arising. The responsibility of the Christian is contentment. Money is a commodity which one should use to serve others (λειτουργία), an attitude which varies from the Greek and Roman approach that one displays one's virtue by giving. The reward, contrary again to Greco-Roman ideas but in keeping with the Old Testament, comes from God, not from the receiver. Likewise the thanks for the blessing of receiving financial help goes to God.[199] Such sharing is defined as κοινωνία. Finally, the defence and confirmation of the gospel is the all-encompassing goal of sharing. In 2 Corinthians 9 sharing proves the truthfulness of one's confession of the gospel and this fact is not far away from Paul's assertion in Philippians that sharing is κοινωνία εἰς τὸ εὐαγγέλιον.

Expanded paraphrase

In an attempt to integrate the findings of this chapter, we offer the following paraphrase of Philippians 4.10–20:

> [10] I rejoiced in the Lord greatly that, after all this time, you have been able to express your concern for me again with another gift. Of course, I know that you have been concerned about me all along but have not been able to show it. [11] Now I am not complaining because of my needs, for I have learned how to live as a Christian in the midst of all life's financial changes. [12] I know how to respond if I am made poor and I know how to respond if I am made rich. [13] And for all that I have been able to learn I must give credit to the Lord who strengthens me to do it.
>
> [14] Yet, despite all that, you are to be commended for your display of real solidarity with me in my troubles. [15] You know that just after I had preached to you, when I left Macedonia, yours was the only church willing to identify with the work of the gospel so as to stand together with me in a special relationship of support. [16] You did this even when I was in Thessalonica by sending things a few times to help me.
>
> [17] Now please don't get the idea that I am commending

---

you as a way to get more of your support. I am not
anxious to receive your gifts, but I am anxious to see these
expressions of love reap spiritual dividends for you. [18] I
received everything you sent and have been made rich. I
am full to overflowing, for I have received your gift from
Epaphroditus, a true Christian offering, a sacrifice bringing
pleasure to God. [19] And my God will reward you by fully
meeting every need of yours from his glorious wealth
which is available for his people in Christ Jesus. [20] To our
God and Father be glory for ever and ever. Amen.

6

GIVING AND RECEIVING ELSEWHERE IN PAUL'S LETTERS

Paul's opportunities for giving and receiving were not restricted to his relationship with the Philippians. Since the exchange of goods and services was woven into the fabric of first-century society, we should expect to see this convention surfacing elsewhere in his letters. Therefore, we shall briefly investigate a few other passages, the understanding of which may be informed by our knowledge of social reciprocity.

We will not attempt a complete exegesis of the texts discussed, for each one offers its own set of exegetical and theological difficulties which could warrant a separate chapter. Our goal is to show that the conclusions drawn from Philippians regarding Paul's adaptation of the metaphor of giving and receiving are both confirmed and illustrated by these other texts.

Social obligations and the Corinthian conflict

In this brief discussion of several passages from the Corinthian correspondence we intend to demonstrate, first, that Paul understands that his reception of the gift offered by the Corinthians would create social dependence. Secondly, that Paul avoided this social dependence because, amongst other reasons, it would be a hindrance to the gospel. Thirdly, that Paul's approach is basically consistent: choices are made on the basis of whether or not they help advance the gospel. Fourthly, that these findings reinforce our conclusions from Philippians.

Some of these goals overlap with the work of Peter Marshall.[1] Though Marshall has given us an enlightening study of Paul's relationship with the Corinthians and has studied in detail how the

---

[1] See especially Marshall's section on Paul's refusal of the Corinthians' gifts (*Enmity*, 233–51).

conventions regarding giving and receiving led to the breakdown of this relationship, there is still work to be done. Marshall's work adds difficulty to an ever present problem concerning Paul's practice regarding financial support. Marshall believes that the apostle has not been entirely consistent in his treatment of the different congregations.[2] After all, Paul received financial support from the Philippians, but he told the Corinthians that he would never receive help from them. Is this behaviour contradictory?[3] Some believe it is.[4] Others, however, offer various theories and reconstructions which demonstrate that the behaviour was not contradictory.[5] In this section we will show how the conventions of social reciprocity help us in our understanding of this apparent apostolic inconsistency.

Our concerns here are very specific and we cannot enter into the debates which have generated a massive amount of literature on Paul's apostolic legitimacy, his arguments with and the identification of his opponents, and the like. We will be concerned only with the reception or refusal of a gift and the motivations for this action which Paul himself gives. We undertake this study in order to compare and contrast Paul's behaviour toward the Corinthians with his behaviour toward the Philippians.

Types of support

Lack of precision with regard to the types of support Paul refers to has evoked erroneous comments from scholars. For example, Furnish asserts:

---

[2] *Enmity*, 255–7.

[3] Several other scholars assert that the apostle exhibits inconsistent behaviour in different areas (e.g., Peter Richardson, 'Pauline Inconsistency: 1 Corinthians 9: 19–23 and Galatians 2: 11–14', *NTS* 26 (1980): 347–62. See the response by D. A. Carson, 'Pauline Inconsistency: Reflections on 1 Corinthians 9: 19–23 and Galatians 2: 11–14', *Churchman* 100 (1986): 6–45). Thus it appears that serious consideration of contradiction in the area of support warrants study.

[4] J. H. Schütz comments (*Paul and the Anatomy of Apostolic Authority* (Cambridge: Cambridge University Press, 1975): 235 n. 1): 'Paul's decision not to accept support in Corinth is not a consistent feature of his apostolic behaviour (II Cor. 11: 7f.; Phil. 4: 10).' Cf. Morton Smith, 'Pauline Problems apropos of J. Munck, "Paulus und die Heilsgeschichte"', *HTR* 50 (1957): 111 n. 10 and Bassler, *God & Mammon*, 64, 75.

[5] E.g., R. F. Hock, *The Working Apostle: An Examination of Paul's Means of Livelihood* (Ph.D. Yale, 1974): 126–7; David L. Dungan, *The Sayings of Jesus in the Churches of Paul* (Oxford: Basil Blackwell, 1971): 31–2.

It may have been Paul's custom to decline aid from every congregation while he was still present (see 1 Thess 2: 9) and to accept aid only in the form of 'missionary' support . . . If so, that policy did not operate in the case of Corinth, for Paul declares emphatically not only that he never has accepted aid from the congregation there, but also that he has no immediate plans to do so (11: 9b; 12: 13).[6]

Furnish's comment fails to account for Paul's use of προπέμπειν[7] and blurs the distinction between support received when absent and that received when present. Thus, in order for us to see clearly how selected texts from Corinthians help to confirm our findings from Philippians, we shall distinguish between the various types of support Paul could have or did receive from his churches.

First, Paul refers to being supported while present with a congregation. Paul emphatically says he has the right to be supported (1 Cor. 9.11–12), which we take to mean he has the right to receive financial assistance from the church which he is making the direct object of his ministry efforts. Further, it is this rightful support which Paul has not utilized.

Paul's statements make plain that the support offered by the Corinthians was offered while he was present with them. He says he will not receive help from the Corinthians and constantly talks about refusing this help while *with them* (2 Cor. 11.9). In 2 Corinthians 12.14 he mentions that he will visit them again and when that time comes he *will not be* a burden to them. These statements show that the support Paul refused was that which was offered while he was present. If we assume that the apostle's statements in 1 Corinthians 9 and 2 Corinthians 11–12 form different parts of one discussion, then we must conclude that Paul refused the very type of support which he insists he has the right to receive. Whether for pastoral, ethical or missionary reasons, he does not make use of his right.[8]

Secondly, Paul refers to accepting travel expenses or to receiving support at his departure from a congregation. Although Paul says that only the Philippians had established a relationship of giving and receiving with him, he certainly received material help, in the

---

6 V. P. Furnish, *II Corinthians* (Garden City: Doubleday, 1984): 507.
7 See the comments on προπέμπειν below, p. 165.
8 In his defence, Paul uses ἐξουσία repeatedly (1 Cor. 9.4, 5, 12a, 12b, 15). Yet even in mentioning the giving and receiving involved (1 Cor. 9.11) ὀφείλη (or ὀφείλημα) does not appear.

form of travel expenses, from other churches. This point is often overlooked by scholars.

Paul tells the Corinthians more than once that he expects them to send him on his way (προπέμπειν, 1 Cor. 16.6; 2 Cor. 1.16); as others have pointed out, this verb frequently has the meaning of helping materially.[9] It is probably best understood to have that meaning in 1 Corinthians 16.6.[10] The indefinite final clause, οὗ ἐὰν πορεύωμαι, does not imply that some of the Corinthians will escort Paul, for his further destination is uncertain. Rather it implies that the Corinthians can supply him with travel provisions no matter where his destination may be.

This use of προπέμπειν in Corinthians is significant. It shows that the issue with regard to Paul accepting help from the Corinthians did not revolve around the simple question of whether he did or did not receive material aid. He refused their gifts, but expected their help with travel expenses.[11] We should assume that the aid they offered and he refused in such texts as 2 Corinthians 11.9 and 12.13–16 was qualitatively different from that which he asked for in such texts as 1 Corinthians 16.6 and 2 Corinthians 1.16.

This qualitative difference is implied by the apostle's words in 2 Corinthians 11.9b and 12.13. In these texts Paul claims never to have been a burden to any of the Corinthians. How can this statement be true if he is requesting and taking money for travel expenses? His claim can only be true if aid in the form of προπέμπειν does not cause one to become a burden.[12]

---

9 Bauer/Aland, *Wörterbuch*, 1420–1; L. Michael White, 'Social Authority in the House Church Setting and Ephesians 4: 1–16', *ResQ* 29 (1987): 217. C. E. B. Cranfield (*The Epistle to the Romans*, 2 vols. (Edinburgh: T & T Clark, 1975–9): 769), in addition to NT texts, cites Herodotus 1.111; 3.50; Xen. *An.* 7.2.8; 1 Macc. 12.4; Ep. Aristeas 172. See also Joseph. *BJ* 1.456, 512, 2.104.

10 Gordon D. Fee, *The First Epistle to the Corinthians* (Grand Rapids: Eerdmans, 1987): 819. Fee states: 'In light of the tensions over his refusal to accept monetary support while among them . . . this has all the earmarks of a peace offering on this matter'. *Contra* A. Robertson and A. Plummer, *A Critical and Exegetical Commentary on the First Epistle of Saint Paul to the Corinthians* (Edinburgh: T & T Clark, 2nd edn, 1914): 388: 'He is not asking for money or provisions; the verb does not necessarily mean more than good wishes and prayers.'

11 W. Meeks, *The First Urban Christians: The Social World of the Apostle Paul* (New Haven: Yale University Press, 1983): 66.

12 White, however, blurs the distinction, calling the acceptance of travel expenses a form of patronage ('Social Authority', 217). We know that Paul requested travel expenses from the Corinthians, but White asserts that Paul refused to accept their patronage ('Social Authority', 220). See our discussion of βαρέω below, pp. 168–71.

Thirdly, there is missionary support, or support given while absent. The help Paul says he received from the Philippians was always sent while he was away (Phil. 4.16; cf. 2 Cor. 11.9). It was support used to advance the message of the gospel in other regions (cf. 1.5). We have already seen how Paul links the support he received from the Philippians with the advance of the gospel.[13]

We must contrast mission support with the offer of help described above, which Paul says he will always refuse from the Corinthians. The latter is that which is offered *while he was in Corinth*. The distinction appears to be between presence and absence.[14] This distinction lends support to the view that Paul did not accept help from churches while he was working with them.

Regarding financial support, Marshall claims that by adopting different attitudes toward the Corinthians and the Philippians Paul is inconsistent. He also states that scholars have failed to demonstrate that there is a difference between the Philippian gifts and the Corinthian offers of aid.[15] Marshall's views result from a misunderstanding of Paul's gospel partnership with the Philippians and from a blurring of the distinctions between support received while present and that received while absent.

Marshall rejects the view of Hock that Paul did not accept support from those he was converting.[16] Marshall rightly notes that, long after the Corinthian church had been founded, Paul insisted that he would continue to refuse support. On the other hand, though citing Dungan, Marshall apparently does not see what is unique to Dungan's view. Dungan asserts that the critical issue for Paul regarding support is whether the apostle is present or absent and correctly cites Philippians 4.15, that Paul received aid from the Philippians *after he went out* from Macedonia.[17]

The above discussion makes clear that Paul refers to three types of material aid in his letters: support while present with a congregation

---

[13] See pp. 99–103 and 150–1 above.
[14] Pratscher, 'Der Verzicht des Paulus', 284–98, esp. 290–2; cf. Hock, *The Working Apostle*, 126–7; Reumann, 'Contributions', 441, following Holmberg, *Paul and Power*, 92–3.
[15] Marshall, *Enmity*, 237, 255.   [16] Hock, *The Working Apostle*, 126–7.
[17] Dungan, *The Sayings of Jesus*, 31–2. Dungan's view requires modification, however. For he asserts that Paul's acceptance of the Philippians' aid was one instance where the apostle received the support owing to him which is described in 1 Cor. 9. Properly understood, however, 1 Cor. 9 only refers to support Paul is due while making a congregation the direct object of his efforts. The Philippian support does not fit this qualification.

(the support due him as an apostle), travel expenses, and mission support. The evidence shows that he rejected the first, asked for the second, and gladly received the third. The significance of Paul's practice will become clearer as we look at his motivations for this practice.

Paul's motivations

With these different types of support delineated, we can now proceed to the motivations Paul expressed for refusal or acceptance.[18] It has been pointed out by several scholars that the reasons Paul gives for his refusal of support are confused, inconsistent and bound up with his apostolic self-legitimation against his rivals in Corinth. We cannot enter into debate with the vast number who have written on the subject.[19] We shall only outline the motivations Paul gives and seek to show how our social model provides fresh light for understanding these motivations.

(i) Paul and the deceitful workers

Much has been written on Paul's opponents in 2 Corinthians.[20] We cannot enter into investigation concerning their identity and practice, but will restrict ourselves to Paul's mention of them with regard to support.

Paul says that he will continue to refuse money from the Corinthians. He will do so in order to distance himself from the false apostles, to avoid appearing to be their equal (2 Cor. 11.12).

---

[18] We shall only deal with reasons Paul himself gives, though it would be fruitful to discuss other possible motivations. See, e.g., A. E. Harvey, '"The Workman is Worthy of his Hire": Fortunes of a Proverb in the Early Church', *NovT* 24 (1982): 209–21; Abraham J. Malherbe, '"Gentle as a Nurse": The Cynic Background to 1 Thess 2', *NovT* 12 (1970): 203–17.

[19] See, e.g., Ernst Käsemann, 'Die Legitimität des Apostels: Eine Untersuchung zu 2 Korinther 10–13', *ZNW* 41 (1942): 33–71; Gerd Theissen, 'Legitimation und Lebensunterhalt: Ein Beitrag zur Soziologie Urchristlicher Missionäre', *NTS* 21 (1975): 192–221.

[20] For larger or more significant treatments see Dieter Georgi, *Die Gegner des Paulus im 2 Korintherbrief: Studien zur religiosen Propaganda in der Spätantike* (Neukirchen: Neukirchener, 1964); C. K. Barrett, 'Paul's Opponents in II Corinthians', *NTS* 17 (1971): 233–54; E. E. Ellis, 'Paul and his Opponents: Trends in Research', *Christianity, Judaism and Other Greco-Roman Cults; Part 1*, ed. Jacob Neusner (Leiden: E. J. Brill, 1975): 264–98; Jerry L. Sumney, *Identifying Paul's Opponents. The Question of Method in 2 Corinthians* (Sheffield: JSOT Press, 1990).

There is some debate on the syntax and meaning of this verse.[21] The general message, however, is clear. Sumney draws out Paul's point with his comment:

> The opponents want to force Paul either to admit that he does not have a right to support or to accept it from the Corinthians. Either way they gain ground. If Paul renounces his right, they are shown to be his superiors. If he accepts support, he puts himself on their level, and thus, they can claim, admits that they are his equals.[22]

Paul seeks to destroy, or at least not to enhance, the position of the false apostles. These workers are described in quite scathing terms. Paul believes that they do not serve God but Satan (vv. 13–15).[23] As such they are deceitful workmen, not those who carry forth the work of God as Paul does. Their work cannot advance the gospel, for they preach a false gospel (11.4).[24] In presenting himself as different from them, Paul hopes to strengthen his own position and what he considers to be the work of God against the work of Satan. To put it another way, refusal of support on Paul's part will help advance the gospel. Refusal has a missionary motivation.

(ii)   Support and being a burden

Paul says he does not want to be a burden (2 Cor. 11.9, 12.13–14, 16). In this context the term *burden* is a financial one. As we demonstrated earlier, in the Greco-Roman world financial dependence yielded social dependence and inferiority.[25] Thus, Paul's repeated insistence that he will not be a burden appears to reflect a resolution on his part not to contract social obligations with the Corinthians through money. The arguments for this understanding may be summarized as follows.

First, as several scholars have shown, βάρος and related words

---

[21] Marshall, *Enmity*, 334; Martin, *2 Corinthians*, 348–9. Winter suggests that Paul, in refusing to accept support, seeks to distance himself from the practice of sophists who accepted money for their teaching (B. W. Winter, *Paul and Philo Among the Sophists* (Ph. D. diss., Macquarie University), 1988).

[22] Sumney, *Identifying Paul's Opponents*, 161.

[23] *Contra* Margaret E. Thrall, who asserts, on the basis of 1 Cor. 11.23, that Paul labels the same group both servants of Satan and of Christ ('Super-Apostles, Servants of Christ, and Servants of Satan', *JSNT* 6 (1980): 42–57).

[24] Martin, *2 Corinthians*, 350.

[25] See Seneca *Ben.* 2.13.2 and pp. 71–3, 80–2 above.

(καταβαρέω, 2 Cor. 12.16; ἀβαρῆ, 2 Cor. 11.9) are often used to speak of financial burdens.[26] In addition to their evidence, Seneca uses the concept 'burden' with respect to social obligations. For example, in *Ep.* 50.2 Seneca mentions Harpasté, his wife's female clown. Harpasté has become part of Seneca's household, for she is a burden incurred from a legacy (*hereditarium onus*).[27] Here we have *onus* used as a label for a *person* who is a financial and social dependant.

We recall our treatment of Oxyrhynchus Papyri 3057 (1st–2nd AD).[28] In that letter Ammonius mentions being burdened (βαρύνειν) with the many kindnesses (φιλανθρωπίαις) he has received from Apollonius. This use of βαρύνειν helps demonstrate that social obligations or responsibilities which have been incurred through giving and receiving could be spoken of as burdens.

Secondly, the desire not to be a financial burden to the Corinthians would be praiseworthy if the Corinthians were indeed experiencing financial hardship. The precise financial status of the Corinthians cannot be established easily.[29] But we know for certain that it is the Corinthians who have attempted to take on this financial burden being spoken of. They have been the initiators. Financial hardship is not foremost in their minds. Therefore, Paul's response to them is less relevant if it is solely a reference to causing financial hardship.[30] We have reason to believe, then, that in using βάρος Paul is making a veiled reference to his desire to avoid social dependence.

Thirdly, if being a burden is simply equivalent to receiving financial help, we may well ask if Paul is being a burden to the Philippians. If not, what are the criteria to distinguish the two relationships? If so, why should Paul insist that he can burden the Philippians but not the Corinthians? If being a burden is simply

---

[26] J. C. Strelan, 'Burden-Bearing and the Law of Christ: A Re-examination of Galatians 6: 2', *JBL* 94 (1975): 266–76; Kiley, *Colossians*, 49; Hock, *Social Context*, 30. Hock cites the following texts: Dio Chrysostom *Or.* 40.7; Philostratus *V. Soph.* 600; P.Oxy. 487.10–11, 1159.2–3, 1481.13; P.Mich. 347.21. See also Sirach 13.2.

[27] Cf. Seneca *Ep.* 17.1–2; *Ben.* 3.31.2, 6.41.1; Cic. *Planc.* 72, 78.

[28] See pp. 80–2 above.

[29] There were, however, some powerful (i.e., wealthy) members of the congregation (Dieter Sänger, 'Die *dynatoi* in 1 Kor 1: 26', *ZNW* 76 (1985): 285–91). See also Marshall, *Enmity*, 214–18; Gerd Theissen, 'Soziale Schichtung in der korinthischen Gemeinde: Ein Beitrag zur Soziologie des hellenistischen Urchristentums', *ZNW* 65 (1974): 232–72.

[30] *Contra* Dungan, *The Sayings of Jesus*, 30.

equivalent to receiving financial help, how can Paul require that the Corinthians be burdened with his travel expenses and yet insist that they must not be burdened with his living expenses? The difficulty of these questions shows that there is more involved with being a burden than simply receiving aid. What is involved is social obligations. These obligations become an issue only when Paul is present with the givers.

Fourthly, this understanding of the 'burden' concept is supported by the apostle's comment in 2 Corinthians 11.9–10. He says he will keep himself from being a burden and that no one will remove this boasting of his. The anticipated retort of v. 11, 'Why (will I keep myself from being a burden to you)? Because I do not love you?' is difficult. But if burden here only refers to a financial hardship, then the anticipated retort is less clear. If, on the other hand, burden here refers to the contraction of a relationship of social dependence, then the retort takes on new and clear significance. We might expand the meaning in a paraphrase: 'I will not enter into a relationship with you that is based on money. Why do I not want to be your social dependant? Do I not wish to have a relationship with you because I do not love you? No! God knows that I do love you.' As Marshall has shown, the refusal of support was a refusal of friendship, which was also a refusal of the giver's affection.[31]

Fifthly, the apostle's discussion of work and being a burden in 1 Thessalonians supports this understanding. In 2.9 he reminds them (μνημονεύετε) of his labour night and day so as not to be a burden (ἐπιβαρῆσαι) to them. The implication is that Paul brought his practice to their attention while he was with them. In 4.11 he again reminds them of his previous instruction to work with their own hands. They should engage in labour so that they will not be dependent on anybody (μηδενὸς χρείαν ἔχητε, 4.12). Because in this respect Paul puts himself forward as an example for the Thessalonians to imitate,[32] we can draw a connection between these two texts: at least in part, Paul desires to avoid being a *burden* so that he will not be *dependent* on anybody.

Sixthly, in the last two decades scholars have come to realize that social obligations created through money played a significant role in the Corinthian conflict.[33] E. A. Judge asserts correctly that in the

---

[31] Marshall, *Enmity*, 13–18.
[32] Malherbe, *Paul and the Thessalonians*, 13 n. 33; cf. 2 Thess. 3.7–9.
[33] See Marshall, *Enmity*, e.g., 218–51; A. D. Clarke, *Secular and Christian Leadership at Corinth. A Socio-Historical and Exegetical Study of 1 Corinthians 1–6*

case of the Corinthians Paul refused aid in order to avoid contracting social obligations with them.[34] In light of the division and party conflict at Corinth Paul's actions become quite understandable.[35]

(iii) Hindering the gospel

Paul does not want to hinder the gospel (1 Cor. 9.12). This desire appears to be the overarching consideration on his part. Though he only makes direct reference to support hindering the gospel in 1 Corinthians and not in his discussion in 2 Corinthians, yet in the latter the idea appears to be latent in his reasoning. It is the impact that acceptance or refusal of support will have on the advance of the gospel which guides the behaviour of the apostle.

In 1 Corinthians 9.12 Paul says he has not made use of his right to support, but has put up with anything rather than hinder the gospel. In this context the hindrance is not spelled out explicitly. It should be seen as significant, however, that this first reference to justifying his method presents the hindrance to the gospel. He will have recourse to other arguments in 2 Corinthians, but his first statement puts forward the priority of the gospel and its advance as Paul's primary consideration. Texts such as 2 Corinthians 11.12 and 12.14–18 should be seen as unpacking the message of 1 Corinthians 9.12.

As we mentioned earlier, in 2 Corinthians 11.12 Paul states that he will continue to refuse support in order to destroy the position of the false apostles.[36] If he accepts support, then in one area he will be seen as their equals. This appearance of equality he cannot allow, for it means their destructive work as servants of Satan will be forwarded.

In 2 Corinthians 12.14–16 Paul claims that his only giving to the Corinthians, and not taking from them, is a reflection of his

(Leiden: E. J. Brill, 1993): 31–6, 85–6, 93–4; E. A. Judge, 'The Social Identity of the First Christians: A Question of Method in Religious History', *JRH* 11 (1980): 214.

34 'The Reaction against Classical Society in the New Testament', *Evangelical Review of Theology* 9 (1985): 172.

35 Jeffrey A. Crafton comments: 'it is probable that, in the light of the divided and competitive situation in the Corinthian community, Paul did not want to be bound to any single person or faction' (*The Agency of the Apostle: A Dramatistic Analysis of Paul's Response to Conflict in 2 Corinthians* (Sheffield: JSOT, 1991): 56 n. 1).

36 See the treatment of Paul and the deceitful workers, pp. 167–8.

parental love. Parents give, children receive. 'His refusal of their offers of financial aid was in line with his parental duties.'[37] To Paul's mind reception of the Corinthians' gifts implies denial of his role as a giving, beneficent parent.[38] Further, we know from our study of the dynamics of giving and receiving that denial of this role, implied by the reception of gifts from the Corinthians, would entail a lowering in Paul's social status and thus his apostolic authority.[39]

The parental metaphor

Above we had brief recourse to Paul's use of the parenthood metaphor in 2 Corinthians 12.14–16. There Paul used his role as a parent to support his decision not to receive the Corinthians' offers of gifts: acceptance would be contrary to the norm that parents give and children receive. In another text, 2 Corinthians 6.13, Paul uses the metaphor of parenthood to solicit from the Corinthians a return for his parental affection. The grounds for their obligation to love in return is Paul's spiritual relationship to them as a father.

In his earlier letter Paul told the Corinthians that he was their father via the gospel (1 Cor. 4.15). In that context this statement is a method to get them to do his will, viz., to imitate him as children should imitate their parents. Thus, the Corinthians should be familiar with the use and meaning of Paul's metaphor. More pointedly in the next letter, Paul says he has opened his heart to them (ἡ καρδία ὑμῶν πεπλάτυνται, 2 Cor. 6.11b). He has not withheld his affection from them, but they have withheld theirs from him. Then v. 13 harks back to v. 11b: τὴν δὲ αὐτὴν ἀντιμισθίαν, ὡς τέκνοις λέγω, πλατύνθητε καὶ ὑμεῖς. Paul is explicitly requesting that the Corinthians make a return and give to him what he has given them.[40] Barrett comments: 'Paul appeals for a response; there is no apostolic authority by which he can compel it.'[41] Yet in the social context of Corinth this appeal will carry

---

[37] See Marshall, *Enmity*, 250–1, for the same line of reasoning with regard to this text.

[38] On parents as benefactors see pp. 48 and 73 above and the comments below on Phlm. 17–19 (pp. 185–91) and on 2 Cor. 6.13 following (pp. 172–3).

[39] On giving and receiving elevating or lowering social power, respectively, see Arist. *Eth. Nic.* 4.1.7; 4.3.24; Seneca *Ben.* 2.13.2; 2.33.1–2; 8.14.3–4; Plut. *Mor.* 808D; Sirach 7.27–8; Jos. *AJ* 4.266; Philo *Decal.* 166–7.

[40] Martin, *2 Corinthians*, 186.

weight, but only if they acknowledge what they have received from him (which they apparently had difficulty doing, 1 Cor. 4.7).[42] What neither Martin nor Barrett considers significant is the force of ὡς τέκνοις λέγω. According to Barrett, 'Paul may mean simply that he is speaking as he would to children.'[43] By referring to 1 Corinthians 4.14 and Galatians 4.19, however, Barrett apparently understands Paul to mean: 'I am speaking as I would to *my* children.'[44] Yet, we have two reasons to question such a view. First, this type of expression is common in Paul[45] and yields a different meaning. In 1 Corinthians he says οὐκ ἠδυνήθην λαλῆσαι ὑμῖν ὡς πνευματικοῖς ἀλλ' ὡς σαρκίνοις (3.1), ὡς φρονίμοις λέγω· κρίνατε ὑμεῖς ὅ φημι (10.15), and ὅτε ἤμην νήπιος, ἐλάλουν ὡς νήπιος (13.11); and all these convey the idea of how one speaks or even what one says. Second, elsewhere Paul prefers the pronoun when referring to his converts as his children.[46] Therefore, we suggest that understanding the phrase as: 'I am speaking as one would to children'[47] deserves more consideration. We have seen from Seneca that asking for a return on benefits is a very sensitive social act.[48] In accord with such a view, Paul states that speaking in such a way as to demand back a return for parental affection is speaking as one would to children.[49]

This understanding is strengthened by the language of reciprocity in the context. The apostle states that through the gospel he has

---

[41] C. K. Barrett, *A Commentary on the Second Epistle to the Corinthians* (London: A & C Black, repr., 1986): 192.

[42] According to Seneca it is a disgrace to have received greatly prized gifts yet to say one has not received them and is not in debt for them (*Ben.* 4.6.2–3).

[43] Barrett, *2 Corinthians*, 192.

[44] That is, what distinguishes this type of speech is its appropriateness to Paul's special filial relationship with the Corinthians.

[45] In parenthesis (BDF, par. 465.2): Rom. 3.5; 2 Cor. 11.21; also 2 Cor. 7.14; Gal. 3.16; 1 Thess. 2.4. The very similar κατὰ + Accus. + λέγω may bear the same meaning: 2 Cor 11.17; Gal. 3.15.

[46] Always with τέκνον in the plural (1 Cor. 4.14, 17; Gal. 4.19; 1 Thess. 2.11), with the singular in Phlm. 10 (but cf. 1 Tim. 1.2, 18; 2 Tim. 1.2; Tit. 1.4).

[47] That is, what distinguishes this type of speech is its appropriateness to children generally.

[48] See *Ben.* 2.11.1, 2.17.7, 5.25.1, cf. 6.27.2. In 1.1.3 Seneca asserts: 'It is not easy to say whether it is more shameful to repudiate a benefit or to ask the repayment of it.'

[49] There is still a further question to be asked, but unfortunately the context does not provide much evidence for an answer: is this an appropriate way to speak to children because they need to be taught reciprocity, because in their immaturity they neglect the responsibilities they have learned, or because it is *only* appropriate to ask repayment from *children*?

become the Corinthians' father; they owe their spiritual life, their new existence (cf. 2 Cor. 5.17), to him. Further, as a dutiful parent should, he has loved them and nurtured them. The reasonable response they should make in return for these great benefits is to give back the equivalent (ἀντιμισθίαν, v. 13a), to love him in return. This response is the discharge of a debt on their part. We have seen that according to first-century Jewish and Greco-Roman convention, children owe the greatest debt of gratitude to their parents.[50] It appears that Paul took very seriously his role as a spiritual parent to his converts. As such he was their benefactor and could require a return on his affection for them.[51]

This interpretation does not deny the filial relationship of Paul with the Corinthians. That relationship must be assumed and indeed would be assumed in light of 1 Corinthians 4.14–15. Rather, it asserts that ὡς refers to τέκνοις, not to an implied μοῦ.

In light of these texts from the Corinthian correspondence we see that Paul believes his reception of the gift offered by the Corinthians would create social dependence. His use of βαρέω and related words or concepts makes this clear. The apostle tells us why he avoided this social dependence. It was because, amongst other reasons, dependence would hinder the gospel, for this dependence would usurp his role as the giver in the relationship. Paul's approach is basically consistent: all is done with a studied consideration to see his choice of behaviour help the advance of the gospel.

This studied consideration is in harmony with our conclusions from Philippians. All language of social dependence on Paul's part is missing from the text of Philippians. Rather, Paul states that because of the Philippians' support, he has a unique relationship of giving and receiving with them. This relationship is partnership in the gospel (Phil. 1.5).

---

[50] See pp. 48, 73. According to Philo none can be more truly called benefactors than parents in relation to their children (*Spec.* 2.229; *Decal.* 112; cf. Arist. *Eth. Nic.* 8.11.1–4; Seneca *Ben.* 5.5.2; SelPap. 1.121.27–8 (2nd AD); Sir. 7.28 (LXX)).

[51] See further the comments on Phlm. 17–19 below. Register also contends, in part correctly, that by working for his living, thus giving the gospel freely, Paul was enabled to claim the honour due to a benefactor or patron, whereas if he had accepted patronage he would have been required to give that honour to the wealthy among the Corinthians (*Giving and Receiving*, 110; see his discussion, 109–12).

Romans 15.25–31: the collection[52]

Romans 15.25–31 is included in our study for three reasons. First, it demonstrates that Paul considers the gospel to be a gift which brings about an obligation of gratitude in the form of a material return. Secondly, this obligation is consistent with the less explicit language of Philippians, where no direct reference to obligation is made. Thirdly, the use of κοινωνίαν τινὰ ποιήσασθαι in 15.26 confirms our conclusion that Paul has a special relationship with the Philippians as a result of giving and receiving.

In Romans 15.25–9 Paul informs the church about his plans for the future. Currently he is on his way to Jerusalem with the collection (v. 25). The churches of Macedonia and Achaia have been pleased to send, through Paul, some financial aid to the saints in Jerusalem. Commentators are agreed that κοινωνίαν τινὰ ποιήσασθαι in v. 26 should be rendered 'make a contribution'.[53] Generally they follow Seesemann who asserts that the verb ποιήσασθαι forces us to take κοινωνία concretely, giving it the meaning 'contribution' or 'alms'.[54] Some commentators cite Bauer/Aland as support for their view that κοινωνία here means contribution.[55] In doing so, however, they have chosen to ignore the other rendering Bauer/Aland offer. In an earlier paragraph, Bauer/Aland offer this translation of Romans 15.26: 'sie haben sich vorgenommen, e. enges Gemeinschaftsverhältnis herzustellen mit d. Armen.'[56] It is surprising that this alternative rendering has been virtually ignored by scholars.[57]

---

[52] The following material is a slightly revised version of the author's 'Romans 15.26: Make a Contribution or Establish Fellowship?' *NTS* 40 (1994): 457–63.

[53] E.g., Cranfield, *Romans*, 772; James D. G. Dunn, *Romans 9–16* (Dallas: Word, 1988): 875; Otto Michel, *Der Brief an die Römer* (Göttingen: Vandenhoeck & Ruprecht, 5., bearbeitete Auflage, 1977): 461, 464 n. 9; John Ziesler, *Paul's Letter to the Romans* (London: SCM Press, 1989): 345. The translation of Ulrich Wilckens, 'eine Gemeinschaftsaktion zu veranstalten für die Armen', is not essentially different (*Der Brief an die Römer*, 3 vols. (Zürich: Benziger, 1982) 3: 123).

[54] Seesemann, *KOINΩNIA*, 29. Seesemann is followed by Hauck, 'κοινωνός', 808, and Keith P. Nickle, *The Collection: A Study in Paul's Strategy* (London: SCM Press, 1966): 124 n. 204; cf. Hainz, *KOINONIA*, 145 n. 121.

[55] E.g., Dunn, *Romans*, 875; Leon Morris, *The Epistle to the Romans* (Grand Rapids: Eerdmans, 1988): 520 n. 129; cf. Bauer/Aland, *Wörterbuch*, 'κοινωνία', para. 3.

[56] Bauer/Aland, *Wörterbuch*, 'κοινωνία', para. 1

[57] Substantially the same alternative translation is offered by Bauer as far back as

Bauer/Aland's alternative rendering has much more to commend it than is commonly recognized. For, in our view, scholars have overlooked the social significance of the construction κοινωνίαν τινὰ ποιήσασθαι in Romans 15.26.[58] We suggest that there are several good arguments in favour of understanding κοινωνίαν ποιήσασθαι as 'to establish fellowship'. The reasons are as follows.

Greco-Roman social convention

We have already seen above that the social practice of Paul's day employed benefaction to create and maintain interpersonal relationships.[59] Here we briefly summarize some of the evidence presented earlier.

According to Seneca it is kindness that establishes friendships. For the giving of a benefit should gain the goodwill of the recipient. Consequently, it is possible to make someone a friend by doing him a service. Since only the wise man knows how to bestow a benefit properly (*Ep.* 81.10–11), the wise man is a master in the art of making friendships (*Ep.* 9.5).[60]

Seneca is not the only writer who tells us of the usefulness of money in establishing friendships. This social practice can be seen as far back as Homer (*Od.* 21.31–41) and other subsequent authors as well.[61]

The language of Romans 15.26 is consistent with the commonly received view of the Greco-Roman world that giving was a way to establish a relationship with someone.

---

the second edition of his *Wörterbuch* (Walter Bauer, *Griechische-Deutsches Wörterbuch zu den Schriften des Neuen Testaments und der übrigen urchristlichen Literatur* (Gießen: Töpelmann, 1928): para. 1): 'sie haben sich vorgenommen, e. Art engen Verhältnisses herzustellen zu d. Armen'. Yet, to our knowledge only Keck mentions the rendering, calling it 'a masterpiece of ambiguity' (Leander E. Keck, 'The Poor among the Saints in Jerusalem', *ZNW* 56 (1965): 119 n. 65). Likewise none of the major translations (e.g., NIV, NASB, NEB, RSV, JB, AV) even inform the reader of any alternative rendering.

[58] No social significance is mentioned by Cranfield, Dunn, Käsemann, Keck, Michel, Morris, Wilckens, Zeller, Ziesler, Georgi, Nickle or Seesemann.

[59] See pp. 66–7 above; Marshall, *Enmity*, 1–23; Mott, 'Giving and Receiving'.

[60] Motto, *Seneca Sourcebook*, 89.

[61] E.g., Thuc. 2.40; Dio Cass. 48.16.3, Arr. *Epict. Diss.* 2.22.34, Plut. *Sull.* 3.1.

Romans 15.26 in context

In Romans 15.27 Paul makes clear the obligation of the Gentiles toward the Jews. This mention of obligation reflects the language of social reciprocity which is fundamental to the Greco-Roman world.[62] The Gentiles, because they have shared spiritual things from the saints in Jerusalem, are debtors (ὀφειλέται) to return material things. In short, because the Gentiles have received, they must give.

Few scholars refer to the fact that the collection is a social debt; that it is the required return of thanks for sharing in spiritual things.[63] Cranfield rightly says that 'the idea of obligation to someone on account of a benefit received from that person is definitely involved'.[64] Unfortunately, however, Cranfield does not discuss social reciprocity nor does he provide any texts to illustrate his point. Nevertheless, his observation is a good one, for we have seen above that material gratitude was the expected result of benefits in Greco-Roman society.[65] Seneca asserts that 'not to return gratitude for benefits is a disgrace and the whole world counts it as such' (3.1.1). When a person receives a benefit it is considered a social obligation to show gratitude.[66] This gratitude is primarily displayed in a counter gift or favour.

Sampley offers a different social context for the collection. According to Sampley, Paul understands his meeting with the Jerusalem pillars to end in a *societas*.[67] He has a formal obligation to take up the collection for the poor in Jerusalem. 'The force of the agreement constituted in the Jerusalem *societas* may be tested in the Pauline corpus . . . The same Paul who has boasted of preaching a gospel free of charge (1 Corinthians 9: 18) returns to his converts and attempts to take up a collection. One can imagine the consternation. Some misunderstand. Others oppose . . . Despite all this Paul persists. Remembering the poor is not an option for Paul.'[68]

---

[62] Register, *Giving and Receiving*, 105.

[63] See, e.g., Ernst Käsemann, *An die Römer* (4., durchgesehene Auflage; Tübingen: J. C. B. Mohr, 1980): 385; We note that mention of the collection as a debt of thanks is lacking in Dodd, Dunn, Michel and Morris.

[64] Cranfield, *Romans*, 773.   [65] See pp. 68–71 above.

[66] Conzelmann, 'εὐχαριστέω', *TDNT*, 9: 407.

[67] Sampley, *Partnership*, 27–32. See pp. 123–7 for our response to Sampley's views on Philippians.

[68] Sampley, *Partnership*, 35.

We must beware of arguments from silence, but when Paul discusses the collection directly, *societas* never enters the picture. In the context of Romans, social debt is the only reason Paul gives for the collection. Social debt is not mentioned in Paul's lengthy discussion of the collection in 2 Corinthians 8–9, and understandably so. For in 2 Corinthians Paul addresses those whom he is encouraging to engage in the offering.[69] Mention of debt to them could well be socially awkward.[70] But nevertheless, also absent from Corinthians is any talk of debt on Paul's part. The reasons he gives there are the blessing of God on the givers, the proof of the Corinthians' love in relieving the saints and the thanksgiving which will accrue to God (2 Cor. 9.10–14).[71] Paul's reason is not based on a Roman *societas* but on the general social convention of giving and receiving. Sampley refers briefly to Paul's assertion that the collection is a debt owed by the Gentiles, but sees no conflict with it also being an obligation on Paul.[72]

The emphasis in Romans 15.26–7 on the free giving of the Macedonians and Achaians does not militate against the view that the gift is a social debt.[73] Besides the fact that the apostle, with no apparent discomfort, can put εὐδόκησαν and ὀφειλέται side by side, we also have the comments of Seneca who asserts that the return is a social obligation (3.1.1) and nevertheless should be given willingly (1.4.2–3; cf. Arist. *Eth. Nic.* 8.13.8).

Though the elements of the discussion overlap quite a bit here, we have seen in the section above that gratitude for benefits received is an expected social convention. Ingratitude is seen as a heinous social evil. In light of these observations Paul's words to the Romans take on fresh significance.

---

[69] Whether or not Paul intended to extend his collection efforts to the Romans is debated. In any case, he does not explicitly solicit the participation of the Romans. See A. J. M. Wedderburn, *The Reasons for Romans* (Edinburgh: T & T Clark, 1988): 70–5.

[70] Likewise, in 2 Corinthians no mention is made of the collection failing as in Rom. 15.31.

[71] See our discussion on 2 Cor. 8.4 and 9.12–14 below.

[72] Sampley, *Partnership*, 32.

[73] *Contra* Nickle, who asserts with regard to the Corinthians: 'Only if their participation was a free act of Christian love could their gift be a vehicle for the blessings of God' (*The Collection*, 122).

The semantic range of κοινωνία

The rendering 'make a contribution' gives κοινωνία a rare, if not unknown, concrete sense. Certainly κοινωνία figures in many financial contexts, but such placement is not to be equated with a concrete sense for the term.

First, as we saw above, in the Greco-Roman world κοινωνία implied financial sharing. The mere passing of money between two people, however, does not imply κοινωνία. Κοινωνία labels a wide range of relationships in the ancient world.[74]

Secondly, examples of a concrete sense for extra-biblical instances of κοινωνία are yet to be found. Dunn asserts that our construction (κοινωνίαν τινὰ ποιήσασθαι) would not be strange to a Greek speaker, citing for support Liddell/Scott/Jones.[75] LSJ, however, provide no examples of the construction. They assert that κοινωνία can have the meaning contribution or alms, citing Romans 15.26, Hebrews 13.16 and a second-century inscription discussed by Rostowzew.[76] In this inscription (post AD 161), however, κοινωνία is not used with ποιέω, nor can it have the meaning 'contribution'. Rather it designates Pogla as without its own city government. Pogla has only the κοινωνία, the constitution of a κοινόν, in relationship with the imperial government.[77]

Thirdly, Hebrews 13.16 also employs κοινωνία in the context of financial sharing. The author says that εὐποιΐα and κοινωνία are sacrifices which are pleasing to God (v. 16b).[78] Εὐποιΐα should be understood as the doing of good, namely, beneficence.[79] Κοινωνία, however, need not be understood as alms, but as generosity.[80] This generosity entails financial sharing, but that is not to be equated

---

74 W. Popkes, 'Gemeinschaft', *RAC* 9 (1976): 1100–45.

75 Dunn, *Romans*, 875.

76 Liddell/Scott/Jones, 'κοινωνία', III.1.; cf. M. Rostowzew, 'Die Domäne von Pogla', *Jahreshefte des österreichischen archäologischen Instituts in Wien* 4 (1900): beiblatt 37–46.

77 Rostowzew, 'Die Domäne', 39.

78 Cf. Phil. 4.18, where the Philippians' financial support of Paul is called ὀσμὴν εὐωδίας, θυσίαν δεκτήν, εὐάρεστον τῷ θεῷ. Benevolence is considered a sacrifice among the fathers as well, e.g., Polycarp *Ep. Phil.* 4.3; Hermas *Sim.* 5.3.3, 7–8; 2 Clement 16.4. On the spiritualization of sacrifice see Ferguson, 'Spiritual Sacrifice', 1151–89.

79 E.g., Lucian *Abd.* 25. Also 'to do good' (εὖ ποιεῖν) often refers to the social act of benefiting another (cf. Mark 14.7; Arist. *Eth. Nic.* 4.1.7, 4.3.24, 8.12.5; Plato *Rep.* 332D; Xen. *Mem.* 2.3.8; M. Aur. 7.73).

80 William L. Lane, *Hebrews 9–13* (Dallas: Word, 1991): 552.

with a concrete sense for κοινωνία. Since εὐποιΐα and κοινωνία share the same article, it is best to view both as activities, rather than a concrete sense for κοινωνία being linked so closely in thought with the abstract εὐποιΐα.

Fourthly, likewise, κοινωνία does not have a concrete meaning elsewhere in Paul. Scholars commenting on Romans 15.26 frequently cite two examples (2 Cor. 8.4, 9.13).[81] Though these texts certainly contain κοινωνία in the context of discussion about the collection, nevertheless κοινωνία is not used concretely, but retains the meaning of fellowship or sharing.

In 2 Corinthians 8.4, κοινωνία is the object of the verb δεόμενοι. The Macedonians requested from Paul that they might have *participation* in the collection, here called service to the saints. The implication is that Paul had not solicited their support, but rather they sought to take part on their own (αὐθαίρετοι, v. 3b). Here κοινωνία cannot be understood concretely.

In 2 Corinthians 9.13, though κοινωνία may be understood to mean 'financial sharing', it does not have the concrete sense of 'alms.'[82] Our decision on κοινωνία is partially determined by the meaning given to ἁπλότης. Scholars debate whether ἁπλότης can have the meaning generosity.[83] But it certainly does have that meaning here. For in 9.11, it is generosity, and not simplicity, which results from enrichment and produces thanksgiving.[84] If the generosity of the Corinthians' contribution is meant, then the cause for thanks lies in the amount of the collection, which does not seem to be the apostle's point. Rather, Paul stresses that the fact of their contribution is a service which yields thanksgiving to God. Further, the final part of v. 13 is more difficult if κοινωνία is taken as concrete. Are we to understand that thanks will arise because of

---

[81] Cranfield, *Romans*, 772; Dunn, *Romans*, 875; Wilckens, *Römer*, 125.

[82] See H. D. Betz, *2 Corinthians 8 and 9* (Philadelphia: Fortress Press, 1985): 122–5 for discussion on possible legal background to the terminology in 2 Cor. 9.13–14. Betz asserts that κοινωνία in Gal. 2.9; Phil. 1.5, 4.14–15; 2 Cor. 9.13 and Rom. 15.26 has a legal meaning. Although such a meaning is possible, Betz provides no argumentation to prove that these texts have a legal context.

[83] The possibility is rejected by Joseph Amstutz, *ΑΠΛΟΤΗΣ: Eine begriffs-geschichtliche Studie zum jüdisch-christlichen Griechisch* (Bonn: P. Hanstein, 1968): 103–11; Karl Prümm, *Diakonia Pneumatos. Theologie des zweiter Korintherbriefes. Zweiter Teil: Das christliches Werk. Die apostolische Macht* (Rome: Herder, 1962): 40–3; H. Bacht, 'Einfalt', *RAC* 4 (1959): 828–30.

[84] Betz, *2 Corinthians 8 and 9*, 116; Martin, *2 Corinthians*, 292; cf. Otto Bauernfeind, 'ἁπλοῦς, ἁπλότης', *TDNT*, 1.387.

the Corinthians' generosity in their *contribution(s)* toward (εἰς) the saints in Jerusalem and toward all (others)? Or does it arise because of the generosity of the special Christian relationship which they have with them and with all? The later of these is preferable and argues for an abstract meaning for κοινωνία.

Fifthly, the argument that the presence of ποιεώ forces us to take κοινωνία as concrete is manifestly false.[85] Although the construction κοινωνίαν ποιήσασθαι is rare we have found no instance where it should be understood as 'make a contribution'. On the other hand, we do find it in Polybius 5.35.1 and Plato *Rep.* 371B5–6 with the sense of creating fellowship.[86]

Polybius says that Cleomenes the Spartan had established a relationship (ἐποιήσατο τὴν κοινωνίαν τῶν πραγμάτων) with Ptolemy Euergetes. He did this with the constant belief that he would receive help from Ptolemy to recover the throne. Here our construction occurs in the context of social reciprocity and κοινωνία clearly has an abstract meaning.

In the dialogue of Plato, Socrates asserts that sharing with one another the products of labour is the very reason why, by establishing fellowship, the city is founded (ὧν δὴ ἕνεκα καὶ κοινωνίαν ποιησάμενοι πόλιν ᾠκίσαμεν). We are not required to discern the precise relationship between the participle and the finite verb in order for us to see that κοινωνία here in *Rep.* 371B5–6 need not be understood concretely.

Furthermore, a very similar construction, φιλίαν ποιήσασθαι, is slightly more common.[87] Certainly this construction does not force us to understand φιλίαν as concrete. In many examples that may be cited, φιλίαν has the abstract meaning 'friendship'. Therefore, as a syntactical argument, there is no good reason to insist that the verb ποιεῖν in Romans 15.26 forces us to understand κοινωνία concretely.

The purpose of the collection

As many scholars have recognized, Paul sees the collection, at least in part, as an attempt to *establish* fellowship or unity between the

---

85 *Contra* Nickle, *Collection*, 124 n. 204; following Seesemann, *ΚΟΙΝΩΝΙΑ*, 28, 67 and Hauck, 'κοινωνός', 809.
86 Compare also κοινωνίαν ἐργαζόμενον, Plut. *Mor.* 957A.
87 See, e.g., Polyb. 21.30.4; Plut. *Thes.* 30.2, *Rom.* 23.5, 25.4, *Sol.* 5.1–2; Josephus *AJ* 5.55, 7.107, 12.414, 13.259, 269, 14.10; *BJ* 1.38.

Jewish and Gentile portions of the church.[88] Our alternative rendering would fit well in this scheme.

First, the apostle does not state clearly the goal of the collection in 2 Corinthians. There are, however, texts from which the goal can be implied.

In 8.13 Paul contends that he does not mean the collection to entail relief for Jerusalem and hardship for the Corinthians. Rather, he declares it is a matter of equality. This reference to equality evokes ideas of reciprocity which are further seen in v. 14: the Corinthians' current abundance can supply the Jerusalem Christians' lack in order that the Corinthians' subsequent lack may be provided by the Jerusalem Christians' abundance. Several scholars rightly have questioned the likelihood that a material lack at Corinth could ever be relieved by the generosity of the church in Jerusalem. Thus the thought appears to be parallel to Romans 15.27: there is a material response to spiritual goods. The Corinthians, despite their spiritual wealth, may still receive blessings from Jerusalem. These Gentile Christians should give, therefore, in order that there might be a reciprocal relationship of giving and receiving.

Perhaps further reasons for the collection are seen in 2 Corinthians 9.12–14. First, the collection fills the needs of the saints. This statement requires no explanation. Secondly, the collection produces thanksgiving to God (9.12b). Paul explains this statement in v. 13: God will be glorified because of the Corinthians' obedience to the confession of the gospel and because of their generosity of sharing (ἁπλότητι τῆς κοινωνίας). In this context it is the Church at Jerusalem which praises God. If they indeed utter praise for obedience to the gospel, it is implied that they have acknowledged the Gentiles' reception of that Gospel. In short, they confess Christian fellowship between the Gentile and the Jewish portions of the church.

Secondly, we can see a further purpose for the collection in Romans. There Paul is very concerned that the collection be acceptable to the saints (15.31b).[89] The implication is that Jeru-

---

[88] F. C. Baur, 'Beiträge zur Erklärung der Korinthierbriefe', *Theologische Jahrbücher* 9 (1850): 181–2; Nickle, *Collection*, 119, 122 n. 188, 124; Betz, *2 Corinthians 8 and 9*, 123–4; Martin, *2 Corinthians*, 251, 257.

[89] This concern is most consistent with the view that Paul's collection is not to be wholly connected with aid requested by the Jerusalem church in Gal. 2.10 (Wedderburn, *Reasons*, 39; *contra* Sampley, *Partnership*, 30–1).

salem's acceptance of the collection is crucial and rejection of it would imply a breach between the mother church of Judea and Paul's congregations.[90] Achtemeier comments that, 'If the church in Jerusalem accepted the offering, it would be an acknowledgment that just as they have rightfully received a share of the material blessing of the gentiles so the gentiles have rightfully received a share of the spiritual blessings of Israel . . . that they are mutually indebted to one another and are on an equal footing within the people of God.'[91] To put Achtemeier's words another way, acceptance implies a special relationship.

Partnership in Philippians

We have seen from Paul's letter to the Philippians that a special relationship was created between the apostle and this church as a result of their offering and the apostle accepting financial support. We need only summarize our findings here.[92]

Paul employs two phrases in Philippians which are unique to the New Testament. First, he mentions partnership in the gospel (κοινωνία εἰς τὸ εὐαγγέλιον, 1.5). He and the Philippians work together in the advance of the gospel.[93] Second, when Paul comes to give a concrete response to the Philippians' gifts, he mentions that no other church entered into giving and receiving with him (ἐκοινώνησεν εἰς λόγον δόσεως καὶ λήμψεως, 4.15). This phrase points up the importance of reciprocity in their relationship.

We should add one last observation on the nature of this relationship. It was not simply Paul's giving the gospel to them which has caused this relationship to be formed. Rather, it is his giving, their receiving, their giving in return and finally his acceptance of their return which has established their partnership in the gospel. We see this same pattern of events depicted in Romans 15.26. The gospel has gone out from Jerusalem. The Gentiles have received. But κοινωνία has not been established merely as a result of these two events. The last links in the process are the return which the Gentiles owe and the acceptance of this return by the church in Jerusalem. The giving of the Gentiles, therefore, fits into

---

[90] Dunn, *Romans*, 879; Wedderburn, *Reasons*, 41.
[91] Paul J. Achtemeier, *Romans* (Atlanta: John Knox Press, 1985): 230–1.
[92] See pp. 91–107, 144–52 above.
[93] *Contra* Seesemann, *KOINΩNIA*, 74. On εὐαγγέλιον as an *nomen actionis* in Philippians see O'Brien, 'The Gospel in Philippians', 213–33.

this scheme as an *attempt* to establish fellowship. We can see that it is an attempt which Paul is very concerned to see succeed (15.31).

The significance of τινά

If we can proceed on the assumption that κοινωνίαν ποιήσασθαι should best be understood as 'to establish fellowship', we need now ask what is the function of τινά: the Macedonians and Achaians have been pleased to establish a *certain* fellowship with the poor among the saints in Jerusalem. Many scholars pass over τινά with little or no comment.[94]

If κοινωνία is understood concretely, what is the significance of the certain contribution? Käsemann asserts that τινά weakens the force of κοινωνία: it does not involve a fixed sum.[95] Such an explanation for τινά finds no support in the context, yet it is hard to avoid Käsemann's assertion if one accepts a concrete meaning for κοινωνία. What is a certain type of alms? Hainz asserts that τινά restricts the fellowship being referred to, in contrast to the unrestricted fellowship expected by Jerusalem.[96] Certainly τινά does function to restrict the meaning of κοινωνία, but that τινά refers to the expectation of the Jerusalem church is also not found in the context.

On the other hand, if κοινωνία is allowed to have its more natural meaning as fellowship or association, the problem is solved. The Macedonians and Achaians have chosen to establish fellowship with the saints in Jerusalem, but it is fellowship of a certain kind; it is a fellowship which the Romans should be informed of at this point. It is a fellowship in giving and receiving; material goods given for spiritual goods. It is a fellowship which acknowledges the debt of the Gentiles toward the Jews for the spiritual things they have enjoyed.

The qualifier τινά could be inserted for the purpose of drawing attention to Paul's designation of the goods exchanged in the fellowship. The creating of friendship through the giving of goods or favours was an integral part of a Roman's life. But the κοινωνία being established through the collection must not be understood in purely social terms.

---

94 No explanation is offered by Cranfield, Dodd, Dunn, Michel, Morris, Schlier or Wilckens.
95 Käsemann, *Römer*, 385.   96 Hainz, *KOINONIA*, 147.

In light of the above discussion Bauer's rendering of Romans 15.26 does not appear to be such a 'masterpiece of ambiguity' after all.[97] Rather, the social context of giving and receiving, and particularly the practice of creating relationships through the giving of a gift, suggests that Bauer's alternate rendering has much to commend it.

This text supports our conclusions drawn from Philippians. First, we see that a gift of money is understood to play a significant role in the establishment of a relationship. In the case of Paul and the Philippians and in the case of Jerusalem and the Gentiles, the gospel has been the initial gift which has initiated the relationship. But in both cases the material return has been called for. Secondly, Paul has adapted the social metaphor for his theological and missionary purposes.

Philemon 17–19: commercial terms

From our study of Philemon 17–19 we hope to show, first, that Paul considers the gospel a gift which brings obligations on the part of the receiver, as we saw especially in Romans 15.26, but also implicitly in Philippians 4.15. Second, Paul uses this obligation when he believes it will help advance the gospel. Here the advance of the gospel is taken more broadly to refer to the living out of the message in the life of one receiver: Philemon.

Although some details of the circumstances surrounding this letter are hard to discern, in general the historical situation is easy to reconstruct. Onesimus has fled from his master.[98] Paul has met up with the slave while in prison, and, as a result of the apostle's witness, Onesimus has become Paul's child in the faith (v. 10).[99]

---

97 *Contra* Keck, 'The Poor', 119 n. 65.

98 Whether Onesimus should be classed as a *fugitivus* is debated. Some scholars believe that Onesimus was not a runaway slave (J. Knox, *Philemon among the Letters of Paul* (Chicago: University Press, 1935): 10; S. Winter, 'Paul's Letter to Philemon', *NTS* 33 (1987): 1–15). John G. Nordling ('Onesimus Fugitivus: A Defense of the Runaway Slave Hypothesis in Philemon', *JSNT* 41 (1991): 97–119) offers a defence of the traditional view that Onesimus was a *fugitivus* in the light of extra-biblical sources. On balance the best view is given by Peter Lampe ('Keine "Sklavenflucht" des Onesimus', *ZNW* 76 (1985): 135–7), who argues cogently that Onesimus did not run away, but sought out Paul, as a friend of Philemon, to act as a mediator between himself and his estranged master. See further defence of this view by B. M. Rapske, 'The Prisoner Paul in the Eyes of Onesimus', *NTS* 37 (1989): 187–203.

99 For a discussion of begetting a convert in Jewish literature see J. Duncan M. Derrett, 'The Functions of the Epistle to Philemon', *ZNW* 79 (1988): 63–91;

Paul must send the slave back to his master. Here the problem arises: Onesimus may face severe punishment. This the apostle wants to prevent. As a result, we have this letter to the master, a tactful yet forcible bit of social coercion.[100]

We will pass quickly over the early parts of the letter. It is certainly significant that the apostle addresses the letter not only to Philemon, but also to the church which meets in his home (v. 2). Thus Paul makes a personal letter an embarrassingly public one.[101] For the public reading of the letter will mean that the coercion contained in it will be doubly effective. If Philemon does not carry out Paul's request, he will feel the social pressure exerted by the others.[102]

Paul makes an emphatic recount of Philemon's past benevolence and mercy in refreshing the hearts of the saints (v. 7). He will return to this language in v. 20. In the immediate context this rehearsal is put as the basis on which he now makes his appeal rather than a command (v. 8). Philemon has already been in the habit of doing good and so the good about to be requested of him will not be out of keeping with his habit. Nevertheless, by merely making reference to the fact that Paul might command Philemon's compliance, he exerts great pressure on him to comply, perhaps even more than a command itself. For this exhortation and appeal is ostentatiously based on Philemon's good service in the past. If Philemon fails, he calls into question Paul's encomium on his record of good.

By referring to Onesimus taking Philemon's place in service to Paul (v. 13), the apostle implies two things: first, that it would be considered proper for Philemon, despite his probable high social status,[103] to serve Paul as the mere slave Onesimus is doing.

David Daube, 'Onesimus', *Christians among Jews and Gentiles*, ed. G. Nickelsburg and G. MacRae (Philadelphia: Fortress Press, 1986): 40–3.

[100] Norman R. Petersen, *Rediscovering Paul: Philemon and the Sociology of Paul's Narrative World* (Philadelphia: Fortress Press, 1985): 99.

[101] Derrett, 'Functions', 66; Stuhlmacher, *Philemon*, 24; cf. U. Wickert, 'Der Philemonbrief – Privatbrief oder apostolisches Schreiben?' *ZNW* 52 (1961): 230–8, who asserts that canonical Philemon is not a private letter, but an open apostolic message concerning a particular person.

[102] Stuhlmacher, *Philemon*, 24.

[103] The scholarly consensus recognizes Philemon as well-to-do because the Christians there are meeting in his house (e.g., Lohse, *Colossians and Philemon*, 186; Stuhlmacher, *Philemon*, 20, citing F. V. Filson, 'The Significance of the Early House Churches', *JBL* 58 (1939): 111. See also J. Gnilka's excursus, 'Haus, Familie und Hausgemeinde', in *Der Philemonbrief* (Freiburg: Herder, 1982): 17–33).

Second, that Philemon may be properly considered in debt to Paul for a service.

At this point we come to the primary pericope of our interest. We divide our comments into three sections.

The request: v. 17

The exact request which the apostle has for Philemon finally appears in v. 17: Philemon should receive Onesimus back as he would receive Paul.[104] Beginning here there is a high degree of identification between the apostle and the slave.[105]

Paul bases his request on his relationship as partner to Philemon. If Philemon considers Paul to be his partner then he should receive the slave as he would Paul (v. 17).[106] The nature of this partnership is not defined explicitly for us here. But in light of Paul's addressing Philemon as συνεργός (v. 1), we take it to be partnership in the work of the gospel.[107] Compare the same type of partnership referred to in 2 Corinthians 8.23. Titus is Paul's partner, in that he is a co-worker and partaker in, not only personal faith, but also service in spreading the gospel.

Now if Philemon considers Paul his partner in the work of the gospel, then he should do more than the mere negative act of cancelling Onesimus' indebtedness (v. 18). Positively, he should receive Onesimus as he would receive Paul himself (v. 17).[108]

Thus far Paul has mentioned two relationships which could ground his request. First, he refers to his position of authority to command (v. 8). Ostensibly he renounces this method. Second, he has referred to the partnership he has with Philemon and the relationship of equality which they have as fellow-workers in the gospel. He holds firmly to this position in his request. There is a further category in the next two verses.

---

[104] F. F. Bruce further asserts that Paul intends Philemon to send Onesimus back to be the apostle's helper ('St Paul in Rome, II: The Epistle to Philemon', *BJRL* 48 (1965–6): 81–97). We consider this interpretation too conjectural.

[105] Stuhlmacher, *Philemon*, 49.

[106] Notice the necessary connection between being κοινωνοί and the giving and receiving of favours (cf. Arist. *Eth. Nic.* 5.5.6; 5.5.14: οὔτε γὰρ ἂν μὴ οὔσης ἀλλαγῆς κοινωνία ἦν).

[107] Cf. P. T. O'Brien, *Colossians, Philemon* (Waco: Word, 1982): 299: 'κοινωνός in this context may have the added nuance of "co-worker"'.

[108] J. D. Pentecost, 'Studies in Philemon. Part IV: Charge That to My Account', *BSac* 130 (1973): 56.

Verses 18–19

It is at this point that Paul supports his request by referring to the relationship of social reciprocity existing between himself and Philemon. He urges Philemon, if Onesimus has wronged him or owes him anything (εἰ δέ τι ἠδίκησέν σε ἢ ὀφείλει), to charge that to Paul's account (τοῦτο ἐμοὶ ἐλλόγα, v. 18). Whether or not Onesimus had actually stolen from his master is not important for our purpose.[109] We are not concerned with these words as they apply to Onesimus, but as they apply to the apostle and the slave owner.

Martin asserts that the terms used in Philemon 18 (ὀφείλω and ἐλλογέω) are technical.[110] They refer to commercial business. Unfortunately, Martin relies on the evidence provided by Hauck and Preisker,[111] and does not provide evidence from the primary sources. Though primarily concerned with the rhetorical use of these terms, and therefore not with their social significance, Martin nevertheless errs because her reconstruction is based on false conclusions regarding ὀφείλω and ἐλλογέω.[112] From what we have seen above, terms like these, when used in social contexts, need not be understood commercially.[113] They can be used to refer to social reciprocity. Indeed, ἐλλογέω is so rare as to make us question the ubiquitous reference to it as a commercial technical term.[114]

Similarly, scholars assert that ἀποτίνω is a legal, technical term

---

[109] See the balanced discussion in O'Brien, *Colossians, Philemon*, 299–300. Pentecost asserts that no slave could have saved enough to pay for travel from Colossae to Rome and concludes that Onesimus must have stolen at least this amount ('Studies in Philemon. Part IV', 51). An Ephesian imprisonment would alter this requirement.

[110] Clarice J. Martin, 'The Rhetorical Use of Commercial Language in Paul's Letter to Philemon (Verse 18)', *Persuasive Artistry. Studies in New Testament Rhetoric in Honour of George A. Kennedy*, ed. Duane F. Watson (Sheffield: JSOT Press, 1991): 321–37; White, 'Social Authority', 218: 'Paul finally resorts to an economic metaphor (vss. 18–20) to cajole Philemon into compliance.'

[111] Hauck, 'ὀφείλω', *TDNT*, 5.559–66 and Preisker, 'ἐλλογέω', *TDNT*, 2.516–17.

[112] In addition to her rhetorical conclusions, Martin errs (following Meeks, *First Urban*, 66–7) in asserting that these terms suggest an ethos where artisans, merchants and persons with some economic assets were possibly the rule rather than the exception (*Rhetorical Use*, 322). From the presence of terms commonly found in commercial contexts one cannot draw conclusions regarding the person's vocation, for we have seen that such terms often refer to relationships of social reciprocity.

[113] See pp. 47–8, 63–4 above.

[114] E.g., Bauer/Aland, *Wörterbuch*, 509; O'Brien, *Colossians, Philemon*, 300; Stuhlmacher, *Philemon*, 49, n. 120; Preisker, 'ἐλλογέω', *TDNT*, 2.516–17.

referring to damages or compensation paid.[115] Again, scholars have relied most heavily on the evidence of selected papyri, and on the work of each other, rather than on the actual use of the term in a range of primary sources. Ἀποτίνω also occurs in literary sources in the context of social reciprocity. For example, Plutarch, in his discussion of self praise, asserts that even the flatterers and those who are socially dependent on the powerful find it hard to stomach the self praise of the rich. Such is a high price to pay for their support.[116] In a speech to his native country, Dio Chrysostom responds to the honours that are proposed for him. He mentions the honours already conveyed to his family and ancestors and then asserts: 'I feel that I myself owe you the thanks for these honours, and I pray the gods that I may be able to discharge the debt' (*Or.* 44.4).[117]

According to Petersen, 'the metaphor of debt is peculiar to' Philemon.[118] From what we have seen above this is not quite correct. Paul does employ talk of debt elsewhere.[119] Yet we can certainly say that in Philemon the metaphor is used more strongly than anywhere else. This letter is certainly a conspicuous example of the use of social pressure to gain the desired action.[120] Moreover, here Paul implicitly calls on Philemon to return a benefit.[121] We consider this letter to be a masterpiece of tact, but one which uses a high degree of social force. Paul is not heavy handed or crass. Nevertheless, his arguments taken together are extremely powerful from a social point of view.[122]

Now we recall that in his request Paul appeals to his relationship

---

[115] Bauer/Aland, *Wörterbuch*, 203; Stuhlmacher, *Philemon*, 50; O'Brien, *Colossians, Philemon*, 300; Wolfgang Schenk, 'Der Brief des Paulus an Philemon in der neueren Forschung', *ANRW* II.25.4: 3476 n.86.

[116] καὶ συμβολὰς ταύτας ἀποτίνειν μεγίστας λέγουσιν, *Mor.* 547B; cf. 1087A.

[117] καὶ οἶμαι τὰς ὑπὲρ τούτων χάριτας αὐτὸς ὑμῖν ὀφείλειν, καὶ εὔχομαι τοῖς θεοῖς ἱκανὸς γενέσθαι ἀποτίνειν; cf. Dionysius Hal. 4.9.3; 11.3.1.

[118] Petersen, *Rediscovering Paul*, 128.

[119] See our comments on 2 Cor. 6.13 and Rom. 15.27, pp. 172–4 and 177–8 respectively.

[120] Petersen, *Rediscovering Paul*, 99. *Contra* Derrett, who considers Paul's talk of debt to be 'playful' ('Functions', 85). Compare similar criticisms of commentators on Phil. 4.15 who considered Paul's language there to be 'humorous' (e.g., O'Brien, *Philippians*, 540; Silva, *Philippians*, 238).

[121] We recall Seneca's claim that asking for a return on benefits is only to be done in rare circumstances (1.1.3; 2.11.1, 2.17.7, 5.25.1).

[122] These observations lend support to Houlden's view that Philemon was a 'rather fiery character' (J. L. Houlden, *Paul's Letters from Prison* (Harmondsworth: Penguin, 1970): 226). For Paul uses an unusually high degree of social pressure on him to achieve the desired end.

with Philemon. If Philemon considers Paul to be his partner, then he should receive the slave as he would Paul (v. 17). If the slave owes anything to Philemon, Philemon should charge that to Paul's account, which the apostle himself will repay (vv. 18–19a). But Paul should not have to remind Philemon that he owes the apostle his very self (σεαυτόν μοι προσοφείλεις).[123] How did it come about that Philemon owes Paul so much? Doubtless it is because, as a convert of the apostle, Philemon is indebted to Paul's spiritual benefits.[124]

In this context the apostle already referred to Onesimus' relationship to him as his child, a relationship which has come about because the slave was converted through Paul's preaching. With this passing remark Paul sparks Philemon's memory. The owner has the same relationship with Paul as the slave since he has also been converted under the preaching of the apostle.[125] Thus, as a beneficiary, Philemon owes a great deal to Paul, and he owes this debt in a way that Paul considers to be very real.[126]

Scholars are wont to refer to Onesimus' literal debt to Philemon and Philemon's metaphorical debt to Paul.[127] Though we understand the distinction being drawn, we must not assert that because Philemon's debt to Paul is metaphorical it is any less real. Paul certainly is wrestling with the problem of reconciling his brotherly role as an equal with his other role as a superior. But we should not conclude, as Petersen does, that at v. 15 he began to see a new way of dealing with the problem by using the idea of obligation (debt).[128] We have seen elsewhere that Paul can view himself as a

---

[123] In his discussion of Phil. 4.15 Gnilka notes the similarity of debt metaphor in that verse and Phlm. 19 (*Philipperbrief*, 178 n. 142) but makes no reference to the Greco-Roman background.

[124] On Paul's spiritual parenthood see our section on the parental metaphor above, pp. 172–4. Cf. Arist. *Eth. Nic.* 8.11.1–4; Sen. *Ben.* 5.5.2.

[125] Bassler, *God & Mammon*, 83; J. D. Pentecost, 'Studies in Philemon. Part V: The Obedience of a Son', *BSac* 130 (1973): 166; Stuhlmacher, *Philemon*, 37; N. T. Wright, *The Epistles of Paul to the Colossians and to Philemon* (Leicester: Inter-Varsity Press, 1986): 188; White, 'Social Authority', 219.

[126] White correctly mentions the tension between Paul's authority as the one who brought Philemon to Christ and Philemon's authority as Paul's host and patron. In using the word *patron*, however, White creates this very tension. Whether Paul had a personal relationship of social dependence and obligation to Philemon cannot be established merely on the basis of the church meeting in Philemon's home.

[127] Petersen, *Rediscovering Paul*, 75; Martin, 'Commercial Language in Philemon', 337.

[128] Petersen, *Rediscovering Paul*, 77.

benefactor and parent in relationship to his converts.[129] As such his converts owe him a spiritual, though very real, debt. The apostle sees no problem with placing Onesimus' so-called literal debt next to Philemon's so-called metaphorical debt. We are not dealing with two divergent forms of debt which cannot be combined. Both of these debts can be entered into the same account book with the result that Onesimus enjoys the profit.

Verse 20

At the end of his appeal Paul is still on the same theme, although his terms allude back to his praise for Philemon's past good work (v. 7). In that praise he had referred to Philemon's past record in refreshing the hearts of the saints. One might think, as the letter progresses and its business becomes clear, that the person who needs refreshing in this case is Onesimus. An appeal is clearly being made on his behalf. But reading v. 20 we see that the case is very different. Philemon has refreshed the hearts of other Christians and now it is not Onesimus' turn but Paul's. Again the apostle puts himself in the place of the slave, thus making Philemon's response a personal one directed toward himself.

Paul states that he wants to receive some benefit from Philemon. Others have noticed that he employs a formula with ὀναίμην which is frequent in current usage.[130] This formula is modified in a significant way: with ἐν κυρίῳ. Paul requests a benefit in the Lord, stressing that the slave owner's debt lies in his new existence as a Christian. We might paraphrase v. 20: 'Yes, that's right brother Philemon, I am asking for a return on the debt you owe me as a Christian. As you have done good to others, so now pay me back with a good deed.'[131]

The forcefulness of vv. 8–20 can hardly be over-emphasized.[132] Paul certainly desires Onesimus to be treated with the utmost respect befitting a brother in Christ. At every turn this respect is called for because of the respect that is due the apostle. This respect

---

[129] See the comments above on 2 Cor. 12.14 and 2 Cor. 6.13, pp. 172–4 and Register, *Giving and Receiving*, 109–12.

[130] O'Brien, *Colossians and Philemon*, 301; Lightfoot, *Colossians and Philemon*, 342; Stuhlmacher, *Philemon*, 51 n. 12.

[131] Lightfoot, *Colossians and Philemon*, 341; Wright, *Colossians and Philemon*, 188: 'If it is a matter of debts, then Paul has the right to claim a dividend on his investment in Philemon.'

[132] Stuhlmacher, *Philemon*, 49.

is due to Paul, however, not on the basis of his apostolic position and authority, but on his position as spiritual benefactor to Philemon.

To conclude on Philemon 17–19, we see that the gospel is a gift which brings obligations on the part of the receiver. This obligation has been referred to explicitly in Romans 15.26, but also implicitly in Philippians 4.15. Paul uses this obligation when he sees that it will be helpful for the advance of the gospel. Here the advance of the gospel is taken more broadly to refer to the living out of the message in the life of one receiver: Philemon.

1 Timothy 5.4: repaying ancestors

Regardless of its authorship we see the same conventions of social reciprocity operating in the church at the time of the writing of 1 Timothy. According to this author, children should learn to put their religion into practice by caring for their own family, thus repaying their ancestors (5.4, ἀμοιβὰς ἀποδιδόναι τοῖς προγόνοις).[133]

Our general treatment of social reciprocity did not detail individual types of relationships. One of the relationships which warrants the most discussion in the literary authors is that of the child to the parent. According to Philo none can more truly be called benefactors than parents in relation to their children (*Spec.* 2.229).[134] We have mentioned this aspect of social reciprocity in our discussion of 2 Corinthians 6.13 above.

Several scholars on 1 Timothy 5.4 refer to the obligation of gratitude (ἀμοιβή) which is owed to parents,[135] and others even go so far as to say this debt is owed in response to the labour the parents invested in rearing children.[136] None of the authors cited,

---

[133] Ἀμοιβή and ἀποδιδόναι often occur in contexts of social reciprocity. E.g., Arist. *Eth. Nic.* 9.1.7; Diod. Sic. 1.90.2; 15.26.1; Dio Chrys. *Or.* 31.27, 53; 44.5; Philo *Spec.* 2.234; P.Oxy. 705.61 (c. AD 200)).

[134] Cf. *Decal.* 112; Arist. *Eth. Nic.* 8.11.1–4; Seneca *Ben.* 5.5.2.

[135] Gottfried Holtz, *Die Pastoral Briefe* (Berlin: Evangelische Verlagsanstalt, 1965): 116; Jürgen Roloff, *Der erste Brief an Timotheus* (Zürich: Benziger, 1988): 288, 288 n. 318; Martin Dibelius and Hans Conzelmann, *The Pastoral Epistles*, trans. Philip Buttolph and Adela Yarbro (Philadelphia: Fortress Press, 1972): 74.

[136] E.g., Gordon Fee, *1 and 2 Timothy, Titus* (Peabody: Hendrickson, 1988): 116; Donald Guthrie, *The Pastoral Epistles* (Leicester: Inter-Varsity, 2nd edn, 1990): 112; Bruce W. Winter, 'Providentia for the Widows of 1 Timothy 5: 3–16', *TynBul* 39 (1988): 90.

however, supplies social background which could illustrate this text.

It is important to note that at the time of the writing of 1 Timothy the expectations of social reciprocity had been accepted into the teaching of the church. One can display their piety by conforming to these social expectations, namely, by repaying the benefits received from one's ancestors.

Romans 5.7 and the good man

As Cranfield points out, the purpose of this verse is clearly to emphasize the extraordinary character of Christ's sacrifice, yet the exact interpretation is disputed.[137] Is the person for whom one may be willing to die, τοῦ ἀγαθοῦ, a benefactor? Cranfield says it is, citing texts that speak of dying for others.[138] Dunn says it is not, citing the same evidence.[139] Both of these approaches take a much too narrow view of the evidence being adduced and both neglect the social world which surrounds this dying for others.

We have already seen that benefactions received cause the receiver to feel obligations to the giver.[140] These obligations are discharged through a counter-gift or favour. A return made in the form of a favour might take the form of a heroic deed. Such deeds are honourable, and the failure to undertake them when the situation arises is shameful.

Andrew D. Clarke notes the distinction being drawn between δίκαιος and ἀγαθός and finds a precedent for it in Greco-Roman usage. Apparently 'in certain contexts the primary meaning of ἀγαθός was a technical description of the wealthy upper classes, and, in these instances, it did not carry strong moral overtones'.[141] Although the one δίκαιος was law-abiding, often the welfare of the city was more important than the injustice of an individual.[142] Link with this the strong sense of obligation that one could feel toward a

---

[137] Cranfield, *Romans*, 264.
[138] Arr. *Epict. Diss.* 2.7.3, Philostratus *VA* 7.12 and a papyrus from Deissmann, *Light*, 118; Cranfield, *Romans*, 265.
[139] Dunn, *Romans*, 256; cf. Morris, *Romans*, 223 n. 26.
[140] See pp. 68–71 above.
[141] 'The Good and the Just in Romans 5', *TynBul* 41 (1990): 136. In *Or.* 31.8, 14, 27 and 65 Dio Chrysostom seems to equate ὁ ἀγαθός with ὁ εὐεργέτης (cf. Plut. *Mor.* 218A, 851D; Seneca *Ben.* 2.17.7; 7.17.2).
[142] A. W. H. Adkins, *Moral Values and Political Behaviour in Greece, From Homer to the End of the Fifth Century* (London: Chatto and Windus, 1972): 124.

generous benefactor, and we can see how one could more readily die for a 'good man' than a 'just man'. We recall the Thankful Letter of Ps-Dionysius in which the author suggests that a thankful letter ought to assert that death would not be able to repay the feeling of debt: 'Even if I give my life for you I could hardly return appropriate thanks for your benefits' (οὐδὲ γὰρ τὸν βίον ὑπὲρ σοῦ προέμενος ἀξίαν ἀποδώσειν χάριν ὧν εὖ πέπονθα).[143]

If this view is correct, it would lend support to Winter's assertion that Romans 13.3–4 speaks of the public praising of benefactors.[144] In addition this would give one more reason to believe that Paul not only was familiar with the social practices surrounding him, but consciously engaged with them or rejected them as the case may be.

Conclusion

The language of social obligation appears with varying degrees in Greco-Roman and Jewish literature contemporaneous with Paul. Within the Pauline corpus the language arises at some interesting and crucial times. We have seen confirmed in these texts our conclusions drawn from the Philippian material. Paul is aware of the conventions of reciprocity and has accepted them to an extent. Paul sees his bringing of the gospel to his converts as an act of beneficence on his part. His converts are his children and owe a great spiritual debt to him for their spiritual life. Though not quick to request repayment, Paul can do so when the situation dictates (Phlm. 17–19, 2 Cor. 6.13). On the one hand, he steadfastly refuses to contract social obligations which he feels will hinder the advance of the gospel (2 Cor. 11.12–15). On the other hand, financial support can be accepted if this giving and receiving helps to advance the gospel (Phil. 1.5) and brings spiritual dividends to the givers (Phil. 4.17).

---

143 This letter is cited in full above, p. 82.
144 Bruce W. Winter, 'The Public Praising of Christian Benefactors: Romans 13.3–4 and 1 Peter 2.14–15', *JSNT* 34 (1988): 87–103.

7

CONCLUSIONS AND IMPLICATIONS

Summary

This study has treated Greco-Roman social conventions regarding reciprocity and the extent to which the apostle Paul accepted or rejected these conventions. Special attention has been given to Paul's financial relationship with the Philippian church as seen in Philippians 4.10–20. Several other passages have been studied which illustrate and expand on the conclusions drawn from the Philippian material.

In the Introduction it was suggested that for a proper understanding of the social conventions of giving and receiving in the ancient world, we needed to establish a model of interaction based on the relevant ancient documents.

Chapter 2 illustrated the conventions of giving and receiving with texts from the Old Testament and selected Jewish literature. Here we saw that social reciprocity has roots in the ancient Jewish world as well as in the Greco-Roman world. Though didactic sections of the Old Testament teach that reward comes *from God* for the good which is done with money, the narrative sections illustrate that social reciprocity operated at the human level: the recipient of good is expected to repay the giver in kind. In didactic sections of extra-biblical Jewish literature we saw that there was ambiguity regarding this reward for doing good. It does indeed come, but the source may be God or the receiver. Further, this literature clearly shows the operation of social reciprocity between individuals.

The clearest and most informative background material was found in chapter 3: 'Giving and receiving in the Greco-Roman context'. This chapter demonstrated that the conventions of giving and receiving were basic to the society from which Paul's congregations were drawn. We saw that patronage, friendship and relations between family members (especially between parents and children) all contain elements of social reciprocity. Also, we sketched out the basic elements of the model used in the investigation of the Pauline texts.

Further, we noted in this chapter the reciprocal obligations and the transactional character that attend giving and receiving. This characteristic of social reciprocity meant that terminology commonly found in commercial contexts to describe commercial transactions was also used in social contexts to describe the transactions of giving and receiving. Thus, we concluded that the phrase ἐκοινώνησεν εἰς λόγον δόσεως καὶ λήμψεως (used in Phil. 4.15) is not primarily a financial expression, but rather a social metaphor. Such expressions are common in the first-century Greco-Roman world.

In chapter 3 we also saw that gratitude, in the form of a return, is very important in Greco-Roman society. Verbal gratitude on the other hand, played quite a different role than it does in twentieth-century western society. An expression of gratitude may be seen as solicitation for further benefits.

Application of findings from the background chapters began in chapter 4. Here we looked at the 'giving and receiving' of Philippians 1–2. We saw that Paul and the Philippian congregation shared a unique relationship of partnership in the gospel. This partnership was established through giving and receiving.

To describe more fully the unique relationship which the apostle enjoyed with the Philippians, chapter 5 was devoted to giving and receiving in Philippians 4. This passage, with its use of what are commonly called technical commercial terms and its lack of the verb εὐχαριστέω, has been a source of vexation to exegetes, which has led many to erroneous theories. We have seen how the conventions of giving and receiving enlighten us as to the meaning and significance of Paul's 'strained' response to the Philippians' gifts. The social conventions regarding gratitude, particularly verbal gratitude, made Paul's written response to their gifts particularly sensitive.

Two full chapters were devoted to canonical Philippians because of Paul's essentially positive relationship of giving and receiving which he enjoyed with the Christians in Philippi. Since Paul's opportunities for giving and receiving were not restricted to his relationship with this particular congregation, chapter 6 expanded our study. There we looked at giving and receiving in selected Pauline writings outside Philippians which help us to draw further conclusions regarding the apostle's acceptance or rejection of the conventions of social reciprocity. These texts were 2 Corinthians 6.13, 11.9–15, 12.14–16, Romans 15.25–31, Philemon 17–19 and 1 Timothy 5.4. From study of these passages we concluded that Paul considers himself a benefactor in relation to his converts. The gift he gives is the gospel. Paul can call for the repayment of a benefit if he sees fit. Further, when the Corinthians offer him gifts, he rejects the inferior role of a receiver in order to avoid hindering the gospel.

Implications and significance

We have seen that the Greco-Roman world in which the apostle Paul worked as a church planter had very clear social expectations with regard to giving and receiving. Cognizance of benefaction, debt and obligation occurred in every relationship we have been able to study. Relationships between equals, or what we may call friendships, were established and carried on through the exchange of goods and services, as were relationships between unequals, or patronage. We should ask where the apostle fits into this social matrix. The letter to the Philippians, with its direct reference to a gift received from this church by Paul, gives us a window through which to view Paul's attitude toward social reciprocity.

At this point, it will be helpful to discuss some of the wider implications of the conclusions drawn in this study.

First, on a general level we see that socio-historical research, when linked with historical-grammatical exegesis, is preferable to simple exegetical work or to pure sociological analysis. Neither approach has presented us with a satisfactory answer to the questions regarding Paul's terminology in Philippians 4. Simple exegetical work has not viewed Paul's relationship with the Philippians in its broader social context. Rather, it has sought to establish the meaning of the phrase ἐκοινώνησεν εἰς λόγον δόσεως καὶ λήμψεως largely through word studies of the noun forms δόσις and λῆμψις. Such studies have led to only a few selected texts, texts which have then been assumed to support the common view that this phrase invariably refers to commercial transactions. This commonly received view has been shown to be patently false.

Likewise, the latter method is too apt to force upon the text false social expectations which are not based on the actual social practice of the Greco-Roman world.

Secondly, κοινωνία is dealt with at such length in Philippians, a church with which Paul had the unique relationship of giving and receiving, that we might ask whether there are implications for our understanding of κοινωνία in other New Testament writings. What role does money play in this fellowship? While some studies of κοινωνία from a theological perspective reach worthwhile, valuable and correct conclusions,[1] our study implies that in other New Testament passages fellowship has financial sharing in mind.

Thirdly, Paul appears to believe that secular power, in the form of financial giving, does not take precedence over the authority structures imposed by the gospel.[2] Though he has received gifts from the Philippians, he never mentions being in debt to them, but rather asserts that they work *with him* in the advance of the gospel (1.5). Though his letter to them is pastorally sensitive, it still contains exhortations and commands. Being the receiver has not usurped his position of apostolic authority.

Paul stresses fellowship to the Corinthians, but it is outside of friendship (φιλία), it is a fellowship in the Spirit (ἐν πνεύματι). Spiritual or religious considerations take precedence over purely social ones. Though it insults them greatly, Paul breaks social convention and refuses to accept their repeated offers of aid. He says acceptance would hinder the gospel.

Philemon is a house church patron, but as such he cannot take precedence over the apostle in authority. Paul not only believes he has the right to command Philemon, but that Philemon is actually a great debtor to him for spiritual benefits.

Fourthly, as we mentioned several times in chapters 4 and 5, our study has implications regarding the unity of canonical Philippians. The extensive use of inclusion in the letter, the great verbal and conceptual similarity between 1.3–11 and 4.10–20, the themes of the gospel's advance and Paul's personal subordination for the progress of the gospel all suggest that the letter as it stands was originally a unified piece of correspondence.

Fifthly, our study leads us to question Neyrey's assertion that Paul was 'fully incarnated in his culture and living out the specific

---

[1] Referring only to biblical studies monographs see Hainz, *KOINONIA* (see also the criticisms of Hainz offered under the treatment of Phil. 4.15, pp. 147–8); Seesemann, *KOINΩNIA*; George Panikulam, *Koinonia in the New Testament – A Dynamic Expression of Christian Life* (Rome: Biblical Institute Press, 1979).

[2] See Clarke, *Leadership*, 109–18.

expectations of that culture'.[3] Just what are the cultural expectations Neyrey has in mind? The evidence gives us reason to believe
that social reciprocity operated both in the Greek and Roman as
well as in the Jewish cultures in which Paul lived. Yet, while Paul
operates with an ideology of reciprocity, it is not the ideology
found in these cultures. Rather, Paul's ideology is informed by the
Old Testament and, most importantly, by the gospel. Paul modifies
the social expectations of his culture because the gospel is an
overriding force which takes priority over the form of social
reciprocity found in his culture.

In line with the above we see that Paul can adapt the language
and metaphors of his culture for his own purposes. Though having
a different application in mind, Koester offers an insightful
comment:

> Adapting certain terms, concepts, and forms of speech –
> whether from his own tradition or from the theological
> vocabulary of his opponents – Paul alters and modifies
> these vehicles of religious language according to his own
> theological criteria. Thus, his own opinion is usually not
> present in the occurrence of a certain term or concept as
> such, but only in the specific modifications which Paul
> introduces in his own usage and which differ from the
> usage of his opponents.[4]

Thus, although ἐκοινώνησεν εἰς λόγον δόσεως καὶ λήμψεως is a
social metaphor used to label the mutual obligations of exchange
relationships, Paul has elevated it to a Christian appellation for
missionary involvement (Phil. 4.15). According to Greco-Roman
thinking, parents become great benefactors to their children by
being the generators of their physical existence and the providers of
all they need over the course of their childhood. Paul, as a preacher
of the gospel, has become a great benefactor to his converts by

---

[3] Neyrey, *Paul, In Other Words*, 18. In the early part of his book Neyrey implies
that Paul would have fully and irrevocably accepted the social expectations of his
culture. He states that his book 'offers some hope of understanding the cultural
viewpoint into which (Paul) was socialized' (12), and that Paul 'was fundamentally
and irrevocably socialized into the purity system of the Judaism of his day' (26).
Neyrey, however, offers no ancient literature to define the expectations of this
culture. Rather his socio-anthropological model is based on the work of anthropologist Mary T. Douglas, *Purity and Danger* (London: Routledge and Kegan
Paul, 1966).

[4] Koester, 'Paul and Hellenism', 193.

being the human instrument through whom the convert has received a new self (Phlm. 19; cf. 2 Cor. 6.13).

This study indicates that the statement recorded in Acts 20.35 is consistent with the practice seen in Paul's letters: it is more blessed to give than to receive. Paul accepts the basic truth of this Greco-Roman aphorism and insists on being a great giver. But according to Greco-Roman thinking one displays virtue by giving goods and favours. Paul, on the other hand, gives something of far greater value and far more costly: he gives himself and the gospel.

Appendix A

A SELECTION OF TEXTS FROM SENECA

Our discussion of social reciprocity in the Greco-Roman world has included frequent reference to the work of Seneca, and especially to his massive treatment of the subject found in *De Beneficiis*. Our references, however, have been scattered throughout chapter 3. Here we present a fuller and more organized collection of texts.[1]

Aspects of giving

Selecting a recipient

Ingratitude is very common because we do not pick those who are worthy of receiving our gifts (*Ben.* 1.1.2).

Although we ought to be careful to confer benefits by preference upon those who will be likely to respond with gratitude, yet there are some that we shall do even if we expect from them poor results (*Ben.* 1.10.4–5).

I must be far more careful in selecting my creditor for a benefit than a creditor for a loan. For to the latter I shall have to return the same amount that I have received, and, when I have returned it, I have paid all my debt and am free; but to the other I must make an additional payment, and, even after I have paid my debt of gratitude, the bond between us still holds; for, just when I have finished paying it, I am obliged to begin again, and the friendship endures; and, as I would not admit an unworthy man to my

---

[1] All texts from Seneca's *De Beneficiis* come from the LCL edition, trans. John W. Basore (London: William Heinemann Ltd, 1935). Those from Seneca's *Epistles* come from the LCL edition, 3 vols., trans. Richard M. Gummere (London: William Heinemann Ltd, 1917–25).

friendship, so neither would I admit one who is unworthy to the most sacred privilege of benefits, from which friendship springs (*Ben.* 2.18.5–6).

Kindnesses establish friendships if they are placed judiciously; it is more important who receives than what is given (*Ep.* 19.11–12).

Superiority of the giver

The gifts that please are those that are bestowed by one who wears the countenance of a human being, all gentle and kindly, by one who, though he was my superior when he gave them, did not exalt himself above me, but, with all the generosity in his power, descended to my own level (*Ben.* 2.13.2).

Aspects of receiving

The obligatory return

We are, as you know, wont to speak thus: 'A has made a return for a favour bestowed by B.' Making a return means handing over of your own accord that which you owe. We do not say, 'He has paid back the favour'; for 'pay back' is used of a man upon whom a demand for repayment is made, of those who pay against their will, of those who pay under any circumstances whatever, and of those who pay through a third party. We do not say, 'He has "restored" the benefit', or 'settled' it; we have never been satisfied with a word which applies properly to a debt of money. Making a return means offering something to him from whom you have received something. The phrase implies a voluntary return; he who has made a return has served the writ upon himself (*Ep.* 81.9–10).

The ungrateful man tortures and torments himself; he hates the gifts which he has accepted, because he must make a return for them, and he tries to belittle their value (*Ep.* 81.23).

He who receives a benefit with gratitude repays the first instalment on his debt (*Ben.* 2.22.1).

The man who intends to be grateful, immediately, while he is still receiving, should turn his thought to repaying (*Ben.* 2.25.3).

To put it briefly, he who is too eager to pay his debt is unwilling to be indebted, and he who is unwilling to be indebted is ungrateful (*Ben.* 4.40.5).

The giving of a benefit is a social act, it wins the good will of someone, it lays someone under obligation (*Ben.* 5.11.5).

Verbal thanks as solicitation

No single fact earned the goodwill of Augustus Caesar, and made it easy for Furnius to obtain from him other favours than his saying, when Augustus at his request had granted pardon to his father, who had supported the side of Antony: 'The only injury, Caesar, that I have received from you is this – you have forced me both to live and die without expressing my gratitude!' (*Ben.* 2.25.1).

Listen to the words of petitioners. No one of them fails to say that the memory of the benefit will live for ever in his heart; no one of them fails to declare himself your submissive and devoted slave, and, if he can find any more abject language in which to express his obligation, he uses it (*Ben.* 3.5.2).

May his nature that of itself is inclined to pity, kindness, and mercy find stimulus and encouragement from a host of grateful persons (*Ben.* 6.29.1).

Special aspects of social reciprocity

Parents as benefactors

Can there possibly be any greater benefits than those that a father bestows upon his child? (*Ben.* 2.11.5).

And so the greatest of all benefits are those that, while we are either unaware or unwilling, we receive from our parents (*Ben.* 6.24.2).

Repayment to the wealthy

How many ways there are by which we may repay whatever we owe even to the well-to-do! – loyal advice, constant intercourse, polite conversation that pleases without flattery, attentive ears if he should wish to ask counsel, safe ears if he should wish to be confidential, and friendly intimacy (*Ben.* 6.29.2).

Interest

A man is an ingrate if he repays a favour without interest (*Ep.* 81.18).

Appendix B

OTHER EXAMPLES OF ΔΟΣΙΣ ΚΑΙ ΛΗΜΨΙΣ

In chapter 3 the study of the phrase 'giving and receiving' did not present all uses of the phrase, but only those considered most helpful for the exegesis of Philippians 4.15. Here we present several other instances of the phrase which further demonstrate that it was not restricted to commercial contexts.

Physical interaction

According to Philo each part of the body has its appropriate and indispensable use. The hands are made for doing things and for giving and receiving (χεῖρες δὲ πρὸς τὸ πρᾶξαί τι καὶ δοῦναι καὶ λαβεῖν, *Spec.* 1.340; cf. *Immut.* 57). In Diodorus Siculus battle is described as the giving and receiving of wounds (τραύματα διδόντες καὶ λαμβάνοντες, 14.52.4; cf. Seneca *Ep.* 91).

Conversation

Plutarch also uses the phrase as 'to engage in discussion' (λόγον δοῦναι καὶ λαβεῖν, *Mor.* 1B, cf. Xen. *Cyr.* 1.4.3; *Oec.* 11.22).

Contracts and pledges[1]

While attempting to unravel the contradictory tradition regarding Sciron (*Vit. Thes.* 10) Plutarch reports that one strand says Sciron was a violent man. Another opposes this, referring to his family ties: he was the son-in-law of Cychreas, who received divine

---

[1] The examples cited here might well be labelled those which do indeed occur *within a social context*. For the relationships being established between the Greeks and Macronians and between Sciron and Cychreas are certainly social relationships. We have, however, defined these relationships as *xenia* in accordance with Herman (see *Ritualized Friendship*, 10–13 and 31–4 for defining characteristics of *xenia* and pp. 49–50 for a discussion of Xen. *An.* 4.8.7).

honours at Athens, and the father-in-law of Aeacus, the most righteous of all Hellenes. If this latter strand of tradition is true, Sciron's good character is proven, for it is not likely that the best men entered family alliances with the worst, giving and receiving the most valuable gifts (οὔκουν εἰκὸς εἶναι τῷ κακίστῳ τοὺς ἀρίστους εἰς κοινωνίαν γένους ἐλθεῖν, τὰ μέγιστα καὶ τιμιώτατα λαμβάνοντας καὶ διδόντας, 10.3). This text is informative. First, it demonstrates that the giving and receiving of gifts can establish social relationships and obligations. Second, the construction εἰς κοινωνίαν . . . ἐλθεῖν is close to Paul's ἐκοινώνησεν εἰς λόγον (Phil. 4.15).

In *Leges* 774C.3 Plato states with regard to dowries that an equal exchange consists in neither the giving nor receiving of a gift (τὸ μήτε λαμβάνειν τι μήτ᾿ ἐκδιδόναι τι). He proposes a penalty for anyone who disobeys this rule by giving or receiving (ὁ δὲ μὴ πειθόμενος ἢ διδοὺς ἢ λαμβάνων, 774D.1–2; cf. Xen. *Cyr.* 4.6.10).

In Xenophon *Anabasis* 4.8.7 the Macronians objected to the Greek army passing through their territory. The Greeks insisted it was a peaceful journey. The Macronians asked whether they would give pledges to this effect. The Greeks replied that they were ready both to give and receive pledges (δοῦναι καὶ λαβεῖν). From this point the two groups cooperated (4.8.8–9).

Legal proceedings

This use is found several times in Dionysius of Halicarnassus. Injured parties who go to court are directed by law to give and receive satisfaction (διδόναι δίκας καὶ λαμβάνειν, 3.8.5; cf. 4.11.2; 4.36.2; 10.18.4; 15.5.1; Dem. *Or.* 37.37).

Commercial business

In *Anabasis* 7.7.36 Xenophon urges Seuthes to pay quickly the soldiers who have salary due them. Though the total amount is great, it is a petty sum in light of Seuthes' ability to pay. For it is not the number that determines what is much or little but the ability of the one who pays and the one who receives (οὐ γὰρ ἀριθμός ἐστιν ὁ ὁρίζων τὸ πολὺ καὶ τὸ ὀλίγον, ἀλλ᾿ ἡ δύναμις τοῦ τε ἀποδιδόντος καὶ τοῦ λαμβάνοντος).[2]

---

[2] Cf. Arist. *Eth. Nic.* 5.5.6: 'But in the interchange of services Justice in the form of Reciprocity maintains the association: reciprocity, that is, on the basis of pro-

Nearly every scholar who attempts to support a commercial understanding of δόσις καὶ λῆμψις cites Sirach 42.7. Here the author encourages readers not to be ashamed of counting and weighing every deposit, and of recording all that is taken in or given out[3] (ὃ ἐὰν παραδιδῷς, ἐν ἀριθμῷ καὶ σταθμῷ, καὶ δόσις καὶ λῆμψις, πάντα ἐν γραφῇ). The mention of *written* records plainly makes this a reference to a commercial financial transaction. The context as well favours this understanding, owing to references dealing with household management (business expenses, v. 3; accurate scales, v. 4; and bargaining with merchants, v. 5a).

portion, not on the basis of equality' (LCL trans., αλλ᾽ ἐν μὲν ταῖς κοινωνίαις ταῖς ἀλλακτικαῖς συνέχει τὸ τοιοῦτον δίκαιον, τὸ ἀντιπεπονθὸς κατ᾽ ἀναλογίαν καὶ μὴ κατ᾽ ἰσότητα).

[3] Skehan/Di Lella, *Ben Sira*, 477.

Appendix C

THE SUPPORT OF WANDERING PREACHERS AND PHILOSOPHERS[1]

In chapter 3 we examined the place and characteristics of social reciprocity in the Greco-Roman world. In chapters 4, 5 and 6 we considered how these social conventions influenced the apostle Paul with regard to the acceptance of financial support from his churches. In those chapters we did not consider another relevant factor: itinerant preacher/philosophers and how their own personal income fits into the social world. In this appendix we will consider the options that were available to such persons and the criteria different groups (e.g., Cynics, Sophists) used to make their decision.

The information presented here must be seen as supplementary to that presented in chapter 3. We are concerned with the question whether the support of preachers may be seen as taking place outside the matrix of social reciprocity or seen as a sub-set of it; that is, was the reception of support by wandering philosophers (in whatever form it came) seen as purely a commercial transaction or was this support seen as a social transaction?

One item we should note early is that the method of support a wandering preacher chose was significant in terms of public perception.[2] 'A preacher's support method became not only a factor in forming public opinion about preachers but was also a common element in the stock criticisms employed against them.'[3] Paul's choice of a method could well have a significant impact on the view formed of him and his message long before the gospel was actually heard from his own lips.

---

[1] On the itinerant preacher/philosopher generally see also W. L. Liefeld, *The Wandering Preacher as a Social Figure in the Roman Empire* (Ann Arbor: University Microfilms, 1967).

[2] Cf. the stereotyped attacks on various philosophies and their support methods in Lucian, *Philosophies for Sale*.

[3] Liefeld, *The Wandering Preacher*, 246.

Support methods

Ronald Hock has produced a short but well documented sketch of the options open to philosophers.[4] Hock brings to our attention the debate carried on in Paul's day concerning the proper means of support for a philosopher. According to Hock one could charge fees, attach himself to a wealthy household, beg or work at a trade.[5] Each method was, of course, defended by those who selected it. We will present the methods as they have been outlined by Hock and refer the reader in the notes to some of the ancient literature he cites. Then, in an attempt to move the discussion beyond Hock, we will consider some of the social implications of employing these methods. We will be concerned to detect what role, if any, social reciprocity played in the choice and the social consequences of a philosopher's support.[6]

Fees

First, one could charge fees. It is the Sophists who are credited with instituting the practice of charging fees for instruction.[7] The practice did not remain with them, however. Some Stoics felt it was proper to ask fees for instruction.[8] According to Forbes, by the time of the Empire teachers of philosophy were almost unanimously ready to take fees.[9]

Those who spoke out against this method basically used two forms of attack. First, the charging of fees was thought to be inappropriate to the teacher of philosophy.[10] It is not consistent with his message, for he should speak out against greed and attachment to worldly goods. Socrates called Sophists pedlars (κάπηλοι).[11]

[4] *Social Context*, 52–9. Cf. also Liefeld, *The Wandering Preacher*, 246–59.

[5] Hock, *Social Context*, 52. Liefeld (*The Wandering Preacher*, 246–7) presents begging, charging fees, working at a trade and contributions from the group served.

[6] In his otherwise excellent sketch of the various methods of support, Hock neglects any mention of the social obligations that might attend the particular method chosen.

[7] C. A. Forbes, *Teacher's Pay in Ancient Greece* (Lincoln: University of Nebraska Press, 1942): 12.

[8] Quintilian *Inst.* 12.7.9; Lucian *J. Trag.* 27, *Symp.* 32, *Herm.* 9, *Icar.* 5, *Vit. auct.* 24–5; D.L. 4.2.

[9] Forbes (*Teacher's Pay*, 41) cites Lucian *Paras.* 52.

[10] Plato *Ep.* 218.10–11.

[11] Pl. *Protag.* 313C–D; cf. Pl. *Men.* 92A, *Euthyd.* 277B; Xen. *Mem.* 1.2.7. Also

Secondly, as far back as Socrates it was felt that the taking of fees enslaves one to teach any person who has money (Xen. *Mem.* 1.2.6). This citation introduces us to a theme which is recurrent in the discussion of support types: the freedom of the receiver, however it was defined, was of the utmost importance.

Patronage

One could attach oneself to a wealthy household. This method was very popular.[12] The philosopher would be expected to instruct the patron's sons or to serve as a counsellor to the patron.[13]

The social obligations that would attend such an arrangement should be obvious. Not only would the philosopher be under the power of the patron, but according to such authors as Lucian and Juvenal there were social indignities which the philosopher could very well suffer. In *De Mercede* Lucian cautions Timocles against taking up a salaried post in a wealthy household by portraying the great indignities it entails.

Lucian says one begins the process by camping in a crowd on the doorstep of the wealthy (10). Then follows an examination to see if one is learned (11). The past life is pried into (12). At the first dinner one suffers great nervousness and is criticized for being socially inept (15–17). One's salary is finally established at a paltry amount, but only after a laborious and embarrassing discussion (21). In service one rises early and suffers an exhausting day running about the city with the patron's entourage (24). In reality one is only a showpiece to display the patron's nobility (25).[14]

Lucian stresses repeatedly that once one enters the household one gives up all freedom (8, 13, 24). The one who enters a wealthy household has sold himself into slavery. This position as a slave is reiterated every month when one stretches out the hand with the

---

Paul's use of καπηλεύω in 2 Cor. 2.17 is instructive. He asserts that, unlike many others who peddle the word of God (οὐ ... ὡς οἱ πολλοί καπηλεύοντες), he preaches from sincerity (ἀλλ᾿ ὡς ἐξ εἰλικρινείας). The implication is that peddling and sincerity are mutually exclusive.

12 Arr. *Epict. Diss.* 4.1.177; Dio Chrys. *Or.* 77/78.34–6; Lucian *Pisc.* 11–13. See Ronald Hock, 'Simon the Shoemaker as an Ideal Cynic', *Greek, Roman and Byzantine Studies* 17 (1976): 41–53, esp. 45–6.

13 Hock, *Social Context*, 53.

14 Cf. Arr. *Epict. Diss.*: 'If you wish to be consul you must keep vigils, run around, kiss men's hands, rot away at other men's doors, say and do many slavish things, send presents to many persons, and guest-gifts to some people every day' (LCL trans., 4.10.20).

rest of the slaves to take one's earnings (23). After his biting critique of the way patrons entertain their clients at dinner, Juvenal adds: 'You think yourself a free man, and guest of a grandee; he thinks – and he is not far wrong – that you have been captured by the savoury odours of his kitchen' (*Sat.* 5.161–2). Here again we see that the client in a patronage relationship may be viewed as a slave.

There is doubtless much exaggeration in the presentations of Lucian and Juvenal. But we cannot doubt that they convey the feelings of many who accepted this method and of many who observed the life of those who took up the method.[15]

With regard to Paul, as we have mentioned earlier, it is very likely that the factionalism at Corinth arose, at least in part, from power struggles between the wealthy in the Corinthian congregation.[16] Acceptance of gifts from one of these personalities would inevitably cause Paul to be drawn into the struggle and obligate his advocacy for the giver. Therefore, the apostle rejected patronage.[17]

Begging[18]

Begging was another option open to the itinerant philosopher. This method was associated with Cynics and it was appropriate to their lifestyle and teaching which stressed rejection of greed (especially that seen in fee-charging Sophists) and which insisted that people could be content (αὐταρκής) with very little.[19]

As far back as Aristotle, however, begging was considered to be the mark of insincere piety.[20] Since some Cynic teachers needed to defend begging as a practice that was not shameful,[21] we can see that many others considered it to be just that. Dio Chrysostom

---

[15] See Duncan Cloud, 'The Client–Patron Relationship: Emblem and Reality in Juvenal's First Book', *Patronage in Ancient Society*, ed. A. Wallace-Hadrill (London: Routledge, 1989): 205–18.

[16] See pp. 168–71 above and Clarke, *Leadership*, 23–40.

[17] Register asserts that in Paul's declaration of the right to support he is claiming the right to receive patronage (*Giving and Receiving*, 109). Understood in its first-century sense, however, it is doubtful whether Paul ever made such a claim.

[18] See also Bassler (*God & Mammon*, 18–29) for a sketch of the attitudes toward begging in the Greco-Roman world.

[19] Hock, *Social Context*, 55.

[20] Liefeld (*The Wandering Preacher*, 69) cites Arist. *Rhet.* 3.2.

[21] See Diogenes *Ep.* 102.23–7 below and Crates *Ep.* 66.21; Diogenes *Ep.* 142.17–18 (reference is made to page and line in Abraham J. Malherbe, *The Cynic Epistles* (Missoula: Scholars Press, 1977)).

derided such practices implying that it brought ill repute on philosophy in general.[22]

In addition to these criticisms of the method, those who begged were aware of its potential social complications. The Cynic epistles are very enlightening with regard to this problem. We present three examples:

(1)   Crates urges his students only to beg or accept from those who have been initiated into philosophy. 'Then it will be possible for you to demand back what belongs to you and not to appear to be begging what belongs to others.'[23]

(2)   Diogenes advises Metrocles that he should be bold in begging for sustenance, for it is not disgraceful:

> It is all right to beg, if it is not for a free gift or for something worse in exchange (οὐ γὰρ προῖκα οὐδ᾽ ἐπὶ χείρονι ἀνταλλαγῇ), but for the salvation of everyone; that is, to ask people for things that accord with nature, and to ask with a view to doing the same things as Heracles, the son of Zeus, and to be able to give back something much better than you receive yourself (ἀμείβεσθαι πολὺ κρείττονα ὧν λαμβάνεις αὐτος).[24]

(3)   Diogenes reports that some people, after listening to his teaching, responded with gifts:

> some gave me money, others things worth money, and many invited me to dinner. But I took from moderate people what was suitable to nature, but from the worthless I accepted nothing. And from those who felt gratitude toward me for accepting the first time (παρὰ τῶν ἐπισταμένων μοι χάριν ἐπὶ τῷ καὶ τὸ πρῶτον λαβεῖν), I accepted again as well; but never again from those who did not feel thankful. I scrutinized even the gifts (δωρεάς) of those who wished to present me barley meal, and accepted it from those who were being benefited (τῶν ὠφελουμένων). But from others I took nothing, since I thought it improper to

---

[22]   *Or.* 32.9, cf. Martial *Epigrams* 4.53. Malherbe asserts that Paul worked at a trade, and encouraged his converts to do likewise, in order to distance themselves from the practice of Cynics (Malherbe, *Paul and the Thessalonians*, 101).

[23]   καὶ ὑμῖν ἐξέσται ἀπαιτεῖν τὰ ἴδια καὶ μὴ δοκεῖν αἰτεῖν τὰ ἀλλότρια, Crates *Ep.* 54.11–12, 1st–2nd AD.

[24]   Diogenes *Ep.* 102.23–7 (post 200 BC).

take something from a person who had himself not received anything.[25]

These texts help demonstrate two points. First, even for the begging philosopher, issues of social obligation loomed large. One had to consider the social consequences (i.e., obligations) that resulted from accepting a gift from a giver. Secondly, the Cynics begged to obtain the necessities of life. In their letters we find no thought of money being used to support mission work.[26] Whether money is accepted or rejected entirely revolves around what impact this decision will have on their individual social lives.

Working

Finally, one could work.[27] One problem with earning a living through manual labour or a trade was that such activity was considered degrading by some.[28] According to Claude Moseé manual labour was generally despised in the ancient world.[29] It was not that the actual activity of work was loathed. Rather it was the tie of dependence between the artisan and the person who bought and used the product. Here we see the issue of freedom arising again. For the ancients, there was really no difference between the labourer who hires out his services and the craftsman who sells his own products. Both work to satisfy the needs of others not their own. For this reason then they are no longer free, for they depend on another for their livelihood.

Moseé notes further that, except for a few systematic thinkers such as Aristotle, work on the land does not incur this contempt. 'Life in the fields strengthened body and soul; love for the soil was an essential ingredient in patriotism.'[30] It appears that the real issue is freedom, defined as lack of independence on others.

In Hock's discussion of Paul's occupation, he independently

---

[25] Diogenes *Ep.* 160.30–162.8 (post 200 BC).

[26] Bassler, *God & Mammon*, 29.   [27] Hock, *Social Context*, 56–8.

[28] Though we have argued that in 2 Cor. 11.7 ταπεινῶν refers to Paul's suffering poverty, i.e., not accepting support (see pp. 138–41), in that context we see that his humiliation comes about through working. Certainly the two are not mutually exclusive.

[29] *The Ancient World at Work*, trans. J. Lloyd (London: Chatto & Windus, 1969): 26–8.

[30] Moseé, *Work*, 26. Unfortunately Moseé cites no primary literature to support these assertions.

agrees with Moseé. 'The chief stigma attached to the trades was that they were regarded as slavish.'[31] This regard stemmed from three sources: (a) workshops typically employed virtually no one but slaves; (b) trades left no time to cultivate the soul, education or city life, and; (c) trades catered to the wealthy.[32] Although Hock cites primary literature to support his assertions, at this point he does not refer to lack of freedom and independence as the fundamental ground for this stigma.

In his discussion of the methods of support open to philosophers Hock makes special reference to Musonius Rufus. Hock cites several ancient authors who advocate the various methods and we can see that the arguments used for and against a certain method take freedom as their basis. Hock concludes that Paul's approach is most in line with Cynics, especially Musonius.

For Musonius the most appropriate method of support was farming, for not only did it allow him to be independent, but it also allowed him to speak with his students as he worked.[33] Hock concludes that, for Musonius, farming would not have been the only appropriate form of work.[34] Yet if Moseé is correct we should not be quick to make this assumption. Farming may have been seen as a qualitatively different form of work for it allowed the philosopher to be free from any appearance of dependence on others for his livelihood.

Thus, working enabled the philosopher to escape from some of the social obligations that arise through other methods of support. 'People trading specific goods and services for payments would hardly classify their relationship as one of friendship.'[35] Working did not permit complete freedom, however. Some still insisted that the worker was dependent on the buyer of the goods. Further, the degrading character of work was another socially negative factor to be overcome.

---

[31] Hock, *Social Context*, 35.   [32] Ibid., 35–6.

[33] Hock sees these two considerations as very important in Paul's method of support as well.

[34] Hock, *Social Context*, 57.

[35] Herman, *Ritualized Friendship*, 10, cf. 80: 'goods can also be exchanged outside the context of friendship, and the two types of exchange are mutually opposed. Crudely, the distinction is this. Outside the context of friendship – in trading relationships, for example – the exchange is a short-term, self-liquidating transaction. Once the benefits are obtained, the social relationship is terminated. The transaction does not create moral involvement.'

Conclusions

From our cursory treatment of support for philosophers we can see that issues of social reciprocity were very important in a philosopher's decision regarding a method of support. On all sides the issues of freedom and independence arise, yet the terms are too flexible to allow any one method to win the argument. Nevertheless, working was the least popular option.[36]

[36] Hock, *Social Context*, 59.

BIBLIOGRAPHY

Primary literature

Literary authors: Unless otherwise noted below, Greek and Latin literary authors are cited from the Loeb Classical Library edition.

Papyri: With the exception of Ziebarth (see below), complete bibliographic data for all papyri cited may be found in *Checklist of Editions of Greek Papyri and Ostraca*, John F. Oates et al. eds., 3rd edn, Bulletin of the American Society of Papyrologists, Supplement 4, Decatur: Scholars Press, 1985.

Anthologia Graeca. Gow, A. S. F. and Page, D. L. *The Greek Anthology. The Garland of Philip and Some Contemporary Epigrams*, 2 vols., Cambridge: Cambridge University Press, 1968.

Bell, H. I. and Roberts, C. H. *A Descriptive Catalogue of the Greek Papyri in the Collection of Wilfred Merton, F. S. A.*, London: Emery Walker Limited, 1948.

Bowman, Alan K. *The Roman Writing Tablets from Vindolanda*, London: British Museum Publications, 1983.

Hesiod. von Wilamowitz-Moellendorf, Ulrich. *Hesiodos Erga*, Berlin: Weidmannsche Buchhandlung, 1928. English translation from West, M. L. *Hesiod. Theogony, Works and Days*, Oxford: Oxford University Press, 1988.

IE. Wankel, Hermann, et al. eds. *Die Inschriften von Ephesos*, 7 vols., Bonn: Rudolf Habelt, 1979–81.

Malherbe, Abraham J. *Ancient Epistolary Theorists*, Atlanta: Scholars Press, 1988.

The Cynic Epistles: A Study Edition, Missoula: Scholars Press, 1977.

Marcus Aurelius. Farquharson, A. S. L. *The Meditations of the Emperor Marcus Antoninus*, Oxford: Clarendon Press, 1974.

Ps-Phocylides. van der Horst, P. W. *The Sentences of Pseudo-Phocylides*, Leiden: E. J. Brill, 1978.

Ps-Plato. *Axiochus.* Hershbell, Jackson P. *Pseudo-Plato, Axiochus*, Chico: Scholars Press, 1981.

Definitiones. Burnet, Ioannes. *Platonis Opera*, vol. 5: *Tetralogiam IX Definitiones et Spuria Continens*, London: Oxford University Press, repr., 1975.

Rahlfs, Alfred. *Septuaginta*, 2 vols., Stuttgart: Privilegierte Württemberg-
ische Bibelanstalt, 1935.

SEG 35. H. W. Pleket and R. S. Stroud, eds. *Supplementum Epigraphicum
Graecum*, vol. 35, Amsterdam: J. C. Gieben, 1988.

SIG.[2] Dittenberger, Guilelmus. *Sylloge Inscriptionum Graecarum*, 3 vols.,
Leipzig: Hirzelius, 1898–1901.

Sirach. Smend, R. *Die Weisheit des Jesus Sirach: Hebräisch und Deutsch*,
2 vols., Berlin: Georg Reimer, 1909.

Ziebarth, Erich. *Aus der antiken Schule: Sammlung griechischer Texte auf
papyrus holztafeln Ostraka*, Bonn: A. Marcus und E. Weber, 1910.

Secondary literature

Adams, J. N. '"Friendship" and "Self-Sufficiency" in Homer and
Aristotle', *Classical Quarterly* 28 (1978): 145–6.

Adkins, A. W. H. *Moral Values and Political Behaviour in Greece, From
Homer to the End of the Fifth Century*, London: Chatto and Windus,
1972.

Alexander, Loveday. 'Hellenistic Letter Forms and the Structure of
Philippians', *JSNT* 37 (1989): 87–101.

Alter, Robert. 'How Convention Helps Us Read: The Case of the Bible's
Annunciation Type-Scene', *Proof* 3 (1983): 115–30.

Badian, Ernst. *Foreign Clientelae (265–70 B.C.)*, Oxford: Clarendon Press,
1958.

Barrett, C. K. *A Commentary on the Second Epistle to the Corinthians*,
London: A & C Black, repr., 1986.
'Paul's Opponents in II Corinthians', *NTS* 17 (1971): 233–54.

Bassler, Jouette M. *God & Mammon. Asking for Money in the New
Testament*, Nashville: Abingdon Press, 1991.

Baumert, Norbert. 'Ist Philipper 4: 10 richtig übersetzt?', *BZ* 13 (1969):
256–62.

Beare, F. W. *The Epistle to the Philippians*, 3rd edn, London: Adam and
Charles Black, 1976.

Beet, J. A. 'The Christian Secret', *Expositor* 3rd series 10 (1889): 174–89.
'Epaphroditus and the Gift from Philippi', *Expositor* 3rd series 9 (1889):
64–75.

Berger, Klaus. 'Almosen für Israel: Zum historischen Kontext der paulinischen Kollekte', *NTS* 23 (1977): 180–204.

Betz, H. D. *Der Apostel Paulus und die Sokratische Tradition*, Tübingen:
J. C. B. Mohr, 1972.
*2 Corinthians 8 and 9. A Commentary on Two Administrative Letters of
Paul*, Philadelphia: Fortress Press, 1985.

Black, David Alan. 'Paul and Christian Unity: A Formal Analysis of
Philippians 2:1–4', *JETS* 28 (1985): 299–308.

Bogaert, R. 'Geld', *RAC* 9 (1976): 797–907.

Bolkestein, Heinrich. *Wohltätigkeit und Armenpflege in vorchristlichen
Altertum. Ein Beitrag zum Problem 'Moral und Gesellschaft'*, Utrecht:
A. Oosthoek, 1939.

Bolkestein, H., and Kalsbach, A. 'Armut I', *RAC* 1 (1950): 698–705.

218   Bibliography

Bornkamm, Günther. 'Der Philipperbrief als paulinische Briefsammlung', *Neotestamentica et Patristica*, Leiden: E. J. Brill, 1962: 192–202.

Brewer, R. R. 'The Meaning of *Politeuesthe* in Phil. 1.27', *JBL* 73 (1954): 76–83.

Bruce, F. F. *An Expanded Paraphrase of the Epistles of Paul*, Exeter: Paternoster Press, 1965.

'The New Testament and Classical Studies', *NTS* 22 (1976): 229–42.

Philippians (NIC), Peabody: Hendrickson Publishers, 1983.

'St Paul in Macedonia: 3. The Philippian Correspondence', *BJRL* 63 (1981): 260–84.

'St Paul in Rome II: The Epistle to Philemon', *BJRL* 48 (1965–6): 81–97.

Buchanan, C. O. 'Epaphroditus' Sickness and the Letter to the Philippians', *EvQ* 36 (1964): 157–66.

Burford, Alison. *Craftsmen in Greek and Roman Society*, London: Thames and Hudson, 1972.

Burke, Peter. *Sociology and History*, London: George Allen & Unwin, 1980.

Campbell, J. Y. 'Κοινωνία and its Cognates in the New Testament', *JBL* (1932): 352–80.

Capper, Brian J. 'Paul's Dispute with Philippi: Understanding Paul's Argument in Phil. 1–2 from his Thanks in 4.10–20', *TZ* 49 (1993): 193–214.

Caragounis, C. C. 'Ὀψώνιον: A Reconsideration of Its Meaning', *NovT* 16 (1974–5): 35–57.

Chow, John K. *Patronage and Power: A Study of Social Networks in Corinth*, Sheffield: JSOT Press, 1992.

Christ, K. 'Die Griechen und das Geld', *Saeculum* 15 (1964): 214–29.

Church, F. Forrester. 'Rhetorical Structure and Design in Paul's Letter to Philemon', *HTR* 71 (1978): 17–33.

Clarke, Andrew. 'The Good and the Just in Romans 5', *TynBul* 41 (1990): 128–42.

Secular and Christian Leadership in Corinth. A Socio-Historical and Exegetical Study of 1 Corinthians 1–6, Leiden: E. J. Brill, 1993.

Collange, Jean-François. *The Epistle of Saint Paul to the Philippians*, trans. A. W. Heathcote, London: Epworth Press, 1979.

Conzelmann, H. 'εὐχαριστέω', *TDNT*, 10 vols., ed. Gerhard Kittel and G. Friedrich, trans. G. W. Bromiley, Grand Rapids: Eerdmans, 1964–76: 9.407–9.

Craddock, F. *Philippians*, Atlanta: John Knox Press, 1985.

Cranfield, C. E. B. *A Critical and Exegetical Commentary on the Epistle to the Romans*, 2 vols., Edinburgh: T & T Clark, 1975–9.

Culpepper, R. A. 'Co-workers in Suffering', *RevExp* 77 (1980): 349–58.

Dalton, W. J. 'The Integrity of Philippians', *Bib* 60 (1979): 97–102.

Danker, F. W. *Benefactor: Epigraphic Study of a Graeco-Roman and New Testament Semantic Field*, St Louis: Clayton Publishing House, 1982.

'Bridging St Paul and the Apostolic Fathers: A Study in Reciprocity', *CurTM* 15 (1988): 84–94.

'Menander and the New Testament', *NTS* 10 (1964): 365–8.

'Paul's Debt to the *De Corona* of Demosthenes: A Study of Rhetorical Techniques in Second Corinthians', *Persuasive Artistry. Studies in New Testament Rhetoric in Honour of George A. Kennedy*, ed. Duane F. Watson, Sheffield: JSOT Press, 1991: 262–80.

'Reciprocity in the Ancient World and in Acts 15: 23–9', *Political Issues in Luke–Acts*, ed. Richard J. Cassidy and Philip J. Scharper, Maryknoll: Orbis Books, 1983: 49–58.

'Under Contract: A Form-Critical Study of Linguistic Adaptation in Romans', *Fs. to Honor F. Wilbur Gingrich*, ed. E. H. Barth and R. E. Cocroft, Leiden: E. J. Brill, 1972: 91–114.

Daube, D. 'Onesimus', *Christians among Jews and Gentiles*, ed. George W. E. Nickelsburg and George W. MacRae, Philadelphia: Fortress Press, 1986: 40–3.

Dautzenberg, G. 'Der Verzicht auf apostolische Unterhaltsrecht. Eine exegetische Untersuchung zu 1 Kor 9', *Bib* 50 (1969): 212–32.

de Vaux, Roland. *Ancient Israel: Its Life and Institutions*, trans. John McHugh, London: Darton, Longman and Todd, 1961.

Deissmann, Adolf. *Light from the Ancient East*, trans. Lionel R. M. Strachen, rev. edn, London: Hodder and Stoughton, 1927.

Derrett, J. Duncan M. 'The Functions of the Epistle to Philemon', *ZNW* 79 (1988): 63–91.

Dewailly, L. -M. 'La Part Prise a L'Évangile (Phil., I,5)', *RB* 80 (1973): 247–60.

Dihle, Albrecht. 'Demut', *RAC* 3 (1957): 35–78.

Die goldene Regel; eine Einführung in die Geschichte der antiken und frühchristlichen Vulgärethik, Göttingen: Vandenhoeck & Ruprecht, 1962.

Dillard, R. B. *2 Chronicles*, Waco: Word, 1987.

Dodd, C. H. 'The Mind of Paul: I', *New Testament Studies*, Manchester: University Press, 1953.

Domeris, W. R. 'Honour and Shame in the New Testament', *Neot* 27 (1993): 283–97.

Donlan, W. 'Reciprocities in Homer', *Classical World* 75 (1982): 137–76.

'The Politics of Generosity in Homer', *Helios* 9 (1982): 1–15.

Dorrie, Heinrich. 'Gnade (Nichtchristlich: Griechisch-römisch)', *RAC* 11 (1981): 315–33.

Drummond, R. J. 'Note on Philippians 4: 10–19', *ExpTim* 11 (1899–1900): 284, 381.

Dungan, David L. *The Sayings of Jesus in the Churches of Paul*, Oxford: Basil Blackwell, 1971.

Dunn, James D. G. *Romans 9–16*, Dallas: Word, 1988.

Eckert, Jost. 'Die Kollekte des Paulus für Jerusalem', *Kontinuität und Einheit*, ed. Paul-Gerhard Müller and Werner Stenger, Freiburg: Herder, 1981.

Eichholz, G. 'Bewahren und Bewähren des Evangeliums: der Leitfaden von Phil 1–2', *Hören und Handeln*, ed. H. Gollwitzer and H. Traub, Munich: C. Kaiser, 1962.

Ellicott, C. J. *A Critical and Grammatical Commentary on St Paul's Epistles to the Philippians, Colossians and to Philemon*, London: Parker, Son and Bourn, 1886.

Elliot, John H. 'Patronage and Clientism in Early Christian Society. A Short Reading Guide', *Forum* 3 (1987): 39–48.

'Social-Scientific Criticism of the New Testament and its Social World: More on Methods and Models', *Semeia* 35 (1986): 1–26.

Ellis, E. Earle. 'Paul and his Co-Workers', *NTS* 17 (1971): 437–52.

Ezell, D. 'The Sufficiency of Christ. Philippians 4', *RevExp* 77 (1980): 373–87.

Ferguson, Everett. 'Spiritual Sacrifice in Early Christianity and Its Environment', *ANRW* II.23.2, ed. Wolfgang Haase, Berlin: Walter de Gruyter, 1980: 1151–89.

Fleury, Jean. 'Une Société de Fait dans l'Église Apostolique (Phil. 4: 10 à 22)', *Mélanges Philippe Meylan*, vol. 2, *Histoire du Droit*, Lausanne: Lausanne University, 1963: 41–59.

Forbes, C. 'Comparison, Self-Praise and Irony: Paul's Boasting and the Conventions of Hellenistic Rhetoric', *NTS* 32 (1986): 1–30.

'Paul's Opponents in Corinth', *BurH* 19 (1983): 19–23.

Forbes, C. A. *Teacher's Pay in Ancient Greece*, Lincoln: University of Nebraska Press, 1942.

Ford, H. W. 'The New Testament Concept of Fellowship', *Shane Quarterly* 6 (1945): 188–215.

Foster, G. 'Peasant Society and the Image of Limited Good', *American Anthropologist* 67 (1965): 293–315.

Garland, D. E. 'The Composition and Unity of Philippians: Some Neglected Literary Factors', *NovT* 27 (1985): 141–73.

'Philippians 1: 1–26: The Defense and Confirmation of the Gospel', *RevExp* 77 (1980): 327–36.

Garnsey, Peter and Saller, Richard (eds.) *The Roman Empire: Economy, Society, and Culture*, Berkeley: University of California Press, 1987.

Geoffrion, T. C. *The Rhetorical Purpose and the Political and Military Character of Philippians. A Call to Stand Firm*, Lewiston: Edwin Mellen Press, 1993.

Georgi, Dieter. *Die Geschichte der Kollekte des Paulus für Jerusalem*, Hamburg: Herbert Reich, 1965.

Gillman, F. M. 'Early Christian Women at Philippi', *Journal of Gender in World Religions* 1 (1990): 59–79.

Glombitza, O. 'Der Dank des Apostels. Zum Verständnis von Phil. 4: 10–20', *NovT* 7 (1964–65): 135–41.

Gnilka, Joachim. *Der Philemonbrief*, Freiburg: Herder, 1982.

Der Philipperbrief, Freiburg: Herder, 1968.

Gordis, Robert. *Koheleth – The Man and His World*, New York: Bloch, 1955.

Grant, Robert M. *Early Christianity and Society: Seven Studies*, New York: Harper and Row, 1977.

Gregory, James R. 'Image of Limited Good, or Expectation of Reciprocity?', *Current Anthropology* 16 (1975): 73–92.

Griffin, M. T. *Seneca: A Philosopher in Politics*, Oxford: Clarendon Press, 1976.

Gutbrod, Karl. *Das Buch vom Reich. Das zweitte Buch Samuel*, Stuttgart: Calwer, 1958.

Güttgemanns, E. *Der leidende Apostel und sein Herr: Studien zur paulinischen Christologie*, Göttingen: Vandenhoeck & Ruprecht, 1966.

Hahn, Ferdinand. 'Paulus und der Sklave Onesimus: ein beachtenswerter Kommentar zum Philemonbrief', *EvT* (37 (1977): 179–85.

Hainz, Josef. *Ekklesia. Strukturen paulinischer Gemeinde-Theologie und Gemeinde-Ordnung*, Regensburg: Friedrich Pustet, 1972.

—— *KOINONIA. 'Kirche' als Gemeinschaft bei Paulus*, Regensburg: Friedrich Pustet, 1982.

Hamilton-Grierson, P. J. 'Gifts (Primitive and Savage)', *Encyclopedia of Religion and Ethics*, 7 vols., ed. James Hastings, Edinburgh: T & T Clark, 1908–26: 6.197–209.

Hands, A. R. *Charities and Social Aid in Greece and Rome*, London: Thames and Hudson, 1968.

Harrington, D. J. 'Ben Sira as a Spiritual Master', *Journal of Spiritual Formation* 15 (1994): 147–57.

Harvey, A. E. ' "The Workman is Worthy of His Hire": The Fortunes of a Proverb in the Early Church', *NovT* 24 (1982): 209–21.

Hauck, Friedrich. 'κοινός κτλ', *TDNT*, 10 vols., ed. Gerhard Kittel and G. Friedrich, trans. G. W. Bromiley, Grand Rapids: Eerdmans, 1964–76: 3.789–809.

Hawthorne, Gerald F. *Philippians*, Waco: Word, 1983.

Hemer, C. J. *The Book of Acts in the Setting of Hellenistic History*, Tübingen: J. C. B. Mohr, 1989.

Hengel, Martin. *Property and Riches in the Early Church: Aspects of a Social History of Early Christianity*, trans. John Bowden, London: SCM Press Ltd, 1974.

Hennebush, P. 'Christian Fellowship in the Epistle to the Philippians', *TBT* 12 (1964): 793–8.

Herman, Gabriel. *Ritualized Friendship and the Greek City*, Cambridge: Cambridge University Press, 1987.

Hermesdorf, B. H. D. 'De Apostel Paulus in lopende Rekening met de gemeente te Filippi', *Tijdschrift voor Theologie* 1 (1961): 252–6.

Hertzberg, H. W. *1 & 2 Samuel. A Commentary*, trans. John Bowden, London: SCM Press, 1964.

Hock, Ronald F. *The Social Context of Paul's Ministry. Tentmaking and Apostleship*, Philadelphia: Fortress Press, 1980.

—— 'Paul's Tentmaking and the Problem of His Social Class', *JBL* 97 (1978): 555–64.

—— *The Working Apostle: An Examination of Paul's Means of Livelihood*, Ph.D. diss., Yale University, 1974.

—— 'The Workshop as a Social Setting For Paul's Ministry', *CBQ* 41 (1979): 438–50.

Holmberg, Bengt. *Paul and Power. The Structure of Authority in the Primitive Church as Reflected in the Pauline Epistles*, Philadelphia: Fortress Press, 1980.

Jewett, Robert. 'Conflicting Movements in the Early Church as Reflected in Philippians', *NovT* 12 (1970): 362–90.

'The Epistolary Thanksgiving and the Integrity of Philippians', *NovT* 12 (1970): 40–53.

Jones, C. P. *The Roman World of Dio Chrysostom*, Cambridge: Harvard University Press, 1978.

Jones, J. W. *The Law and the Legal Theory of the Greeks*, Oxford: Clarendon Press, 1956.

Jones, M. 'The Integrity of the Epistle to the Philippians', *Expositor* 8th ser. 8 (1914): 457–73.

Judge, Edwin A. '"Antike und Christentum": Toward a Definition of the Field. A Bibliographic Survey', *ANRW* (1979), pt. 2 vols. 23.1: 3–58.

'Cultural Conformity and Innovation in Paul: Some Clues from Contemporary Documents', *TynBul* 35 (1984): 3–24.

'The Early Christians as a Scholastic Community: Part II', *JRH* 2 (1961): 125–37.

'Paul As a Radical Critic of Society', *Interchange* 16 (1974): 191–203.

'Paul's Boasting in Relation to Contemporary Professional Practice', *AusBR* 16 (1968): 37–50.

Rank and Status in the World of the Caesars and of St Paul, Canterbury: University of Canterbury Press, 1982.

'The Reaction Against Classical Education in the New Testament', *Evangelical Review of Theology* 9 (1985): 166–74.

'The Social Identity of the First Christians: A Question of Method in Religious History', *JRH* 11 (1980): 201–17.

The Social Patterns of the Christian Groups in the First Century: Some Prolegomena to the Study of the New Testament Ideas of Social Obligation, London: Tyndale, 1960.

'St Paul and Classical Society', *JAC* 15 (1972): 19–36.

Käsemann, E. *An die Römer*, Tübingen: J. C. B. Mohr, 4., durchgesehene Auflage, 1980.

'Die Legitimität des Apostels: Eine Untersuchung zu 2 Korinther 10–13', *ZNW* 41 (1942): 33–71.

Keck, Leander E. 'The Poor among the Saints in Jerusalem', *ZNW* 56 (1965): 100–29.

Kennedy, H. A. A. 'The Financial Colouring of Philippians 4: 15–18', *ExpTim* 12 (1900–1): 43–4.

Kidd, Reggie M. *Wealth and Beneficence in the Pastoral Epistles*, Atlanta: Scholars Press, 1990.

Kiley, Mark. *Colossians as Pseudepigraphy*, Sheffield: JSOT Press, 1986.

Kirk, J. Andrew. 'Did "Officials" in the New Testament Church Receive a Salary?', *ExpTim* 84 (1973): 105–8.

Kittel, Gerhard. 'αὐτάρκεια, αὐτάρκης', *TDNT*, 10 vols., ed. Gerhard Kittel and G. Friedrich, trans. G. W. Bromiley, Grand Rapids: Eerdmans (1964–76): 1.466–7.

Koch, E. W. 'A Cameo of Koinonia. The Letter of Philemon', *Int* 17 (1963): 51–87.

Koester, H. 'Paul and Hellenism', *The Bible and Modern Scholarship*, ed. J. P. Hyatt. Nashville: Abingdon Press, 1965.

Koskenniemi, H. *Studien zur Idee und Phraseologie des griechischen Briefs bis 400 n.Chr.*, in *Annales Academiae Scientiarum Fennicae* 102–103 (1956–7): 77–114.

Kötting, Bernhard. 'Euergetes', *RAC* 6 (1966): 848–60.

Kraft, Peter. 'Gratus Animus (Dankbarkeit)', *RAC* 12 (1983): 733–52.

Kurz, William S. 'Kenotic Imitation of Paul and of Christ in Philippians 2–3', *Discipleship in the New Testament*, ed. F. F. Segovia, Philadelphia: Fortress Press, 1985: 103–26.

Lambert, J. C. 'Note on Philippians 4: 10–19', *ExpTim* 11 (1899–1900): 333–4.

Larfeld, Wilhelm. *Handbuch der griechischen Epigraphik*, 2 vols., Leipzig: O. R. Reisland, 1902–7.

Levick, B. M. *Roman Colonies in Southern Asia Minor*, Oxford: Clarendon Press, 1967.

Liefeld, Walter Lewis. *The Wandering Preacher as a Social Figure in the Roman Empire*, Ann Arbor: University Microfilms, 1967.

Lightfoot, J. B. *Saint Paul's Epistles to the Colossians and to Philemon*, London: Macmillan and Co. Limited, 1897.

St Paul's Epistle to the Philippians, London: Macmillan & Co., 1869.

Lohmeyer, E. *Der Brief an die Philipper*, Göttingen: Vandenhoeck & Ruprecht, 1964.

Lohse, Eduard. *A Commentary on the Epistles to the Colossians and to Philemon*, trans. William R. Poehlmann and Robert J. Karris, Philadelphia: Fortress Press, 1971.

Lull, David J. 'The Servant-Benefactor as a Model of Greatness (Luke 22.24–30)', *NovT* 29 (1986): 289–305.

McDermott, M. 'The Biblical Doctrine of ΚΟΙΝΩΝΙΑ', *BZ* 19 (1975): 64–77, 219–33.

McKane, William. *Proverbs: A New Approach*, London: SCM Press, 1970.

MacMullen, Ramsay. *Roman Social Relations, 50 BC to AD 284*, New Haven: Yale University Press, 1974.

Malherbe, Abraham J. '"Gentle as a Nurse": The Cynic Background to 1 Thessalonians 2', *NovT* 12 (1970): 203–17.

'Greco-Roman Religion and Philosophy and the New Testament', *The New Testament and its Modern Interpreters*, ed. E. J. Epp and G. W. MacRae, Philadelphia: Fortress Press, 1989: 1–26.

'Hellenistic Moralists and the New Testament', *ANRW* 2.27.1, forthcoming.

Paul and the Thessalonians: The Philosophic Tradition of Pastoral Care, Philadelphia: Fortress Press, 1987.

Social Aspects of Early Christianity, Philadelphia: Fortress Press, 1983.

Malina, Bruce J. 'The Individual and the Community-Personality in the Social World of Early Christianity', *BTB* 9 (1979): 126–38.

'Limited Good and the Social World of Early Christianity', *BTB* 8 (1978): 162–76.

The New Testament World: Insights from Cultural Anthropology, Atlanta: John Knox Press, 1981.

Malinowsky, Francis X. 'The Brave Women of Philippi', *BTB* 15 (1985): 60–4.

Mannzmann, Anneliese. 'Αὐταρκία', *Der kleine Pauly. Lexikon der Antike*, ed. Konrat Ziegler and Walther Sontheimer, 5 vols., Stuttgart: Alfred Druckenmüller, 1964–75: 1.777–9.

Manson, T. W. 'St Paul in Ephesus. The Date of the Epistle to the Philippians', *BJRL* 23 (1939): 182–200.

Marshall, Peter. *Enmity in Corinth: Social Conventions in Paul's Relations with the Corinthians*, Tübingen: J. C. B. Mohr, 1987.

Martin, Clarice J. 'The Rhetorical Function of Commercial Language in Paul's Letter to Philemon (Verse 18)', *Persuasive Artistry. Studies in New Testament Rhetoric in Honour of George A. Kennedy*, ed. Duane F. Watson, Sheffield: JSOT Press, 1991: 321–37.

Martin, Ralph P. *2 Corinthians*, Waco: Word, 1986.

Philippians (NCB), Grand Rapids: Eerdmans, 1976.

Mauss, M. *The Gift: Forms and Functions of Exchange in Archaic Societies*, trans. I. Cumnison, London: Routledge, 1969.

Mayer, Bernhard. 'Paulus als Vermittler zwischen Epaphroditus und der Gemeinde von Philippi. Bemerkungen zu Phil 2,25–30', *BZ* 31 (1987): 176–88.

Meeks, Wayne. *The First Urban Christians*, New Haven: Yale University Press, 1983.

'The Social Setting of Pauline Theology', *Int* 36 (1982): 266–77.

Meyer, Harold. E. *Lifetime Encyclopedia of Letters*, Englewood Cliffs: Prentice-Hall, Inc., 1983.

Michael, J. H. *The Epistle of Paul to the Philippians*, London: Hodder and Stoughton, repr., 1939.

'The First and Second Epistles to the Philippians', *ExpTim* 34 (1922–3): 107–9.

'The Philippian Interpolation: Where Does it End?', *Expositor* 8th ser. 19 (1920): 49–63.

Michel, O. *Der Brief an die Römer*, Göttingen: Vandenhoeck & Ruprecht, 5., bearbeitete Auflage, 1977.

Momigliano, Arnaldo. 'Biblical Studies and Classical Studies: Simple Reflections about Historical Method', *BA* 45 (1982): 224–8.

Morris, L. *The Epistle to the Romans*, Grand Rapids: Eerdmans, 1988.

'Καὶ ἅπαξ καὶ δίς', *NTS* 1 (1956): 205–8.

Moseé, Claude. *The Ancient World at Work*, trans. J. Lloyd, London: Chatto & Windus, 1969.

Mott, S. C. 'The Power of Giving and Receiving: Reciprocity in Hellenistic Benevolence', *Current Issues in Biblical and Patristic Interpretation*, ed. G. F. Hawthorne, Grand Rapids: Eerdmans, 1975: 60–72.

Motto, A. L. *Seneca Sourcebook: A Guide to the Thought of Lucius Annaeus Seneca*, Amsterdam: Adolf M. Hakkert, 1970.

Moule, C. F. D. *The Epistles of Paul the Apostle to the Colossians and to Philemon*, Cambridge: Cambridge University Press, 1957.

Muffs, Yochanan. 'Abraham the Noble Warrior: Patriarchal Politics and Laws of War in Ancient Israel', *JJS* 33 (1982): 81–107.

Nachmanson, Ernst. 'Zu den Motivformeln der griechischen Ehrenschriften', *Eranos* 11 (1911): 180–96.

Newton, M. *The Concept of Purity at Qumran and in the Letters of Paul*, Cambridge: Cambridge University Press, 1985.

Nickle, K. F. *The Collection: A Study in Paul's Strategy*, London: SCM Press, 1966.

O'Brien, Peter. *Colossians and Philemon*, Waco: Word, 1982.

'The Fellowship Theme in Philippians', *Reformed Theological Review* 37 (1978): 9–18.

'The Importance of the Gospel in Philippians', *God Who is Rich in Mercy*, ed. Peter T. O'Brien and David G. Peterson, Homebush West, Australia: Lancer Books, 1986: 213–33.

Introductory Thanksgivings in the Letters of Paul, Leiden: E. J. Brill, 1977.

'Thanksgiving and the Gospel in Paul', *NTS* 21 (1974–5): 144–55.

Ogden, Graham. *Qoheleth*, Sheffield: JSOT Press, 1987.

Omanson, R. L. 'A Note on the Translation of Philippians 1: 3–5', *BT* 29 (1978): 244–5.

Palmer, D. W. '"To Die is Gain" (Philippians I 21)', *NovT* 17 (1975): 203–18.

Patsch, H. 'εὐχαριστέω', *Exegetisches Wörterbuch zum Neuen Testament*, ed. Horst Balz and Gerhard Schneider, 3 vols., Stuttgart: W. Kohlhammer, 1978–83: 2.219–21.

'εὐχαριστία', *Exegetisches Wörterbuch zum Neuen Testament*, ed. Horst Balz and Gerhard Schneider, 3 vols., Stuttgart: W. Kohlhammer, 1978–83: 2.221–2.

Pearson, A. C. 'Gifts (Greek and Roman)', *Encyclopedia of Religion and Ethics*, ed. James Hastings, 7 vols., Edinburgh: T & T Clark, 1908–26: 6.209–13.

Peifer, C. J. 'Three Letters in One', *TBT* 23 (1985): 363–8.

Pentecost, J. D. 'Studies in Philemon. Part IV: Charge That to My Account', *BSac* 130 (1973): 50–7.

'Studies in Philemon. Part V: The Obedience of a Son', *BSac* 130 (1973): 164–70.

Perkins, Pheme. 'Christology, Friendship and Status: Rhetoric in Philippians', *Society of Biblical Literature 1987 Seminar Papers*, ed. Kent Harold Richards, Atlanta: Scholars Press, 1987: 509–20.

'Philippians: Theology for the Heavenly Politeuma', *Pauline Theology I: Thessalonians, Philippians, Galatians, Philemon*, ed. Jouette M. Bassler, Minneapolis: Augsburg Fortress, 1991: 89–104.

Peterman, G. W. 'Romans 15.26: Make a Contribution Or Establish Fellowship?', *NTS* 40 (1994): 457–63.

'"Thankless Thanks." The Social-Epistolary Convention in Philippians 4.10–20', *TynBul* 42 (1991): 261–70.

Petersen, Norman R. *Rediscovering Paul: Philemon and the Sociology of Paul's Narrative World*, Philadelphia: Fortress Press, 1985.

Pilch, John J. '"Anyone Unwilling to Work Should Not Eat"', *TBT* 32 (1994): 38–45.

Pollard, T. E. 'The Integrity of Philippians', *NTS* 13 (1966): 57–66.

Popkes, W. 'Gemeinschaft', *RAC* 9 (1976): 1100–45.

Portefaix, Lilian. *Sisters Rejoice: Paul's Letter to the Philippians and Luke-Acts as Seen by First-century Philippian Women*, Stockholm: Almquist & Wiksell, 1988.

Pratscher, W. 'Der Verzicht des Paulus auf finanziellen Unterhalt durch seine Gemeinde: ein Aspekt seiner Missionsweise', *NTS* 25 (1979): 284–98.

Price, A. W. *Love and Friendship in Plato and Aristotle*, Oxford: Clarendon Press, 1989.

Prockter, L. J. 'Alms and the Man: The Merits of Charity', *JNSL* 17 (1991): 69–80.

Rahtjen, B. D. 'The Three Letters of Paul to the Philippians', *NTS* 6 (1959–1960): 167–73.

Rapske, B. M. 'The Importance of Helpers to the Imprisoned Paul in the Book of Acts', *TynBul* 42 (1991): 3–30.

Register, David Roy. 'Concerning Giving and Receiving. Charitable Giving and Poor Relief in Paul's Epistles in Comparison with Greco-Roman and Jewish Attitudes and Practices', M. Phil. Thesis. University of Sheffield, February 1990.

Reumann, John. 'Contributions of the Philippian Community to Paul and to Earliest Christianity', *NTS* 39 (1993): 438–57.

'The Theologies of I Thessalonians and Philippians', *Society of Biblical Literature 1987 Seminar Papers*, ed. Kent Harold Richards, Atlanta: Scholars Press, 1987: 521–36.

Rich, Audrey N. M. 'The Cynic Conception of ΑΥΤΑΡΚΕΙΑ', *Mnemosyne* series 4, 9 (1956): 23–9.

Rist, John M. *Stoic Philosophy*, London: Cambridge University Press, 1969.

'The Stoic Concept of Detachment', *The Stoics*, ed. John M. Rist, Berkeley: University of California Press, 1978: 259–72.

Rolland, B. 'Saint Paul et la pauvreté: Phil; 4: 12–14, 19–20', *Assemblées du Seigneur* 59 (1974): 10–15.

Rostowzew, M. 'Die Domäne von Pogla', *Jahreshefte des österreichischen archäologischen Instituts in Wien* 4 (1900): 37–46.

Russell, Ronald. 'The Idle in 2 Thess. 3: 6–12: An Eschatological or a Social Problem', *NTS* 34 (1988): 105–19.

Sahlins, M. *Stone Age Economics*, Chicago: Aldine Publishing, 1972.

Saller, R. P. *Personal Patronage under the Early Empire*, Cambridge: Cambridge University Press, 1982.

Sampley, J. Paul. *Pauline Partnership in Christ. Christian Community and Commitment in Light of Roman Law*, Philadelphia: Fortress Press, 1980.

Schenk, Wolfgang. 'Der Brief des Paulus an Philemon in der neueren Forschung (1945–1987)', *ANRW II* 25.4 (1987): 3135–55.

Die Philipperbriefe des Paulus, Stuttgart: W. Kohlhammer, 1984.

Schubert, Paul. *Form and Function of Pauline Thanksgivings*, Berlin: Töpelmann, 1939.

Schütz, John Howard. *Paul and the Anatomy of Apostolic Authority*, Cambridge: Cambridge University Press, 1975.

Schwer, W. 'Armenpflege', *RAC* 1 (1950): 689–98.

Scroggs, Robin. 'The Sociological Interpretation of the New Testament: The Present State of Research', *NTS* 26 (1980): 164–79.

Seesemann, H. *Der Begriff* ΚΟΙΝΩΝΙΑ *im Neuen Testament*, Gießen: Töpelmann, 1933.

Sevenster, J. N. *Paul and Seneca*, Leiden: E. J. Brill, 1961.

Shelton, J. R. *As the Romans Did. A Source Book in Roman Social History*, Oxford: Oxford University Press, 1988.

Silva, Moisés. *Philippians*, Chicago: Moody Press, 1988.

Skehan, P. W. and Di Lella, A. *The Wisdom of Ben Sira*, New York: Doubleday, 1987.

Smith, H. P. *A Critical and Exegetical Commentary on the Books of Samuel*, Edinburgh: T & T Clark, 1912.

Spencer, A. B. *Paul's Literary Style. A Stylistic and Historical Comparison of II Corinthians 11.16–12.13, Romans 8.9–39, and Philippians 3.2–4.13*, Jackson: ETS, 1984.

Stagg, F. 'The Mind in Christ Jesus: Philippians 1: 27–2: 18', *RevExp* 77 (1980): 337–47.

Stambaugh, John E. and Balch, David L. *The New Testament and Its Social Environment*, Philadelphia: Westminster Press, 1986.

Steen, Henry A. 'Les Clichés Épistolaires dans les Lettres sur Papyrus grecques', *Classica et Medievalia* 1 (1938): 119–76.

Stock, S. G. 'Friendship (Greek and Roman)', *Encyclopedia of Religion and Ethics*, ed. James Hastings, 7 vols., Edinburgh: T & T Clark, 1908–26: 6.134–8.

Stowers, Stanley K. 'Friends and Enemies in the Politics of Heaven: Reading Theology in Philippians', *Pauline Theology I: Thessalonians, Philippians, Galatians, Philemon*, ed. Jouette M. Bassler. Minneapolis: Augsburg Fortress, 1991: 105–21.

Letter Writing in Greco-Roman Antiquity, Philadelphia: Westminster Press, 1986.

'Social Class, Public Speaking and Private Teaching: The Circumstances of Paul's Preaching Activity', *NovT* 26 (1984): 59–82.

Strelan, J. C. 'Burden-Bearing and the Law of Christ: A Re-examination of Galatians 6: 2', *JBL* 94 (1975): 266–76.

Stuhlmacher, Peter. *Der Brief an Philemon*, Zürich: Benziger, 1975.

Stuiber, Alfred. 'Eulogia', *RAC* 6 (1966): 900–28.

'Geschenk', *RAC* 10 (1978): 685–703.

Sumney, J. L. *Identifying Paul's Opponents. The Question of Method in 2 Corinthians*, Sheffield: JSOT Press, 1990.

Swift, R. C. 'The Theme and Structure of Philippians', *BSac* 141 (1984): 234–54.

Talbert, C. H. 'Money Management in Early Mediterranean Christianity: 2 Corinthians 8–9', *RevExp* 86 (1989): 359–70.

Theissen, Gerd. 'Legitimation und Lebensunterhalt: Ein Beitrag zur Soziologie Urchristlicher Missionäre', *NTS* 21 (1975): 192–221.

Psychological Aspects of Pauline Theology, Edinburgh: T & T Clark, 1987.

The Sociology of Early Palestinian Christianity, Philadelphia: Fortress Press, 1978.

The Social Setting of Pauline Christianity, Philadelphia: Fortress Press, 1982.

Thomas, W. D. 'The Place of Women in the Church at Philippi', *ExpTim* 83 (1971–2): 117–20.

228   Bibliography

Thrall, Margaret E. *Greek Particles in the New Testament. Linguistic and Exegetical Studies*, Leiden: E. J. Brill, 1962.

'Greco-Roman Friendship', *ExpTim* 99 (1988): 185.

Treu, Kurt. 'Freundschaft', *RAC* 8 (1972): 418–34.

Veynre, Paul. *Bread and Circuses*, trans. Brian Pearce, London: Penguin Press, 1990.

Vincent, Marvin R. *A Critical and Exegetical Commentary on the Epistles to the Philippians and to Philemon*, Edinburgh: T & T Clark, repr., 1979.

Wacht, Manfred. 'Gütergemeinschaft', *RAC* 13 (1986): 1–59.

Wallace-Hadrill, Andrew (ed). *Patronage in Ancient Society*, London: Routledge, 1989.

Walter, Nikolaus. 'Die Philipper und das Leiden: aus den Anfängen einer heidenchristlichen Gemeinde', *Die Kirche des Anfangs*, ed. R. Schankenburg, Freiburg: Herder, 1977: 417–34.

Watson, Duane F. 'A Rhetorical Analysis of Philippians and its Implications for the Unity Question', *NovT* 30 (1988): 57–88.

Watson, Francis. *Paul, Judaism and the Gentiles: A Sociological Approach*, Cambridge: Cambridge University Press, 1986.

Wedderburn, A. J. M. *The Reasons for Romans*, Edinburgh: T & T Clark, 1988

Weinfeld, Moshe. *Deuteronomy and the Deuteronomic School*, Oxford: Clarendon Press, 1972.

Westermann, Claus. *Genesis 12–36: A Commentary*, trans. John J. Scullion, Minneapolis: Augsburg, 1985.

White, John L. *Light from Ancient Letters*, Philadelphia: Fortress Press, 1986.

White, L. Michael. 'Morality Between Two Worlds: A Paradigm of Friendship in Philippians', *Greeks, Romans & Christians*, ed. D. L. Balch, E. Ferguson and W. A. Meeks, Minneapolis: Fortress Press, 1990: 201–15.

'Social Authority in the House Church Setting and Ephesians 4: 1–16', *ResQ* 29 (1987): 209–28.

(ed). *Social Networks and Early Christianity*, Decatur: Scholars Press, 1988.

Wickert, U. 'Der Philemonbrief – Privatbrief oder apostolisches Schreiben?', *ZNW* 52 (1961): 230–8.

Wilckens, Ulrich. *Der Brief an die Römer*, 3 vols., Zürich: Benziger, 1978–82.

'ὕστερος κτλ', *TDNT* 8.592–601.

Wiles, G. P. *Paul's Intercessory Prayers. The Significance of the Intercessory Prayers in the Letters of St. Paul*, Cambridge: Cambridge University Press, 1974.

Wilpert, Paul. 'Autarkie', *RAC* 1 (1950): 1039–50.

Winter, Bruce W. '"If a Man Does Not Wish to Work . . ." A Cultural and Historical Setting for 2 Thessalonians 3: 6–16', *TynBul* 40 (1989): 303–15.

Philo and Paul among the Sophists: A Hellenistic Jewish and Christian Response, Ph.D. diss., Macquarie University, 1988.

'The Problem with "Church" for the Early Church', *In the Fullness of Time: Biblical Studies in Honour of Archbishop Donald Robinson*, ed. D. Peterson and J. Pryor, Sydney: Lancer Books, 1992: 203–17.

'Providentia for the Widows of 1 Timothy 5: 3–16', *TynBul* 39 (1988): 83–99.

'The Public Praising of Christian Benefactors: Romans 13.3–4 and 1 Peter 2.14–15', *JSNT* 34 (1988): 87–103.

Winter, J. G. 'In the Service of Rome: Letters from the Michigan Papyri', *Classical Philology* 22 (1927): 237–56.

Winter, S. C. 'Paul's Letter to Philemon', *NTS* 33 (1987): 1–15.

Wiseman, T. P. 'Competition and Cooperation', *Roman Political Life 90 BC–AD 69*, ed. T. P. Wiseman, Exeter: Exeter University Publications, 1985.

Wright, N. T. *The Epistles of Paul to the Colossians and to Philemon*, Leicester: Inter-Varsity Press, 1986.

Ziesler, J. *Paul's Letter to the Romans*, London: SCM Press, 1989.

INDEX OF GRECO-ROMAN AUTHORS, PAPYRI AND INSCRIPTIONS

Greco-Roman authors

Aeschylus
  Pr. 700, 124
  Ch. 481, 124
Anthologia Graeca
  9.546, 60
  12.204, 60
Aristotle
  Eth. Nic. 2.7.4, 58
    4.1.1–30, 58–9, 125, 147
    4.1.1–29, 65
    4.1.1–25, 15
    4.1.1, 58, 65
    4.1.7, 58, 61, 140, 156
    4.1.8, 58
    4.1.15, 58, 59, 65
    4.1.24–5, 58
    4.1.29–30, 88
    4.1.29, 58
    4.1.30, 59, 65
    4.3.24, 58, 72, 116, 140, 172, 179
    5.5.6–7, 88
    5.5.6, 102, 117, 187, 206–7
    5.5.14, 47, 102, 187
    8.1.1, 116
    8.7.2, 88
    8.11.1–4, 41, 73, 174, 190, 192
    8.12.5, 58, 179
    8.13.2, 72, 116, 117
    8.13.8, 178
    8.13.9, 71
    8.14.2, 72–3
    8.14.2–4, 149
    8.14.3–4, 73
    9.1.7, 40, 192
    9.8.9, 116
  Magna Moralia
    1211A46, 117
  Politics
    1302A32–4, 109

1302B4, 109
1303A15, 109
8.2.1, 140
Arrian
  Epict. Diss.
    1.1.27, 142
    1.4.32, 71
    1.6.1–2, 95
    1.6.29, 142
    1.6.40, 142
    1.9.7, 137
    1.9.19–20, 134, 141
    1.16.6, 95
    1.16.15–21, 128
    1.22.3, 145
    2.7.3, 193
    2.9.11–12, 56
    2.9.12, 56–8, 71, 147
    2.9.13, 57
    2.9.15, 57
    2.11.4, 145
    2.14.7, 137
    2.16.42, 57, 131
    2.19.26, 131
    2.22.24, 131
    2.22.34, 66, 176
    2.23.23, 71
    3.3.15, 137
    3.8.2, 137
    3.24.8, 137
    3.24.54–6, 141
    3.25.1, 137
    3.26.2, 139
    4.1.54, 141
    4.1.177, 210
    4.4.18, 95
    4.10.20, 210
    4.12.20, 141
    4.72.7, 95
Cicero
  Amic. 8.2663–4, 65, 147

Papyri and inscriptions

Papyri

INDEX OF BIBLICAL BOOKS WITH
APOCRYPHA AND FATHERS

The Fathers and other early Christian works

GENERAL INDEX

Abraham, 49

Alexander, Loveday, 15, 18, 19, 80

anthropology, 3, 20–1

Aristotle, 58–9, 72, 109, 113, 115–16

Barrett, C. K., 5, 167, 172–3

Bassler, Jouette M., 10, 14–15, 102, 147, 151, 163, 190, 211, 213

Beare, F. W., 11, 17, 19, 20, 99, 104, 114, 121, 122, 132, 134, 158

Bell, H. Idris and Roberts, C. H., 75.

benefaction, 44, 45, 46, 67, 70, 73, 83, 84, 85, 86, 87

benefactors, 25, 44, 47, 48, 70, 72, 73, 83, 84, 85, 86, 87, 193–4

    God as, 49, 104

    parents as, 40, 45, 48, 73, 192–3

    Paul as, 171–4, 188–91, 197

Betz, H. D., 180, 182

blessing (as gratitude), 29, 31, 32–3, 36, 37

Bolkestein, H., 4, 51, 140, 150, 156

Bolkestein, H. and Kalsbach, A., 139

Bruce, F. F., 62, 145, 187

Buchanan, Colin O., 12, 133, 144

Burford, Alison, 7

Capper, B. J., 122, 133

Chow, John K., 6

Cicero, 63–4, 71

Clarke, Andrew D., 72, 113, 170, 193, 198, 211

Collange, Jean–François, 12–13, 122, 134, 135, 158

collection, 99, 110, 118, 148, 175–85

commercial terminology

    in Greco–Roman friendship, 15, 58–9, 63–5, 89

    in OT, 24–5, 47–8

    in Philemon, 185–91

    in Philippians Four, 10, 123–4, 142–4, 147, 196

Conzelmann, H., 36, 61, 83, 129, 177.

Corinthians

    Paul's relationship with, 6, 8, 126, 162–74

Cranfield, C. E. B., 117, 165, 175, 177, 180, 184

Danker, F. W., 5, 84

David, 30–2

De Beneficiis, 52–5, 117, 126, 201–4

debt

    and expressions of gratitude, 70, 74, 76, 81, 82

    created by receiving, 39, 47, 54, 69, 71, 85

    of converts to Paul, 174, 188–91

    of Gentiles to Jews, 177–8

    of God to benefactors, 25

    of Philippians to Paul, 15, 148

    to parents, 40, 73, 174

Dewailly, L.-M., 99, 101

Deissmann, Adolf, 1, 13, 143, 144, 193

Derrett, J. D. M., 185, 186, 189

Dihle, Albrecht, 141

Dio Chrysostom, 70, 87, 113, 132, 140

Dodd, C. H., 11, 103, 122, 147, 168, 177

Δόσις και λήμψις

    equivalents in *De Beneficiis*, 53–5

    in Greek literature, 55–65

    in Philippians Four, 8, 10, 101, 124, 125, 143, 146–51, 196

    in non–reciprocity contexts, 205–7

Dungan, David L., 163, 166, 169

Dunn, James D. G., 175, 176, 177, 179, 180, 183, 184, 193

Elisha, 33–4

Epictetus, 56–8

equity, 72, 75, 77

Esau, 28–9